# THE FIGHTERS

# THE FIGHTERS

THE MEN AND MACHINES OF THE FIRST AIR WAR / BY THOMAS R. FUNDERBURK

"In the case of a European war between two countries, both sides would be equipped with a large corps of aeroplanes, each trying to obtain information of the other and to hide its own movements. The effort which each would exert in order to hinder or prevent the enemy from obtaining information would lead to the inevitable result of a war in the air, for the supremacy of the air, by armed aeroplanes against each other. This fight for the supremacy of the air in future wars will be of the first and greatest importance . . ."

CAPTAIN MURRAY F. SUETER, RN
*(From a speech to a technical sub-committee of the Committee of Imperial Defense, February 5, 1912)*

**GROSSET & DUNLAP**
**A Filmways Company**
**Publishers • New York**

TO
WILLIAM ERIC BARNES
FIRST LIEUTENANT, 147th AERO SQUADRON
FIRST PURSUIT GROUP, U.S.A.S.
AND
FOR THE GRANDEST OLD SOLDIER OF THEM ALL,
MY FATHER.

In acknowledging the help he has received in the preparation of this book, the author expresses a debt he cannot adequately repay. In gratitude he can but list the names of those friends from whom he has received encouragement, and whose time and effort have been freely and graciously given.

In the first instance, Oscar Dystel, who made the book possible; Mrs. Frieda Taliga and John Kirbach, who surmounted language barriers; and Conrad Brown, the editor, who guided the book to completion.

The author's colleagues of *Cross & Cockade,* Peter Grosz, O. A. Sater, Russell Manning, and Frank W. Bailey were his conscience, and their advice eliminated a number of errors from the manuscript. The errors that remain are the author's own.

For the labor of typing the entire manuscript (most of it twice), and for innumerable sound criticisms, the author is grateful to his wife.

The kind consideration shown by the following persons and institutions was of inestimable value in a number of ways: Col. Paul A. Rockwell; Lt. Col. T. M. Hawker; Mrs. Frances Lewis of the Aeronautical Chart and Information Center, U.S. Air Force; Lt. Col. Milton K. Kegley of the Office of Information, U.S. Air Force; Leonard Joseph Patrick Leone; William E. Morse, Jr.; Alfred Friedrich of the *Gemeinschaft der Alten Adler*; the British Imperial War Museum; the French *Musée de l'Air*; and the Belgian *Musée Royal de l'Armée et d'Histoire Militaire*.

Last on this list and foremost in the author's esteem are the aviators themselves, to whom he is indebted and grateful for their own words and thoughts, given in letters and interviews, and for the patience with which they endured his queries: Charles J. Biddle, Douglas Campbell, Reed McKinley Chambers, Brig. Gen. Everett R. Cook, Capt. Edward Vernon Rickenbacker, George A. Vaughn, Jr., Air Vice Marshal John Oliver Andrews, Air Vice Marshal Raymond Collishaw, Air Marshal Wilfred Austin Curtis, Air Marshal Hugh W. L. Saunders, Hermann Becker, Generalleutnant Hermann Dahlmann, Werner Junck, Carl-August von Schoenebeck, Oberstleutnant Ehrhardt von Teubern, Oberstleutnant Walter von Teubern, Baron Theobald von Zastrow, Joseph Frantz, Jacques Leps, Gilbert Sardier, Paul Tarascon, and Robert Waddington.

THE GREAT WAR, as every schoolboy knows until he forgets, began on July 29, 1914, when the armies of Austria-Hungary invaded the Slav state of Serbia with the aim of redressing a long series of "indignities" by a crushing humiliation. Russia, as self-appointed protector of Slavic interests in Europe, immediately declared war on Austria. Germany, as ally of Austria, declared war on Russia. Great Britain and France, in entente with Russia, declared war on Germany. It was the grotesque old joke about "some fool thing in the Balkans."

The fuse was lit and the ensuing explosion nearly destroyed not only the fact of the Old World but obliterated the dream of a Better World as well. Within six weeks the Western Front defined itself as an entrenched battle line that stretched from Switzerland to the North Sea, the mass grave of an entire generation. For four years the armies slaughtered each other by turns in futile frontal assaults that withered in machine gun fire and drowned in mud. No-man's-land became an unspeakably foul waste of wreckage and human debris that could not be crossed save in the air. Yet so new was the element of the air that the first men to fly were long in carrying the war into it.

*         *         *

WHEN THE GREAT armies took the field in August of 1914, they numbered about six million men. France mustered 62 divisions, Germany, 87. In the same month, France had 120 aeroplanes, not all of which were owned by the military, and none of which were even military types. Britain had 113, and Germany had as many, precisely, as the two put together. To say that this was a small beginning for air power is to say the desert is sandy.

There are many cogent reasons for the general lack of preparedness for war in the air, doubtless, but the air services reflected the attitude of the armies of which they were an inconsiderable adjunct. Almost to a man the commanders believed in the infallibility of the general plans, and that a limited, inexpensive war could be fought and won before Christmas. France planned to launch her offensive with a smashing drive through the German center—"We'll cut them in half!"—and Germany planned to wheel around the French left and cut straight down to Paris in 39 days. That both Plan 17 and the Schlieffen Plan failed because the premises upon which they were based were unrealistic has been explained many times. It would have taken a historically unique set of circumstances to have conferred upon the commanders the will to originate or the prescience to appreciate a vital and integrated role for anything so new as aviation.

Aeroplanes were noisy, fussy, gimcrack novelties that few military men were willing to consider capable of performing any useful purpose. They were slow, unarmed, defenseless, fragile, hopelessly subservient to the weather, and too feeble to carry any load other than a pilot and passenger. What good were they?

To tell the truth, they weren't much good. Not when we consider the endless and amazing variety of jobs today's aircraft can perform. But they could execute one tactical function, one that required no armament, no particular range, speed, or ceiling, or ability to lift any load other than a pilot and passenger: reconnaissance. If the passenger were a professional soldier, a Regular Army officer able accurately to interpret and report what he saw from the air, one aeroplane and its crew could do the work of a regiment of cavalry.

While the armies had experimented with aerial reconnaissance during manoeuvres before the war, and the aeroplane had won a limited acceptance, the vision of the war being won in a grand style by sweeping corps movements and dashing cavalry charges had been too glorious a one to be forsaken lightly in the interest of a handful of greasy mechanics.

So the nations marched, or rode, to war. The Air Service went along almost as an afterthought. Like the tail of the donkey it had its function, but no one expected it to draw any of the load.

The background of Britain's Royal Flying Corps presents a typical example of the slowness and apparent reluctance with which an aerial service was given an official endorsement. By August 1914 there were an even dozen aerodromes in England, none of which were owned or operated by the military. On these fields some 30 civilian flying schools were operating. These schools, subsidized in part by the Government, had trained about 660 officers, all of whom had had to pay their own tuition (£ 75), which was returnable from the War Office in the case of officers on active duty who joined the RFC on passing out of the school.

In Germany, Belgium and France the situation was identical; the United States will be passed over in silence. The situation was a joke.

*        *        *

WHEN THE SHOOTING started in earnest in August 1914 Britain's Aerial Arm was ready to help, eager to take part, and for the first week, uninvited. The aviators fretted and fumed, fearful that the war would end before they could make that contribution which would prove their worth. Their chance came, however; the first squadrons went to France on August 13, following the four-division BEF commitment. While the German armies of the north were wheeling through Belgium and northern France, the British were feeling for a firm contact with their ally the French. The BEF at Mons lay square in the path of General Alexander von Kluck's First Army, the German right wing. The Royal Flying Corps spotted von Kluck's army and kept it under surveillance, and the British were ready when battle was joined. In his dispatch for September 7, 1914, Sir John French, the British Commander-in-Chief, cited the RFC in the following terms: "I wish particularly to bring to your lordship's notice the admirable work being done by the Royal Flying Corps under Sir David Henderson. Their skill, energy, and perseverance have been beyond all praise. They have furnished me with the most complete and accurate information, which has been of incalculable value in the conduct of operations. Fired at constantly, both by friend and foe, and not hesitating to fly in every kind of weather, they have remained undaunted throughout."

The four squadrons of the RFC billed to go to France had assembled at Dover on August 12, landing in parks and on playing fields. The one-night camp was astir at dawn—most of the pilots and ground crew had slept under the wings of their machines—and the order was passed that everything was to be ready for the start to an undisclosed destination at six o'clock.

The engines were started up and Lieutenant Colonel F. H. Sykes, then Chief of Air Staff, came to see the aeroplanes and crews off. He told the pilots their destination, Amiens, and pointed out the approximate route on a map. Straight across the Channel to Cap Gris Nez, then down the coast of France to the mouth of the Somme, then along the course of the river to Amiens. One hundred twenty miles; two hours. Piece of cake, really. Then Sykes shook hands with each man in turn. The handshake was a bit of bad judgement, and most of the pilots felt it had been better left out for it imparted a depressing "God be with you" tone to the operation. Aviators, like actors, are a superstitious lot in spite of themselves, and the most sincere expression of good wishes is better left unsaid; rather, you must say *"Hals und Beinbruch,"* that is, "Break your neck and your legs," or "I'll be slapping you in the face with a shovel, Buddy." Something delicate.

The mixed company of aeroplanes bumped across the ground, lifted into the air, and turned their noses toward Britain's ancient bulwark, the Channel.

Lieutenant H. D. Harvey-Kelly of No. 2 Squadron, flying a B.E.2a, was the first to leave and the first to arrive, setting down at Amiens about twenty minutes past eight. One by one the others came in, although not necessarily in the order of their departure. One pilot force-landed with engine trouble, and several others, seeing his machine in a field, supposed that they had arrived and landed beside him. Much annoyed, they then continued their flight to the correct destination.

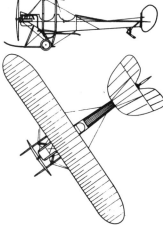

*B.E.2a*

Not all of the aeroplanes and crews made it, however. One machine, a Blériot two-seater of No. 3 Squadron piloted by a Lieutenant Skene, leveled off abruptly on leaving the ground and, instead of climbing to join its fellows, continued on a level course that soon took it out of sight behind the trees girding the field. The men who had been watching from the ground exchanged glances, then froze as the engine suddenly cut out. An appalling silence endured for a fraction of eternity, then there came a splintering crash and the men began to run toward the sound.

They found the wreck in a clump of trees, the early morning sun slanting across the shattered wood and bloodied linen.

The Royal Flying Corps had lost the first of six thousand.

\*　　　　　　\*　　　　　　\*

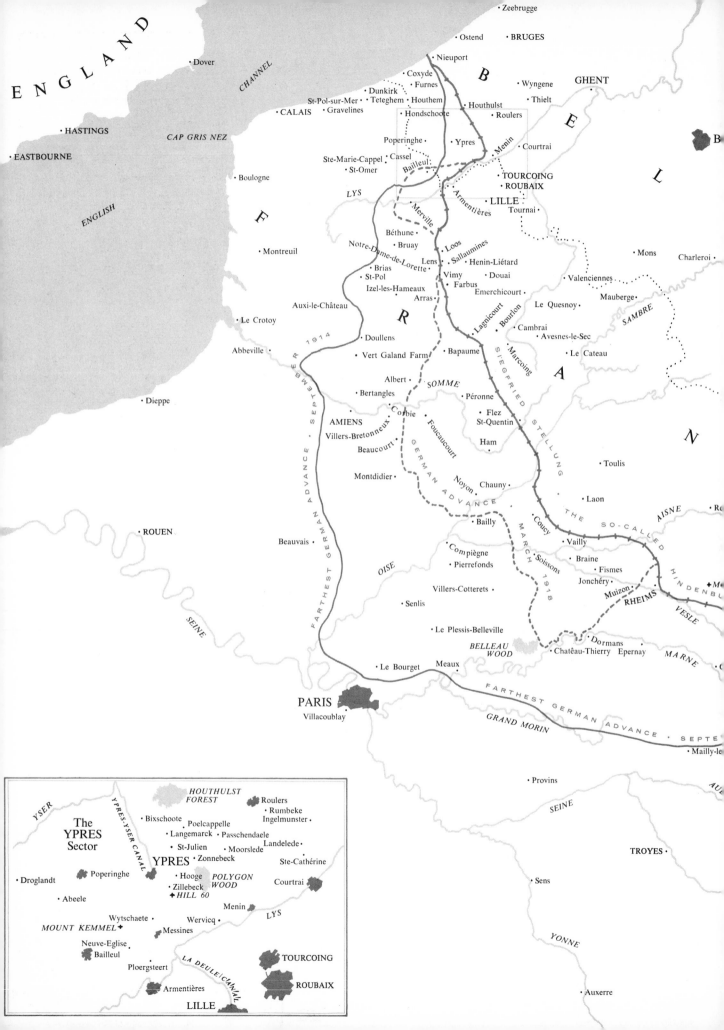

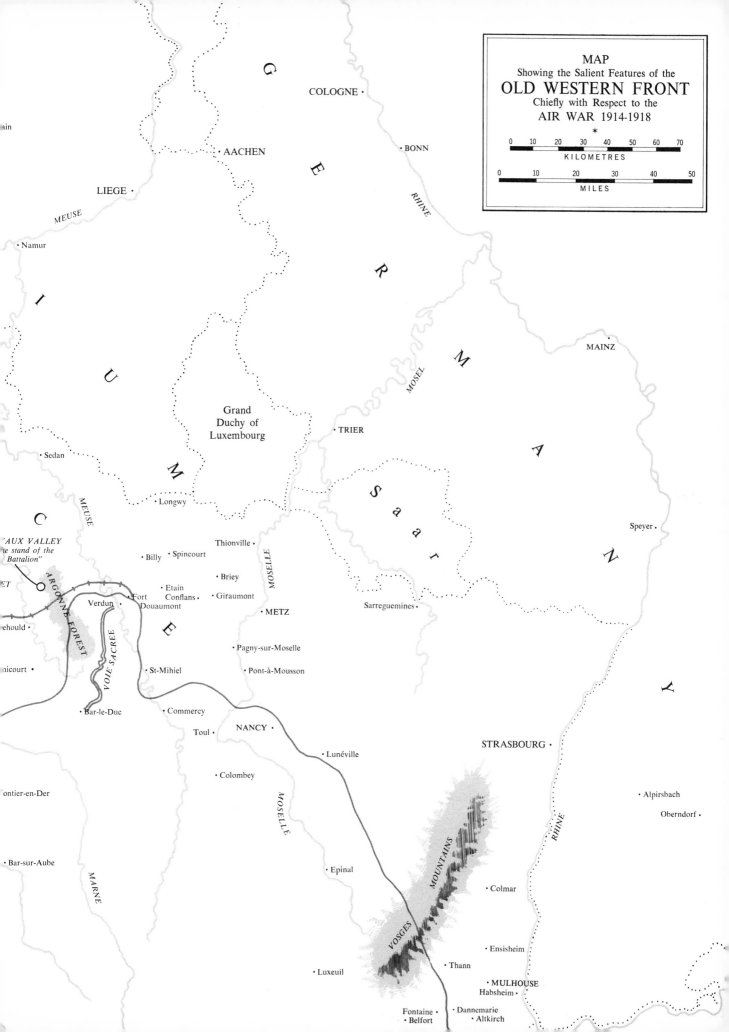

MAP
Showing the Salient Features of the
**OLD WESTERN FRONT**
Chiefly with Respect to the
AIR WAR 1914-1918

KILOMETRES

MILES

COLOGNE

BONN

AACHEN

RHINE

LIEGE

MEUSE

Namur

MAINZ

Grand
Duchy of
Luxembourg

TRIER

MOSEL

Sedan

Longwy

Speyer

'AUX VALLEY
e stand of the
Battalion"

MEUSE

Thionville

Billy · Spincourt

Briey

MOSELLE

Sarreguemines

Etain
Conflans · Giraumont

Fort
Douaumont

Verdun

METZ

ARGONNE FOREST

ehould

Pagny-sur-Moselle

nicourt

VOIE SACREE

St-Mihiel

Pont-à-Mousson

Bar-le-Duc · Commercy

Toul  NANCY

STRASBOURG

Lunéville

Colombey

ontier-en-Der

MOSELLE

Alpirsbach

Oberndorf

Bar-sur-Aube

MARNE

Epinal

Colmar

MOUNTAINS

Ensisheim

VOSGES

Thann

RHINE

Luxeuil

MULHOUSE
Habsheim

Fontaine ·  · Dannemarie
· Belfort  Altkirch

# CONTENTS

·

"A EUROPEAN WAR"
PAGE 3

·

"THE INEVITABLE RESULT"
PAGE 56

·

"THE SUPREMACY OF THE AIR"
PAGE 143

·

## "A EUROPEAN WAR"

*"Never before the war of 1914 did I envisage piloting aeroplanes—so extraordinary did flying seem to me."*

JACQUES LEPS

AN AMERICAN, Charles J. Biddle, of Andalusia, Pennsylvania, was a man who could not wait for the United States to end her shivering on the brink. He entered the war by way of the French Foreign Legion, the conventional way for men who were not French nationals to fight without relinquishing their home country citizenship. Notified that he had been accepted, he was required to report for a physical examination at a recruiting office near the *Invalides* in Paris. The office was one of those shabby, slightly sour *bureaux* where France's *petit fonctionnaires* nest in their coils of red tape, living out their drab, devoted lives in an extravagantly quaint setting that made one think of nothing so much as a Daumier lithograph. Awaiting his turn, Biddle fidgeted on a hard, official bench.

One man ahead of him was being examined for the infantry of the Foreign Legion. He was very nervous and inadvertently signed his own name to the papers. He had had his documents all made out with an alias and then got excited at the last minute. The officer in charge smiled and glozed over the inadvertent exposure, which was nothing new in the Legion.

Biddle was sent to Avord, one of the larger air training establishments in France. The flying school at Avord was operated on the principle of the "Blériot school." The students learned to fly in single-seat machines, going up at no time

with an instructor. Although this sounds dangerous, it wasn't, because the classes progressed by easy stages from non-flying to flying machines. The beginners— *débutants*—started out on "Penguins." The Penguin was a Blériot monoplane powered with a 35-horsepower Anzani engine, incapable of flight because its wings were clipped. Sitting in a Penguin, the student got a good idea of what it was like to sit in a real aeroplane. After a brief instruction on the engine and a few rudiments of flight, the student climbed into the cockpit and strapped the seat belt across his lap. With ignition off and chocks against the wheels, the propeller was rotated once or twice by hand to draw fuel into the cylinders. The ignition was switched on and the mechanic spun the prop. The motor burst into life . . . sometimes. Sometimes several tries and a considerable amount of earnest swearing were necessary. When the engine was running, the chocks were removed and the Penguin rolled forward. The student shoved the stick forward and the tail came up, then if he could get the "feel" of the rudder bar with his feet he could keep the machine rolling on course. When the student had mastered the knack of steering with his feet he was able to zip along the ground at a speed of 35 or 40 miles an hour keeping to a more or less straight line across the field.

Passing out of the Penguins, the student moved up to the *rouleur* (roller) class. In this class real aeroplanes were used, Blériot monoplanes without clipped wings, powered by 60 to 80 horsepower rotary engines. The student repeated his Penguin lesson, racing back and forth along the ground trying to describe a perfectly straight line. When the instructor was satisfied that the student was able to keep the machine under control he was considered to be in the next class, the *décolleur* (unsticker). In this class the student was allowed to "unstick" himself from the ground. Starting up the motor as usual he rolled forward over the ground, holding to a straight course by controlling the rudder bar with his feet, holding the aeroplane in a level position with the stick at the center. Then, easing back a shade on the stick, the student caused the aeroplane to rise off the ground. His altitude, if you can call it that, was not to exceed three feet. In what he fondly hoped was his element, the student sailed along at full throttle, three feet off the ground, endeavoring to hold to the familiar straight course. That's all there was to it, and in wartime the program was gradually speeded up, the students who looked fairly promising being passed through in a few days. Biddle went through all the courses thought necessary to train him as a combat pilot inside of five months.

The "Blériot system" in use at Avord when Biddle went through the school was expensive since it used up a great many machines. There were accidents every day, but hardly anyone got hurt. The steps were gradual; the student who paid attention was not likely to get himself in trouble. The system had the advantage that a few instructors could handle masses of students.

Metre by metre the students ventured into the air, ten, 100, 500, 1000 metres; five minutes, 15 minutes, half an hour. Ten kilometres, 25, 50. Then the cross-country flight—Avord to Chateauroux to Romorantin—225 kilometres per leg with a stop at each aerodrome for gasoline and oil and a signature on the dotted line just to show that you have really been there, *mes enfants, n'est-ce pas?*

4

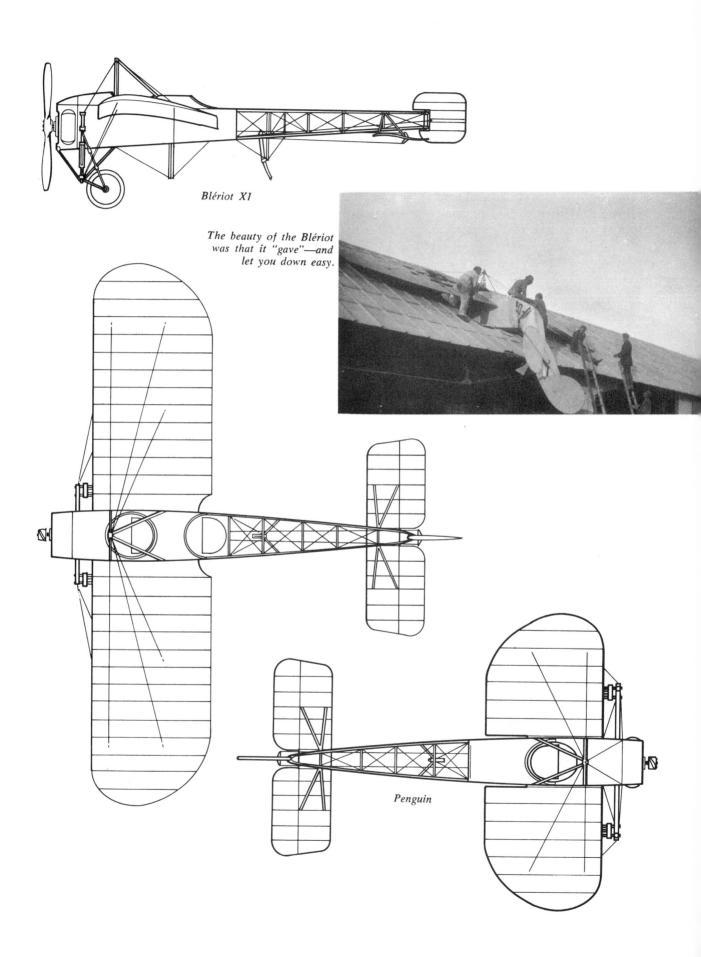

*Blériot XI*

*The beauty of the Blériot was that it "gave"—and let you down easy.*

*Penguin*

From 1300 metres the country is spread out below exactly like a map—the canals and rivers, towns and villages, roads and railroads, even the ponds, are there exactly where they are supposed to be.

One last flight—an endurance test. The student must climb above 2000 metres and remain there for an hour. Although it is chilly, even in June, the flight is no strain on the student; the endurance being tested is that of the temper. To hold the frail, underpowered, and not particularly stable Blériot above 2000 metres for an hour was an exasperating chore. Even so, for Biddle, the hour was soon up, and the student had won his wings.

Biddle's first real test as a pilot was an honest-to-God forced landing during an endurance flight, out of which he brought himself and his machine most commendably.

His motor had been behaving badly one day and cut out abruptly at an altitude of 450 metres, or about 1500 feet. He immediately pushed the stick forward to put the nose down so as to maintain flying speed. Glancing rapidly about the terrain below, he picked out a promising-looking field. He glided toward the field, but just as he was going into it over the trees, the engine caught and roared back to life. He decided to continue his assigned flight and eased back on the stick to begin to climb back to the proper altitude. He had no sooner passed over the field he had chosen than the engine died again, this time permanently.

There was little time to be choosey about a spot to land. He was too low to glide very far and the country below was much cut up with hills, hedges, and trees. One field presented itself as being the most promising, a narrow strip full of wild flowers with a stream bordering it on one long side. There was a chance that the field would be marshy because of the stream, which appeared to have no banks, but mud is better than trees, so in he went. Holding the Blériot's tail low he glided down at near stalling speed. Just before he touched he pulled the stick back further and the machine mushed down, the tail settling into the tall grass and hitting the ground before the main wheels. Mud and water sprayed in all directions, but the machine stayed right side up, rolling only about 15 feet before it stopped, the wheels six inches deep in the goo.

Biddle clambered out of the dripping aeroplane and walked around it to make sure nothing was broken. The usual crowd of French peasants soon began to collect and with their help he pushed the machine to dryer ground. After changing the spark plugs from his tool kit he instructed the most intelligent-looking man how to spin the prop without decapitating himself, climbed back in and got a start from his extemporaneous ground crew. The ground was still pretty soft and he had a job to get up flying speed, but he horsed the aeroplane off and got home safely.

The authorities probably want these little emergencies to crop up, Biddle reflected, just to see how a man takes care of himself.

*                    *                    *

ADOLPHE PÉGOUD was born June 13, 1889, at Monferrat (Isère), France. His father, an infantryman, had been interned in Germany after the Franco-Prussian War of 1870. In 1907, at the age of 18, Adolphe Pégoud enlisted in the 5th Regiment of the *Chasseurs d'Afrique,* passed to a hussar outfit, then to a regiment of colonial artillery. With this latter, while stationed at Toulon, he made the acquaintance of a military aviator, *Capitaine* Carlin, who took him for his first ride in an aeroplane. Pégoud summed up the experience in one word—joy. Under the aegis of *Capitaine* Carlin, he was inscribed an assistant mechanic and rode regularly with Carlin who taught him to fly. Discharged from the service in February 1913, Pégoud was uncertain what career to follow. He had hoped to make the military his profession, but flying had fired his ambition and he could not devote himself to any career that did not involve aviation. To be a military pilot he would have had to become an officer, since it was only the luck of *Capitaine* Carlin's patronage and interest that had made it possible for him to fly in the army. He unsuccessfully offered his services to Serbia and Rumania, where some soldiers of fortune had reputedly done well as aviators, but finally managed to land a job with Louis Blériot, the famous flyer and aeroplane constructor.

He test-flew factory aeroplanes for a few months and in August 1913, got a chance to do something that promised a bit of celebrity. He demonstrated a parachute, the invention of a Monsieur Bonnet.

This parachute was of the familiar silk canopy construction and was packed in a canvas container that was attached to the outside of the aeroplane, behind the cockpit. The pilot donned a harness before boarding the aeroplane, and the parachute rig was clipped to the harness after he settled himself in the cockpit.

Pégoud took off in a Blériot monoplane and climbed to 100 metres. He unfastened his safety belt and stood up, pulling the rip cord as he did so. The parachute snapped open, actuated by springs, caught the air, and yanked him out of the cockpit. The aeroplane continued on in a straight line then gradually dipped its nose in a dive, leveled out, slid off on a wing, then dipped its nose again, and so on, finally diving into the ground on the estate of a M. Quesnel, whose lands flanked the aerodrome. Pégoud landed in a wood and climbed down the tree, leaving his parachute draped over the branches. He was hoisted to the shoulders of the crowd which had followed him cross-country during his descent.

Watching the pilotless machine while swinging under the 'chute Pégoud determined that his next experiment would be something that he had been thinking about a lot but which he had never seen or heard of—upside-down flying.

No scientist, Pégoud never pretended that he could calculate everything on paper, in advance. But he had an infallible instinct about what he could or could not do, a *feel* for the air and the aeroplane in it that gave him control over the situation at all times. He had a generous complement of self-confidence, but no illusions that he was indestructible: "If I kill myself, so what? One less aviator. But if I succeed, how many valuable lives will be saved for aviation!"

He was struck by the behavior of the pilotless Blériot after he had bailed out. It had described the most perfect curves by itself. It followed that what the aeroplane would do by itself it could be made to do by the pilot. Obviously, the machine, left to its own devices, would follow a set of "natural" responses: if the pilot were sensitive to these he could utilize them to make the machine manoeuvre as he wished, and this included upside-down flying. A pilot could turn an aeroplane upside down by rolling it on its long axis or by going into a steep sideslip and letting it flip itself over by abruptly dropping the high wing.

Pégoud contrived to have a machine slung up in the hangar, himself strapped in, and rolled over to simulate the upside-down flying attitude. When his ears turned red they rolled him back. Satisfied that he had the hang of it, he went out and *did* it. The next day he gave a public demonstration of inverted flight. Sensation. Asked by a reporter to describe how it felt to fly upside down, he replied, "Bizarre, but not at all unpleasant."

Stunting and flying exhibitions aside, the real purpose of his experiments was to *know*. To know just what an aeroplane would do and to know what the pilot should do in any situation. Aerobatics are, after all, insurance. When a gust of wind whips your crate upside down, is it the end? Certainly not. An aviator who has already had the experience of deliberate, *controlled* upside-down flight knows there is nothing simpler than rolling out of an inverted position. Of course, Pégoud did not stop until he had experienced every conceivable position and attitude that he could put the machine, or it could put itself, into.

Pégoud was the star of the day. The Paris newspapers hailed him as a hero. He flew and thrilled spectators from Norway to Italy. In September 1913, at Brooklands aerodrome a few miles southwest of London, he gave a demonstration of calm mastery of the machine. After performing his usual repertoire of stunts he flew by the stands with both hands raised over his head.

He was in Hamburg, prepared to embark with three crated aeroplanes for a tour of America, when "some fool thing in the Balkans" made it imperative that he return to France immediately.

*         *         *

BEFORE THE WAR, Germany, like England, arranged for flying instruction to be given to select military personnel. Regular Army officers were chosen for air observer's and aerial photography courses, and pilots were trained as "chauffeurs." The aviation training was given in civilian schools operated for the most part by established aero-engineers and constructors. At the Halberstadt Aeroplane Works in Halberstadt, for example, Oswald Boelcke learned to fly in the summer of 1914, and at the *Fliegerschule,* or Flying School, operated by the Albatros Works in Berlin, Walter von Teubern took his pilot's training in the autumn of 1913.

In the suburb of Berlin known as Johannisthal was an aerodrome where some of the great firms of German Aviation were located, Albatros, Aviatik, L.V.G., Rumpler. There they maintained their factories and display rooms and gave flying lessons as a side line.

In the autumn of 1913 Pégoud gave an exhibition of stunt flying at Johannisthal that drove the crowds out of their heads. The newspapers reporting on the show informed their readers that man had accomplished feats in the air of which the birds had never dreamed.

One of the spectators at that show was a boy named Theobald von Zastrow, youngest son of Heinrich J. von Zastrow, eighth Baron of Sengerhof in Westphalia. Theobald was born on August 31, 1896, raised on the estate at Sengerhof, and educated at Berlin and at St. Andrew's College near Copenhagen. Taken to see Pégoud at Johannisthal by an older brother, Theobald was so thrilled by the flying that a lifetime interest in aviation was born, and he is today a lively veteran whose vivid recollections and rich fund of souvenirs have contributed much to the writing of this book. Theobald had a cousin named Hellmuth von Zastrow, also interested in aeroplanes, who entered the air service when the war began. Theobald entered the 3rd Guards Regiment of Uhlans as a cadet, switched to the air service at the end of 1916, and, as a Regular Army officer, was trained as an air observer. Between the two of them, the cousins Theobald and Hellmuth knew very nearly the whole experience of the air service, from Eastern Front to Western, from observer to fighter pilot, prisoner of war to the office of the Inspector General for Aviation. Some part of the extraordinary careers of Theobald and Hellmuth will be told at the appropriate time.

At Johannisthal to witness Pégoud's flying exhibition that day was another spectator whose name and career will figure in this account, an enthusiastic young man of Dutch parentage and citizenship named Anthony Herman Gerard Fokker. Fokker operated a flying school at Johannisthal and a small factory at Schwerin in Mecklenburg employing some 50 hands at turning out a series of sport aeroplanes of which he was the designer, but his early fame was to come

*Fokker*

to him as an exhibition pilot. Later, during the war, Fokker was to build some of Germany's finest fighters, but in 1913 he was still the enterprising newcomer who hadn't yet made the big time.

Flying was *the* sport then, and Fokker's flying school was his bread and butter. Poor students and well-heeled bluebloods flocked to the aerodromes, and an occasional crack-up added the spice of danger to what was by its nature an exhilarating sport. Today, when even small and unprepossessing training machines may be spin-proof, closed-cockpit jobs, we feel none of the out-and-out personal challenge to danger that was the reward of flying 50 years ago. The low-powered, cranky machines of the early years are gone now, and few living men can remember when it was a thrill merely to be in an aeroplane.

Fokker watched Pégoud's performance critically. He was good, all right, but Fokker's reaction was not the same as everyone else's. Instead of being overwhelmed, he was stirred by a flood of new ideas. Fokker would do just what Pégoud did, and he would beat him on his own ground—in the air. It was easy to see that Pégoud would be hard to beat. He performed all the standard stunts with terrific flair—vertical banks, split-S's, falling leaves, spins and stalls, and he added ruffles and flourishes of his own. He pulled one at Johannisthal that

10

Fokker had never heard of, a half-loop that ended with a roll-out at the top—
a graceful manoeuvre that was later to be known as the "Immelmann turn."

Well, the Flying Dutchman could do anything that a Frenchman could do.
The show was not so much the spur as the revelation. The spur was Fokker's
ambition, it had always been there; the revelation was that he should stunt himself. What an advertisement. Potential students would be thrilled, not by Pégoud,
but by Fokker himself, and he would stunt in one of his own aeroplanes.
*Wunderbar!* But first he needed a machine that would permit itself to be stunted;
the inherently stable machines he had thus far produced were simply not tractable
enough. Stability, moreover, was not necessarily a virtue, now that such relatively
powerful engines as the 80-horsepower Gnôme rotary were available. Blériot
had crossed the English Channel in 1909 in a monoplane of his own design
pulled by a 35-horsepower Anzani engine. For 1913 the Gnôme offered a lot of
horses, giving the pilot control he had never had before. Fokker would use this
famous engine and build a new aeroplane around it. So was born the M.5, one of
the machines which a year and a half later was to usher in war in the air.

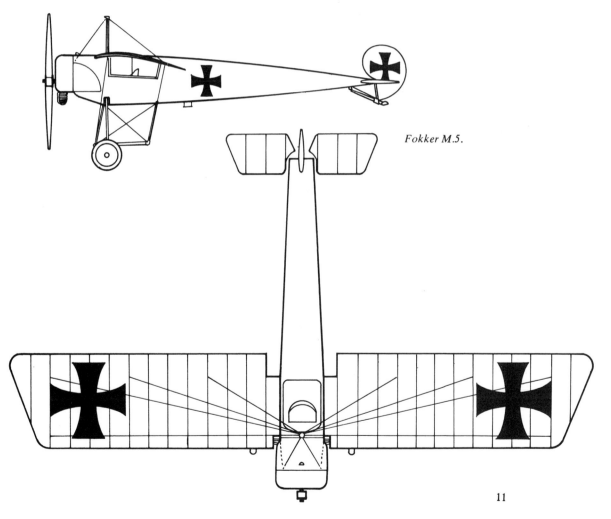

*Fokker M.5.*

11

In layout the new monoplane somewhat resembled the Blériot machine flown by Pégoud, but to its construction Fokker brought a real innovation: the fuselage and wing skeletons were built of welded steel tubing instead of wood. This was eminently characteristic. Fokker usually borrowed ideas, in this case the form of the aeroplane was inspired by the French monoplanes, but he made a stronger aeroplane by using steel tubing. The gifted mechanic could always do something a little better, and in the new M.5, Fokker looped and stunted about Germany, thrilling his audiences, and, what is of particular importance, making a stunning impression on General von Falkenhayn, the Minister of War, who witnessed one of Fokker's flying exhibitions in the spring of 1914.

Fokker's extraordinary flying so moved the newspaper reporters that they called him and his dainty monoplane the "masters of the sky."

\*      \*      \*

BUT THE SKY was dark in the east, the end of the world was near, and there was now no time left for the happy games that had been played in the last bubbly days of peace.

There were no fighter aeroplanes as such and there would not be for some time. But there were fighters. The first man to land at Amiens on the occasion of the RFC fly-over, Lieutenant H. D. Harvey-Kelly of No. 2 Squadron, was flying an observation mission on August 26, 1914, with two other B.E.2a's. Near the front lines the pilots spotted a German reconnaissance machine and impulsively gave chase, banging away at it with pistols. Somehow they forced the machine down and its pilot landed it in a field. As the British machines landed beside it the pilot and observer scrambled out and went tearing for the woods. Lieutenants Harvey-Kelly and Mansfield charged into the woods after them, waving their pistols in the air, but returned in a few minutes hot and out of breath, having been distanced handily by their quarry. They had to be satisfied with setting fire to the enemy aeroplane, a somewhat left-handed victory.

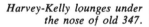

*Harvey-Kelly lounges under the nose of old 347.*

THE AGE OF AIR FIGHTING was inaugurated in the sky near Rheims as the Great War entered its second month.

Joseph Frantz had been flying since 1910, had won his military pilot's certificate (number 363) in January 1911. At the military concourse at Rheims the same year, he piloted a Savary biplane, the engine of which had been constructed by the firm of Labor-Aviation. That company sent a young mechanic named Louis Quénault to attend to the servicing of the engines. Quénault and Frantz formed a team for the duration of the military trials, and in August 1914, when Frantz joined Voisin Squadron 24, then forming, it was arranged that Quénault be attached to the same squadron as mechanic.

The squadron was flying Voisin two-seaters—sturdy, dependable aeroplanes in which the pilot and passenger shared a common cockpit in a bathtub-like nacelle, the pilot in front, the passenger behind him. The air crews flew mostly reconnaissance missions, according to the requirements of the army corps to which they were attached. No weapons were carried in the aeroplanes, other than the customary side arms issued to officers, or the cavalry carbines of the enlisted men. Such weapons as were occasionally taken along were not considered to be of any use in the air, the assigned function of the air services at the time being the gathering of information, not fighting.

The pilots of Voisin Squadron 24 encountered German aeroplanes from time to time, and some of the more daring passengers took pot shots at them, but nothing ever came of it. It was harmless, really, and the commanding officers saw no reason to forbid such high-spirited foolishness so long as it did not interfere with the completion of the business at hand.

Gabriel Voisin, of the Voisin Aeroplane Company, and *Capitaine* André Faure, the commander of no. 24, without asking anyone else's opinion or advice, decided to arm the machines of Faure's squadron because it seemed obvious to them, if to no one else, that an aeroplane equipped with a machine gun could shoot down another aeroplane. Why not? The Voisin was a pusher, with its engine in the back. The passenger had a clear field of fire before him, and a machine gun mounted on a tripod would be just about as steady as it would be on the ground. Voisin, in fact, had already improvised a mounting that could be fitted to his aeroplanes. It was a simple tubular affair, the apex of which was over the pilot's head, so that the butt of the gun would be convenient to the passenger who would stand on his seat to shoot. Voisin made a trip to the Hotchkiss armory, and signed for twelve Hotchkiss clip-fed machine guns. He did not, however, sign his own name; he borrowed for this signature the name of General Bernard, who at that time was Director of Military Aviation at French Army Headquarters. The Hotchkiss was chosen because it was reasonably dependable and because it was light in weight.

From the beginning of September 1914 the Voisins of Faure's squadron were armed. In the next few weeks, Frantz and Quénault met German aeroplanes a dozen times but either were unable to get close enough to shoot, or were off their aim. At any rate, no decisive result was achieved. They were determined to succeed, however, and spent much time discussing just how to proceed.

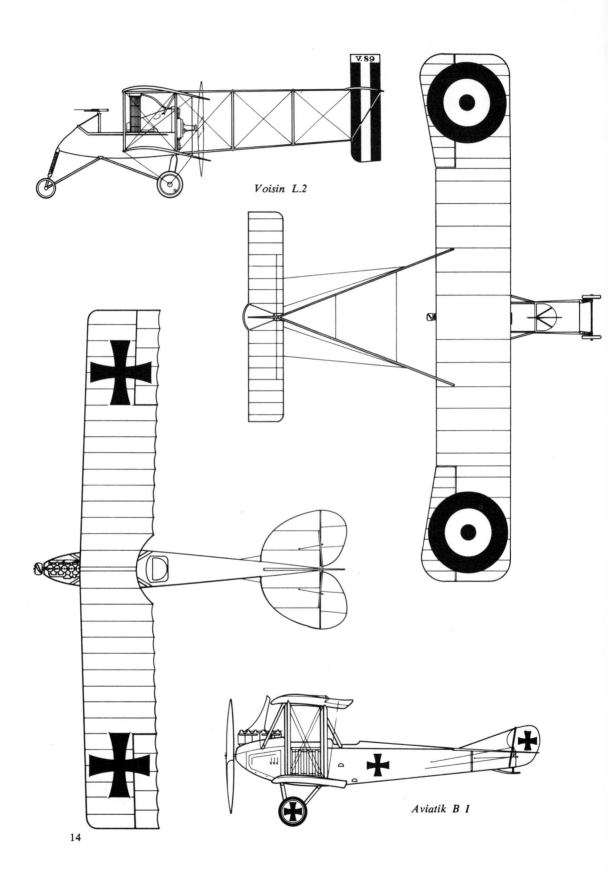

V. 89

Voisin L.2

Aviatik B I

14

On October 5, *Capitaine* Faure sent them on a mission to the region of Rheims where they were to drop six ninety-millimetre artillery shells on enemy troop concentrations. Over the Vesle near Jonchéry, Frantz spotted an Aviatik two-seater returning to the German lines. In his own words, Monsieur Frantz has described the event:

"The Aviatik and, moreover, all German aeroplanes had a fuselage in the fore part of which was the motor and the propeller.

"From this we easily drew some conclusions. It was necessary to attack from the rear, a manoeuvre become classic from the very first combat.

"I therefore dived to cut off the retreat of the Aviatik and manoeuvred to place myself behind the enemy.

"The manoeuvre completed, we had approached to a point at which we could distinguish clearly the movements of the pilot and his passenger.

"At this moment, the man in the front seat, the passenger, shouldered a repeating carbine and opened fire on our machine. The pilot and the tail assembly visibly disturbed his aim, completely masking our position.

"Quénault then opened fire, shooting ahead of him, over my head.

"The Hotchkiss, well steadied by the tripod, was easy enough to manoeuvre, but was subject to stoppages when fired fully automatic.

"We had therefore decided to shoot one round at a time. Quénault fired one by one forty-seven rounds—at the forty-eighth the gun jammed. Quénault, whose composure was astounding, commenced to strip the receiver to clear the jam, when the German lurched before our eyes, began to dive, then turned on its back in its descent and smashed into the ground in a cloud of black smoke."

Witnesses from the ground who had followed the encounter ran to the spot where the aeroplane had gone down. It had landed in a wood beside a small pond, in a marshy bit of ground where the motor had almost completely buried itself. The pilot lay perhaps ten feet away from the twisted fuselage, among shattered fragments of the wings which were scattered about. He had been killed by Quénault's fire and the aeroplane had then fallen out of control bearing the observer to his death. The latter was in his final convulsions when the witnesses came up, and one of them carried away a vivid recollection of how his well-tended hands clawed at the earth.

Frantz and Quénault had landed nearby, and now came up to view their work. An automobile arrived and General Franchet d'Esperey alighted to congratulate them. "I will give you the *Médaille militaire*," he said to Frantz.

"I already have it, *mon Général*," said Frantz.

"Then I will make you *Chevalier* of the *Légion d'Honneur* and award the *Médaille militaire* to your mechanic."

As the other witnesses crowded around to shake their hands, an old woman came out of the wood to offer them bunches of flowers she had gathered.

---

Joseph Frantz, who was born August 7, 1890, at Beaujeu (Rhône), survived the war, serving as chief test pilot for the Voisin company from 1916 to 1918. He is the founder and President of the *Société L'Electrolyse Frantz* and a member and co-founder of the *Vieilles Tiges,* an association of pioneer aviators. He still flies, having recently completed a Mediterranean trip with Madame Frantz in a Jodel two-seater.

GRUDZIADZ IS A TOWN on the Vistula in the old Polish province of Pomorze. It was founded by the Teutonic Knights in the thirteenth century, came under the rule of Poland in 1466 by the Peace of Thorn, and was seized by Prussia in 1772 at the first partition of Poland. It was called Graudenz in German. In 1807 the city and fortress of Graudenz, under the command of General von Courbière, was the only Prussian stronghold that would not capitulate to Napoleon.

Throughout the nineteenth century a fortress—*Festung*—was developed at each of seven fortress towns ringing Germany: Strasbourg, Metz, and Cologne in the Rhineland, Posen in the east, and Königsberg, Lotzen, and Graudenz in the north to secure the enclave of East Prussia. When aeroplanes made their appearance in the first years of the twentieth century, they were grudgingly accepted by the Imperial Staff and the establishment for the fortresses was expanded to include a permanent complement of four two-seaters for each *Festung*. These "fortress squadrons" were called *Festungsfliegerabteilungen,* or Fortress Flying Sections.

Graudenz received its first four aeroplanes in due course, with an enlisted man as pilot for each one and four regular army officers to act as observers. Gradually the flying facilities there were expanded until Graudenz became a major air station for the *Fliegertruppen,* or Flying Troops, the collective name for German air personnel.

*Hellmuth von Zastrow*

By the spring of 1915 the *Fliegertruppen* had grown enough to require the establishment of eleven flight training schools. These were called *Fliegerersatzabteilungen,* or Flying Replacement Sections. Taking the initials of the three words in that impressive compound, *Fliegerersatzabteilung,* a standard abbreviation— *F.E.A.*—was obtained. *F.E.A. 2* was created at Graudenz.

On December 15, 1914, Hellmuth von Zastrow was sent to Graudenz as a pilot with the *Festungsfliegerabteilung* while his father, General Ernst von Zastrow, was in command of the fortress itself. Hellmuth was born in Berlin on November 15, 1890, was raised there and entered the Berlin Realgymnasium in 1910. On September 1, 1914, he entered *Flieger-Bataillon Nr. 1* at Berlin-Döberitz and won his pilot's certificate on October 23. From there he went to Graudenz. On January 19, 1915, Hellmuth made his first flight over the enemy lines on the Eastern Front during the battles at Prasnysz-Ciechanow and Narew. In February 1915 he was commissioned a *Leutnant* and awarded the Iron Cross Second Class in recognition of his arduous flying.

There was a bit of folklore about Hellmuth in the *Fliegertruppen* to the effect that he should have been awarded the Iron Cross for having almost wrecked an aeroplane during training. An altimeter had been installed in his aeroplane by a representative of the manufacturer, and great were the claims made for this marvel of aeronautical instrument technology. Hellmuth, more than a little skeptical, took off to test the new altimeter. "Just keep your eye on that instrument," he had been told. He did as he was bidden and at the end of his flight, brought his ship in to a harsh landing, bounced hard, and rolled to a stop. The

commandant was on his neck immediately. "What the devil were you trying to do, von Zastrow, wreck that machine?" For answer, Hellmuth pointed to the jammed altimeter. According to it, he was still six hundred feet off the ground.

There was a spring of ironic humor in Hellmuth that bubbled to the surface during the cruel years of the war. Possibly Hellmuth was already thinking about a project that was to become very much a part of him, an expression of a sense he shared with Scaramouche "that the world was mad." The project was a series of poems, parodies of the verse of Christian Morgenstern, whose logical improbabilities seem to widen rather than bridge the gap between the romantic nineteenth and the incredible twentieth century.

In the spring of 1915 Hellmuth had little time for reading, and the project waited a year before he was able to devote any time to it. In May 1915 he was transferred to Champagne in France where he served as a pilot in *Fliegerabteilung 60* attached to the Crown Prince's Fifth Army.

A few months earlier, another young officer had been transferred from the Eastern to the Western Front to serve in the Fifth Army, but that young officer had not yet won any medals, nor had he ever given a thought to flying.

Manfred *Freiherr* von Richthofen was a young lieutenant of cavalry when war was declared in 1914. He was an old man not quite twenty-six when he was killed the third Sunday after Easter, April 21, 1918.

The name Richthofen means court of justice and is a kind of title deriving from ancestors who had been councillors, judges and mayors in Silesia since the seventeenth century. Leopold I had granted the family its patent of nobility and Frederick the Great had bestowed upon the males the title of *Freiherr,* or Baron.

Manfred was born on May 2, 1892, the son of Albrecht von Richthofen, a professional soldier. As a child he was small but possessed of a robust constitution and sturdy vitality. He was fond of horses, guns and dogs. At the age of eleven he was sent to the military academy at Wahlstatt. It was customary in most old Prussian families for the oldest son to become a cadet, and Albrecht wanted his son to follow in his footsteps. From Wahlstatt, Manfred went to the Royal Military Academy at Lichterfelde, and from Lichterfelde to the Berlin War Academy, whence he was graduated in the spring of 1911 at the age of 19. He won his lieutenancy in the fall of 1912 with the First Regiment of Uhlans.

At no point had he been consulted as to his own choice in the matter of a career. Not that there was ever any question of his doing as he was bidden, but he was not too keen on the military. He had an idea of what military discipline could be like before he ever experienced it, and he had a strong individualism in his make-up that promised to make such discipline a trial. On the other hand, when the trial came, Manfred found a strength of character that was capable of imposing a more stern discipline from the inside than the Prussians could apply from without. Self-mastery was his chief attribute—he could have walked on fire if he had put his mind to it.

17

Stationed in home country near Breslau in Silesia, von Richthofen spent two years with the Uhlans riding and hunting. In 1913 he entered the Imperial Cross-Country Race for officers. Galloping across an open stretch of meadow, his mount put her foot in a rabbit hole and Manfred took a terrific spill. With agony in one shoulder he remounted and continued the race, which he won. He then submitted himself to a doctor. The medical examination revealed that he had a broken collarbone; the race revealed that he had grit.

When the war began he was sent first to Kielce in Poland, 150 miles east of Breslau, but within two weeks was transferred to the Western Front to be attached to the Crown Prince's Fifth Army in the Ardennes. There he had his first brush with the enemy.

The French, wearing their famous pre-war red pantaloons, had advanced in close order and had been mowed down by the Germans. The Crown Prince called up the cavalry to reconnoitre the enemy's new positions. This was the fundamental tactical role of the cavalry and the simplest, most direct way to execute it was to draw the enemy's fire.

Manfred rode forward with his squadron and scanned the terrain. It was hilly, rolling country with wooded ravines and naked upland wastes. Not the kind of country one would ride into without keeping an eye peeled. The eager young Uhlans made that omission for they ran straight into an ambush. It was probably a spur-of-the-moment affair else none of them would have survived. The lead men pulled up short at a barricade on a forest path and took the first shots from a concealed body of riflemen. Several men and horses fell and Manfred wheeled his mount around and signaled for his men to close up and follow him out.

"They certainly had surprised us," he admitted ruefully.

He rode a number of similar missions after that, but the stabilization of the Front put an end to the tactical use of mounted troops and the cavalry officers were assigned to new duties. To his disgust Manfred became a supply officer; he chafed at rear-echelon inactivity. He was afraid that the war would be over before he could get back into it, and he was envious of his younger brother Lothar who seemed to be in the thick of it. The war dragged on, however, and he began to consider transferring to some other branch of the service in the hope that this would bring him back into action. At the end of May 1915, his application for transfer into the flying service was approved and he was accepted as one of 30 officers to be detached for training at Cologne with *Fliegerersatzabteilung Nr. 7*.

*     *     *

THE AVIATION FIRM of Morane-Saulnier, at Villacoublay near Paris, was famous before the war for a classy series of sport monoplanes. A number of honors was won for the company by Roland Garros, a well-known pre-war aviator, who had established the world altitude record in December 1912, and had been the first man to fly across the Mediterranean Sea, in September 1913. He was a wealthy, polished man of the world, a piano virtuoso, and an exhibition pilot of superlative skill.

Roland Garros and the Morane-Saulnier "N" monoplane were a splendid team.

The Morane machines were a racy-looking family and the "N" was no exception. With a top speed of 100 miles an hour and an ability to climb to 10,000 feet in 12 minutes flat, it was also a racy performer. It required competent handling because it had a high landing speed and, owing to the absence of horizontal stabilizing surface in the tail, was extremely sensitive on the controls. Roland Garros, with his pianist's hands, was sensitive, was capable of handling the most cranky aeroplane. And when war came was capable of killing.

In May 1914 Raymond Saulnier had written a letter to the Inspector-General for Air outlining his conception for an armed single-seat aeroplane. It was an original idea since nothing like that existed in the air service of any country, but it failed to evoke even a flicker of interest in the War Office. Those charged with preparing for war care only for peace—which is either praise or condemnation, and one is unwilling to say which. In any event the letter went unanswered and the project received no government backing until the shooting started. Saulnier had had the idea that a Hotchkiss clip-fed machine gun could be affixed to the aeroplane within reach of the pilot so that he would be able to reload it and clear it if it jammed. He had first tried to synchronize the rate of fire of the gun with the rate of revolutions of the propeller, but soon found that the engine speed could not be controlled precisely enough—it was always speeding up or slowing down that minute degree which would throw the whole works out of whack. So he tried armoring the propeller. At this point, Garros took over.

Garros had offered his services to the *Service d'Aéronautique* when the war began and had been assigned to M-S 23, commanded by *Capitaine* Vergnette. French squadrons—*escadrilles*—were identified throughout the war by equipment and serial number. Thus M-S 23 was *escadrille* 23 which at that time was flying Morane machines.

On August 16, 1914, Garros made his first flight up to the lines. Missions consisted of observation, photography, and the dropping of either hand grenades or *fléchettes* on enemy troop concentrations. The *fléchette* was a primitive missile, a barbed steel dart, packed in boxes and dumped over the side wherever targets seemed to offer themselves in appropriate clusters.

The victory of Frantz and Quénault sparked his imagination and when Raymond Saulnier wrote to him about the idea for an armed single-seater Garros immediately obtained permission from his commander to report to Villacoublay and work with Saulnier on the new weapon. He arrived in November and by the end of January 1915 had perfected a workable "deflector gear." The technique was simplicity itself: a machine gun was bolted to the fuselage of the aeroplane, butt end extending into the cockpit within easy reach of the pilot. Directly in front of the muzzle of the gun, which fired straight forward along the line of flight, steel wedges were affixed to the rear face of the propeller, a wedge for each blade. The wedges presented their points to the muzzle and so deflected any bullets

*Roland Garros*

that struck the propeller. It was estimated that fewer than ten per cent of the bullets would strike the propeller. If it is accepted that the most useful direction of fire in a chase context is straight ahead, then it will be seen that the major problem of an accessible gun firing through the propeller had been solved.

*        *        *

A NEW WEAPON, the fighter, had been forged. Until it was wielded with killing intent, however, the sky was relatively peaceful. A few aviators carried weapons with them when they flew, but they were the exception. In the German air service *Leutnant* Wilhelm Siegert, later Inspector of Flying Troops, carried a carbine with a gramophone horn nailed to the stock—"so that in the event of meeting an enemy I might at least dismay and terrify him with its illusory calibre."

*        *        *

AIR-FIGHTING as a tactical practice was still not foreseen. Or not so much not foreseen as not given more than the briefest consideration. Until the war was going into its fourth month everyone had thought it would be over in three and the air would be superfluous because the battles and the war would be won on the ground.

There was work to be done, of course, but the military staffs did not expect that the aeroplane would ever replace the cavalryman's horse as a means of getting observers out and back. The aeroplane was not considered a weapon in itself any more than the horse was.

The casual armament that was carried in aeroplanes was more for defense in the event of a forced-landing behind the lines than for offensive action in the air. The observers, being usually officers, had their own side arms such as automatic or machine pistols which they carried with them while flying, and the enlisted men were regularly issued carbines. With improvised mountings like that in the Voisin of Frantz and Quénault even machine guns might be taken along. But it was common for crews to fly with no armament at all.

The French were of two minds about the war. Some thought it grand sport, but most were serious about it. After all, the war was being fought in home country. The British, many of them, regarded it as a grotesque and colossal joke. Britain was as usual safely insulated by the Channel. It's a pretty big difference. The Germans were impelled by duty, *Vaterland, Lebensraum* and other large ideas.

All of the airmen had this in common: they flew because it interested them, all were volunteers, and they craved excitement. They were young.

Flying was exciting and different, with or without a war, and many pilots and observers felt a comradeship with enemy airmen. In late 1914 and early 1915 it was still a lark to take along a rifle and have a sporting shot at any opposite numbers one might come across. No one expected to get hurt, no one seriously expected to shoot anyone down. When, on occasion, it chanced that unarmed crews should meet, they could fire colored signal flares at each other.

*        *        *

TWINS JEAN AND PIERRE NAVARRE were born August 8, 1895, at Jouy-sur-Morin (Seine-et-Marne). Jean was fascinated by aeroplanes as a boy and when he was called up at Mobilization he applied for aviation training. Although they had been inseparable as boys, Jean and Pierre went separate ways in the army, Jean to the *Service d'Aéronautique,* Pierre to the *Génie,* or Army Engineers.

Jean was brevetted a pilot in September 1914 and sent to MF 8, a squadron equipped with Maurice Farman machines. The squadron, based near Amiens, was one of the first to see action in the war, and the early exploits of its members were legendary. There was Poinsard, the iron man, who flew back to the base after having been shot clean through the body; there was Perrin de Brichambaut, one of the earliest Aces; there was Sallier, who was shot down in flames, but who managed to destroy his papers before crashing. It was Poinsard who first led Navarre up to the lines.

The first time he ever saw a *Boche,* in December 1914, Navarre was flying alone. The German was flying alone too, and he flew up alongside Navarre and waved. Navarre waved back and then snatched up his carbine, letting go of the controls. He threw a shot at the other man who quickly dived away. The Farman lurched up toward a stall and Navarre dropped the carbine and grabbed the controls. As he continued his flight, his thoughts were abstracted. When he landed back at base he had made up his mind that he must fight. To fly was not enough—one must fly *and fight.* There was a war on.

He immediately requested a transfer to a Morane squadron, for the trim and speedy Moranes were enjoying a reputation as the best machines at the Front. The request was refused because the commander of the squadron did not feel he could spare any pilots. Navarre persisted until the commander tired of his importunities and decided that there was, indeed, one man he could spare. Navarre was sent to the rear and a citation for which he had been named was suppressed.

He was ordered to report to St-Cyr for reassignment and he decided to make his own luck. When he presented himself to the *capitaine* he lied his way into a Morane squadron, figuring that the truth would not catch up with him until he had had a chance to prove himself and he might as well let the red tape work for him instead of against him.

"Ah-ha!" said the *capitaine,* "you have been kicked out of your *escadrille?*"

"I, *mon capitaine?* (with perfect innocence) You must be mistaken. I was proposed for a citation. I have, on the contrary, applied for a transfer to a Morane squadron and have been accepted by the Director of Army Aviation. So here I am."

"Impossible. You come from a Farman squadron and you want to be transferred to Moranes? My poor boy . . ."

"You forget, *mon capitaine,* that for three years in Chile and Argentina I flew every kind of crate. Because there was such a need for Farman pilots I hurried back to offer my services, but I was faithfully promised a transfer to Moranes at the first opportunity."

"Er, well . . . that is, of course, different . . ."

And that, either because the *capitaine* was convinced or indifferent, was that.

22

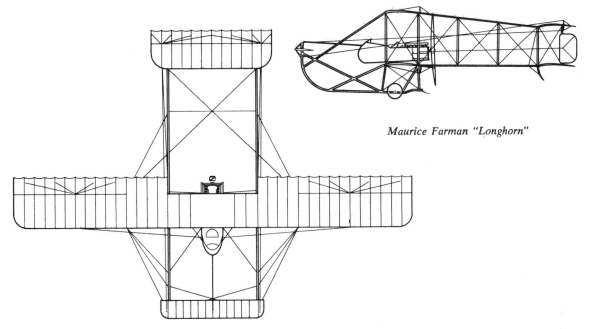

*Maurice Farman "Longhorn"*

Commanding the Morane-Saulnier division at Villacoublay was a professional soldier from the artillery, *Capitaine* Le Révérend, who was known to be as good a judge of men as he was of machines. Largely through his good reports to French Army Headquarters (*Grand Quartier Général,* hereafter GQG) the Chief of Aviation, *Colonel* Barès, had urged the formation of additional Morane-Saulnier *escadrilles* for all army corps. Navarre had staged his pardonable deception at the opportune moment when more M-S pilots were needed.

Sent to the M-S division at Villacoublay to take the usual conversion course (a spot of special instruction is *de rigueur* when one switches from a moving van to a racer), Navarre soon came to the attention of *Capitaine* Le Révérend. Le Révérend's keen intuition told him that Navarre could be a great pilot and he insisted on passing him through against the opposition of the instructor who predicted glumly that Navarre would never achieve anything but to break his own neck because he was over-confident and over-eager. For all his close calls, Navarre didn't break so much as a wire during training. He had a feel for the aeroplane, and when his rash enthusiasm got him into a jam he always managed to find the right thing to do and so lived to make more mistakes and profit by them.

Assigned to M-S 12 at Muizon near Rheims, Navarre bid adieu to Villacoublay with an exhibition of stunting. The new squadron, commanded by *Capitaine* P. de Bernis, flew Morane-Saulnier *parasols* on photography and reconnaissance missions. The *parasol* was so named because the wing, supported by struts, shaded the front seat like a parasol.

By April 1915 Navarre had won the *Médaille militaire* for two confirmed victories and had established a reputation as a stunter among the infantry of the sector. The *poilus* watched for Navarre because he never failed to put on a little stunting show over the trenches.

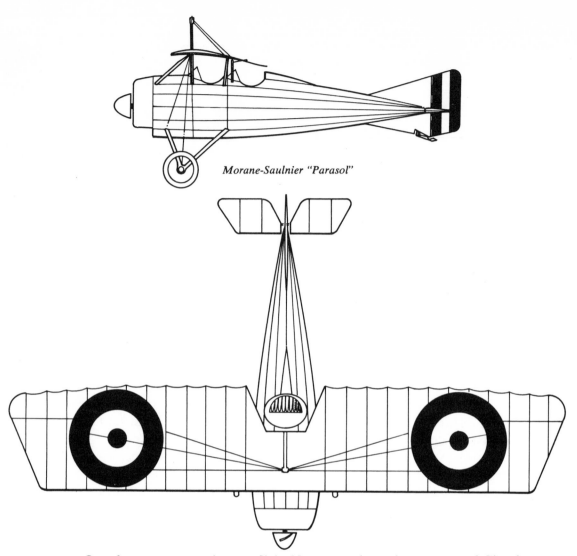

*Morane-Saulnier "Parasol"*

One day on a reconnaissance flight Navarre and an observer named Girard espied another *parasol* harrying two German machines. The French pilot, Pégoud, as it happened, had run out of ammunition and was unable to do more than worry the Germans. Girard stood up in his seat and fired a hand-held Hotchkiss machine gun over the wing while Navarre banged away with a pistol. The motor of the nearer Aviatik was hit and it died, sputtering. The pilot tried to get away by diving. He might have been able to coast to the German lines because he had built up a good turn of speed in the dive, but he pulled out too low over the French trenches and the *poilus* opened up with a fusillade that brought him down for keeps. Navarre turned for the second without following the first one down, but that one had already gotten away by diving.

Navarre and Girard almost shot themselves down, for Girard, in his excitement, had accidentally put a couple of shots through the blades of the propeller which was now vibrating badly. They force-landed at Sainte-Menehould.

＊　　　　　　＊　　　　　　＊

AS A LEADER, an innovator, and an inspiration to his men, one of the great aviators of the war was a Saxon named Oswald Boelcke. He was born in Giebichenstein near Halle on May 9, 1891, and gained his army commission by way of the Prussian Cadet Corps. He first witnessed military aviation before the war while on manoeuvres, and, his interest aroused, applied for flying training. He was accepted and sent to the Halberstadt Flying School, where he obtained his pilot's certificate two weeks after the outbreak of the war, on August 15, 1914.

In September Boelcke reported to a squadron on active service in the field, one in which his brother Wilhelm, a Regular Army officer, was serving as an observer. For the next few months the brothers flew regularly as a team, Oswald as the chauffeur.

The squadron in which the brothers flew was one of 30 German and four Bavarian units of which the German air service's field strength was composed. The equipment for each squadron was six machines, uniformly biplane two-seaters with 100 horsepower motors. They were regularly issued without armament. The squadrons were ancillary to the usual Army Corps service units and were called simply Flying Sections—*Fliegerabteilungen.* (Or Field Flying Sections—*Feld Fliegerabteilungen.*) These six-machine *Fliegerabteilungen* were under the command of an *Inspekteur* or Director at Corps level, and were completely subservient to Army Corps commanders. Their work was reconnaissance, observation, artillery-spotting, photography, and liaison. The latter was pretty simple. It consisted chiefly of shooting pre-arranged signal flares or dropping messages so that ground units could more or less keep in touch with one another.

For the first year of the war all the air services had the same jobs, worked out on manoeuvres before the war, and no improvisation was allowed.

Reconnaissance flights were those whose object was to spy out new developments on the other side of the line; observation and photography were methods of keeping those developments under surveillance. Spotting for artillery meant signalling battery commanders, either visually or by wireless, exactly where their shots were falling. It meant circling one spot for an hour or so, bored and frightened to death, keeping a watch on the shoot and reporting every shot so the gunners would know if they were putting them over or short, waiting for the anti-aircraft guns to blow you to bits. It was the dullest, most dangerous work in the air.

After the war had gone on long enough for everyone to realize it was not going to be over "by Christmas" because Christmas was already past, the air services began expanding. In April 1915 Oswald Boelcke was selected, because of his experience, to help shape up a new Flying Section, *Fliegerabteilung 62,* and get it operational. Boelcke had been awarded the Iron Cross First Class in February 1915 for having completed fifty observation missions, which was very nearly a record.

The standard aeroplanes in use in the German air service up to the spring of 1915 were two-seater biplanes of the "B" class, the Albatros, Aviatik, and L.V.G. being among the more common. These machines had proved their value for observation and artillery-spotting, but were unable to defend themselves.

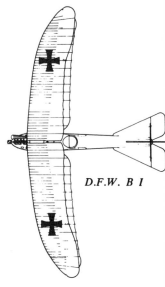

*D.F.W. B I*

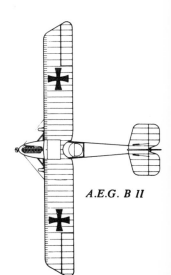

*A.E.G. B II*

25

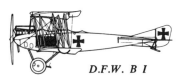

*D.F.W. B I*

*A.E.G. B II*

*Pilot and observer/gunner in Halberstadt CL II, the observer armed with Parabellum. Empty cartridge tape is seen dangling from left side of gun.*

*Twin Lewis gun armament for observer in an R.E.8.*

French pilots chauffeuring armed observers in such handy machines as the Morane-Saulnier *parasol* had created a serious problem for the Germans, forcing the establishment of a new class of machine—the "C" two-seater. This new class was basically the same as the "B" class, but there were three significant improvements. The horsepower was upped to a rating of at least 150, the pilot and passenger traded seats, and a Parabellum machine gun was made standard equipment. The pilot, now seated in the front, enjoyed an improved view uninterrupted by the observer's form, and the latter, in the rear, had some room to swing his Parabellum about.

A word here about that terrifying American invention, the machine gun. Richard Jordan Gatling of North Carolina developed his famous "Gatling gun" in 1862. It saw some use in the Civil War. Its action depended on a hand crank, so it was not a true machine gun, but it was the first successful rapid-fire weapon to use a self-contained metallic cartridge. The modern machine gun utilizes the energy of the expanding combustion gas in the barrel—the "kick." It remained for Benjamin Hotchkiss (1826–1885) of Connecticut, Hiram Maxim (1840–1916) of Maine, John Moses Browning (1855–1926) of Utah, and Isaac Newton Lewis, West Point class of '84, to develop guns in which the recoil energy was harnessed and made to do the job of reloading and firing again in a fully automatic fashion. Most standard machine guns were either designed by these men or based on their designs.

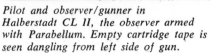

*Hotchkiss*

The Hotchkiss was a smallish weapon, not much larger than a rifle, and was part of the regular equipment of the French and Belgian infantries. It was fed from a rigid spring-loaded clip holding 25 cartridges. It was the first machine gun in the air, being used by Frantz and Quénault and by Roland Garros in the first armed single-seater. The Browning weapons were used mostly by the infantry and had only a very limited application in the air service.

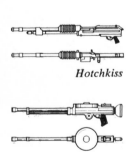

*Lewis (shown with and without water jacket).*

From the point of view of the development of fighter aviation the major weapons are the Lewis and the Maxim. Colonel Lewis patented the gas-operated gun that bears his name in 1911. It was fed from a round, flat drum that rotated as the gun was fired. The cartridges arranged radially inside the drum were driven into the firing chamber by spring-action. It was a light-weight, reliable weapon. In 1916 its capacity was doubled by the development of a larger drum. The Lewis, like most machine guns, was amenable to the attachment of muzzle dampers that retarded the escape of combustion gas and so speeded up the rate of fire.

26

The Maxim gun was manufactured in England by Vickers' Sons and Maxim, Limited, and was known as a Vickers gun. The same gun was manufactured under license by the German Weapons and Munitions Factory, a state arsenal at Spandau, Berlin, and was known as a Spandau gun. A light version of the gun was developed by the Germans for the use of aerial gunners and known as a Parabellum (literally "for war;" from the Latin motto, *Si vis pacem, para bellum*—"If you wish for peace, prepare for war"). The Maxim in all its aviation forms was an air-cooled, belt-fed weapon. The belts were initially made of canvas, but were unsatisfactory because they caused jams when they twisted in the slip-stream or distorted in damp weather. The problem of fool-proof feed was eventually solved by two refinements: the enclosed track and the disintegrating link belt. The former protected the belt against deformation by the slip-stream and the latter, being composed of flat, stamped metal loops, was indifferent to atmospheric conditions.

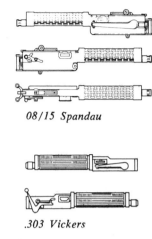

*08/15 Spandau*

*.303 Vickers*

While the Germans armed the big two-seaters purely as a defensive measure, men like Oswald Boelcke were determined to exploit the offensive possibilities of the new arrangement. Instead of being content to fire a shot or two at any enemy aeroplanes that came nosing around in the hope of scaring them off, the born hunters went after them, jockeying the machines about to give the observers a clear shot.

On a number of different occasions during the spring and summer of 1915, Boelcke, flying out of the aerodrome at Douai with various observer-gunners, had offered combat to enemy aeroplanes but had not achieved any decisive result. In July he finally managed to bring off one of Germany's first aerial victories, albeit not *the* first.

Flying an Albatros C I with an observer named *Leutnant* von Wuehlisch, he spotted a Morane *parasol* over Liétard. Boelcke made a pass at the Morane, and the two aeroplanes danced around each other to Valenciennes where Boelcke managed to put his machine into a good position for von Wuehlisch to tear off a burst. The *parasol* heeled over and fell toward a wood, both of its French occupants dead in their seats. The German aviators watched their victim flutter down and disappear amongst the trees, not knowing the ironic conditions of their victory. Many Frenchmen died in sight of their own homes, or in sight of the wreckage that had been their homes. The wood into which the *parasol* had fallen was part of the estate of the *Comte* de Beauvricourt; the observer in the *parasol* had been the *comte* himself.

This was Boelcke's only victory in a two-seater. At the end of May the first two machines of a new one-winger called the Fokker E I had been demonstrated near Verdun, and because Boelcke had already had some experience with Fokker monoplanes, two of the new models were delivered to him at Douai for operational assessment.

But that's another story.

＊　　　　　＊　　　　　＊

*Ehrhardt von Teubern*

*Target practice.
From right to left: Immelmann, von Teubern, Porr, Boelcke, von Wuehlisch, and at the gun, Hauptmann Ritter.*

27

IN FEBRUARY OF 1915 Roland Garros reported back to M-S 23 from Villacoublay with his armed single-seater. For several weeks he flew on the variety of missions that was usual before the days of specialization, but he never got a crack at a *Boche*. The air is a big place and it would be a mistake to suppose that aviators encountered enemy machines every time they went up.

On the first day of April Garros took off alone with 200 pounds of bombs to drop on the railroad station at Ostend. At a point several miles on the other side of the lines he caught sight of a German two-seater that was flying more or less directly over the French lines and drawing the fire of the French anti-aircraft batteries. The enemy machine, an Aviatik, was some 1500 feet above him so Garros immediately began to climb to put himself on the same level. Since he was in a position to cut off the retreat of the Aviatik, Garros allowed himself a considerable length of time—six or eight minutes—to manoeuvre into position. Judging himself to be well placed he rushed straight in. At a range of about one hundred feet he fired. The observer in the two-seater answered with a rifle. Garros fired off the 25-round Hotchkiss clip and quickly reloaded, firing off another clip. The Aviatik dived away, but Garros clung to its tail. As the two machines descended to perhaps 3000 feet Garros closed up and triggered a very short burst from his third clip. The Aviatik suddenly caught fire. An immense flame enveloped it and it fell spinning toward the earth.

"It was tragic, frightful," wrote Garros. "At the end of perhaps 25 seconds (which seemed long) of falling, the machine dashed into the ground in a great cloud of smoke."

In his own words the episode ends on a note of shocked horror: "I went by car to see the wreck; those first on the scene had pilfered souvenirs—side arms, insignia, and the like. I took energetic steps to retrieve them. The two corpses were in a horrible state—naked and bloody! The observer had been shot through the head. The pilot was too horribly mutilated to be examined. The remains of the aeroplane were pierced everywhere with bullet holes . . ."

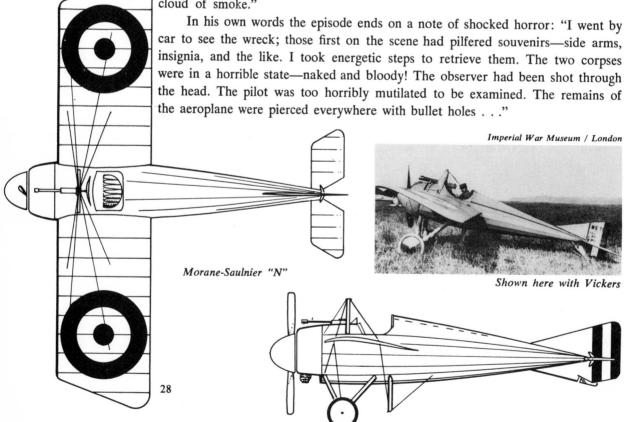

*Imperial War Museum / London*

*Morane-Saulnier "N"*

*Shown here with Vickers*

28

IN THE SAME MONTH, April 1915, in contrast to the grim and terrible experience of Garros, a young man named Fonck knew the clean and innocent joy that flying gives to those who are young enough to have no thought for the future; who fly to fight only the elements, conquer only the air, kill only distance.

Paul-René Fonck made his debut on a Penguin *rouleur* at Le Crotoy the first day of April. The stench of gasoline, castor oil, and aircraft dope was intoxication; the rackety noise of the engines, delight; and for a youth four days past his twenty-first birthday, the knowledge that he would fly was the realization of a dream. As a boy, Fonck had followed the pre-war careers of Pégoud and Garros, and when he soloed about the middle of April the world was no longer big enough for him, for he had seen the stretch of the sky.

AT ABOUT THE TIME that Hellmuth von Zastrow arrived at *Flieger-Batallion Nr. 1* at Berlin-Döberitz, one of the old-timers of the German air service left. This old-timer was about 25 years old, and had served in the *Fliegertruppen* since its inception in 1912. He was a member of an old Saxon military family named von Teubern, and he, Walter von Teubern, had served for some time in the Royal Saxon Light Artillery Regiment Nr. 19 when he was selected for training as an air observer. After completing his special instruction he was assigned to *Festungs-fliegerabteilung Metz,* where he served from June to September 1913. In October he reported to the Albatros Works Flying School at Johannisthal for flying lessons. Learning to fly was Walter's dream and he was delighted with his orders. He soloed in November 1913 and from then to the outbreak of the war served as a pilot in *Flieger-Batallion Nr. 1.*

In February 1914 Walter gave his brother Ehrhardt his first ride in an aeroplane. That aeroplane ride was the big step in Ehrhardt's career, for he became so enthusiastic about flying that he soon decided to make it his profession.

(Both brothers are retired Lieutenant Colonels today, and have served in the German air service for the better part of half a century.)

At the outbreak of the war Walter von Teubern returned to the field in *Fliegerabteilung 29.* Ehrhardt impatiently waited for his transfer to the air service.

Ehrhardt von Teubern was born on February 23, 1890, in Geising, Saxony, where his father was serving as a customs control officer. He was raised in Chemnitz and attended the Realgymnasium there. In October 1904 he entered the Royal Saxon Cadet Corps in Dresden where he met and became friends with a young man named Max Immelmann. Together Ehrhardt and Max passed the happy years at the Cadet Corps, true comrades, and graduated at Easter 1911. Ehrhardt entered the Royal Prussian Infantry Regiment Second Posen Nr. 19 von Courbière. It was while serving with the von Courbière regiment at Berlin that Ehrhardt had the chance to take a ride with his brother Walter and so became enthusiastic about flying. Max Immelmann resigned from the army to enter the Technical College in Dresden, since he had decided he wanted to be an engineer.

At the beginning of 1915 Ehrhardt got his wish and was transferred to the *Fliegertruppen,* taking his air observer's training at Elsenmühle. He was assigned to a new field squadron, *Fliegerabteilung 62,* then in the process of forming up at Berlin-Döberitz. In March 1915 *Fl. Abt. 62* went to the Front, to Douai in northern France. In May Max Immelmann joined Oswald Boelcke and Ehrhardt von Teubern there.

When Max Immelmann joined *Fl. Abt. 62* the morale of some German air service men was low. The victories of Garros had inspired some extravagant rumors, so that before he had been up to the lines once Immelmann had heard all manner of "horror tales." But young Max was indifferent to rumor. He knew that in the army you believe nothing of what you hear and half of what you see. He was sensible, confident . . . and inexperienced. Certainly, until he had seen the war for himself, nobody else's stories were going to worry him.

Immelmann had been born in Dresden, September 21, 1890. At outbreak of war he had reported to his regiment but had been disappointed to learn that his unit was not scheduled to be moved immediately to the Front, so had applied for aviation duty because aeroplanes appealed to his mechanical proclivities. He was accepted for pilot training in late 1914, and passed his flight tests in early 1915. When he reported to Douai and *Fl. Abt. 62* he was still an under officer, his promotion to *Leutnant* coming through at the end of July.

*Immelmann. Any landing you can walk away from is a good landing.*

*Immelmann and von Teubern in an L.V.G. BII prepare for a mission armed with the French machine gun.*

For their first operational flights together, Immelmann and von Teubern flew as pilot and observer in a general-purpose aeroplane of pre-war design. In the spring of 1915 there was still little specialization in aeroplane design and the machines of the first year of the war were not much different from the machines of the years immediately preceding it. Garros and Fokker (and the men who worked with them) changed all that, of course, and Immelmann, as one of the innovators of air fighting, made his contribution as well.

During June and July Immelmann and von Teubern flew the usual variety of observation missions. The first armament they received was a carbine, later a machine pistol for Ehrhardt. Later still, they were given a French machine gun from a captured aeroplane. This gun was rigged up on an improvised mounting on the observer's seat (the front seat), but the benefit derived from it, if any, was largely psychological. It seemed possible, in principle at least, to defend oneself in the air in case one were attacked. The two young men felt themselves to be rulers of the Front and presumably immune to harm. They flew high (a mile) and fast (about 65 miles per hour). What else does it require to be a ruler?

In the evenings Boelcke, Immelmann and von Teubern would join their comrades at the *Kasino* and share a bottle of Burgundy. Immelmann and von Teubern, who did not smoke, would clear out before the air turned blue around the card table. Boelcke was a quiet fellow, but a dangerous man at cards and, according to von Teubern, he always won.

30

Although several times they were attacked by French flyers, von Teubern and Immelmann always managed to make it home. Once they were almost shot down. A French observer armed with a Hotchkiss machine gun put a burst into the aeroplane right between the two cockpits, but did not hit either Immelmann or von Teubern. The bullets did put holes in the fuel tank, or else severed the fuel line, for the engine quickly went dry and died. Immelmann glided down to a smooth landing and the two airmen congratulated themselves on their escape.

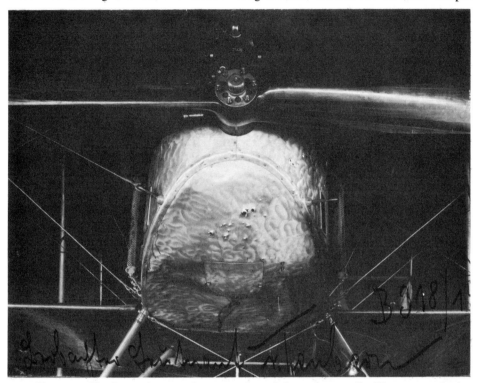

For von Teubern, it was the second and last close call. He was as lucky in the air as Boelcke was at cards. He had been in a crack-up at Elsenmühle with a civilian pilot and the aeroplane was wrecked, but neither man was hurt. His luck never deserted him. Immelmann's did. He was never shot down again, but there are many ways by which fighter pilots may die.

*           *           *

ALTHOUGH HE WEPT at the thought of killing in the air, Roland Garros grimly accepted what he believed to be the necessity of it. He believed his duty lay in killing. France was invaded, engaged in a merciless war no one would admit to having started, Paris trembled under the guns of the invader. Garros wept, but he shot down two more German aeroplanes in the next two weeks.

Toward the end of April, *Kriegszeitung,* the newspaper of the German Fourth Army, published the following account:

"April 18, 1915, at about seven o'clock in the region of Sainte-Cathérine and Landelede, two aeroplanes suddenly appeared flying at a great height. One of them disappeared in the direction of Menin, pursued by our anti-aircraft fire. The other, which was piloted by Roland Garros, headed toward Landelede.

"Precisely at this moment a train was passing on the Ingelmunster-Courtrai line, arriving from the north. Immediately on perceiving the train, Garros made a vertiginous descent, at an angle of some sixty degrees, coming down from 2000 metres to about 40, executing a series of tight turns over the train.

"Garros dropped one bomb which fell upon the rails, digging a crater one metre deep and two across.

"Some sentinels opened fire on him at a range of 100 metres. The aviator dropped a second bomb and climbed to 700 metres.

"Suddenly his motor stopped. The aeroplane wavered and descended in a glide in the direction of Hulste.

"Garros set fire to his machine on touching the ground and took refuge in a peasant homestead. The soldiers who were pursuing him had to look some time for him. They finally discovered him crouching in a ditch behind a thick hedge.

"The soldiers asked him if he did not have a companion. Garros gave them his word of honor that he had been alone in the machine, the engine of which was capable of but 80 horsepower and able, consequently, to carry but a single passenger.

"Garros then explained that at 700 metres his motor had been hit during the shooting and that this had forced him to land."

It was subsequently learned that the soldiers of the *Landsturm* who had effected the capture had been awarded a bonus of one hundred marks. Cheap indeed, considering the value of the prize.

*           *           *

BY HIS MOBILIZATION orders, Adolphe Pégoud was recalled to the Briançon Light Artillery, but as one of Europe's most famous exhibition pilots he was quickly detached to the *Service d'Aéronautique*. He flew the usual army co-operation missions—reconnaissance, observation, photography. He also flew ground attack missions, dropping those beastly *fléchettes* on enemy troops, but here he brought his personal flair into play, for he also dropped them on enemy observation balloons.

The end of January 1915 he was transferred to Ste-Menehould. As a good luck charm he carried a plush doll, a penguin. Since the elementary training machines were called Penguins and Pégoud was one of the most skillful aviators of the day, the little plush penguin was in the nature of a personal joke.

He had scored several victories when he was transferred from the Vosges front to Alsace, *escadrille* M-S 49, stationed then at Fontaine. Previously, he had flown mostly *parasols,* but with M-S 49 he had the opportunity to fly a single-seater type "N" with armored propeller, the same type that Garros had introduced on April first.

32

Matutinal in his habits, Pégoud was up and in his flying togs at the hangar by dawn. He frequently flew voluntary early patrols. If he was not flying he would be found recumbent in a deck chair placed before the hangar, his binoculars in his hand, scrutinizing the sky.

Because the names of Garros and Pégoud were well known by their pre-war achievements, the handful of victories they won (in a day when aerial victories were virtually unknown) was magnified in the newspapers. Pégoud, with his score standing at five was called an *As,* or Ace. The expression "ace" was current sports slang in France; it derived from the high card and meant "champion." Pégoud was a national hero. "Pégoud" became the name of a cocktail and a brand of cigarettes and five victories became the fortuitous standard by which one qualified as an Ace.

In July 1915 Pégoud destroyed a German two-seater while flying the Morane "N". As usual, he had been standing by, ready to go. His diary gives the following account:

"An Aviatik is sighted flying over Dannemarie region. Nine minutes after, see nothing. Continue patrol toward Thann, Belfort, and Swiss frontier. Fly over Dannemarie again. See far off toward Basle a black speck growing. Soon distinguish a superb Aviatik. Try to draw it into our lines. Several feint attacks. Won't come, flies along Front. Seeing this, dive on him and immediately pass under him while he shoots at me with machine gun located in rear. Shooting not accurate, his own fuselage in the way. Try to keep myself right under him. Succeed with quick manoeuvres, following movements of enemy aeroplane exactly. Arrive at a bound about 150 feet below, start firing with first clip of 25 cartridges, aiming a little behind motor, then mow down pilot and passenger. After ten rounds, *Boche* nosedives, flames come out of fuselage. Follow it down, firing and reloading. Finding myself over enemy lines at Altkirch, level off at 5000 feet. Watch fall of Aviatik which crashes on road by Altkirch, between railroad and village. Wreckage remains clearly visible."

At 8:30 in the morning on Tuesday, August 31, 1915, a call came through that a German machine had been spotted high over Montreux, headed for Belfort. Pégoud was ready this morning as he was on all others, and found the *Boche* soon after taking off. Exchanging long bursts with the gunner in the two-seater, Pégoud exhausted his first clip. He banked away to reload then drove in again from the side and a little above. One bullet from the observer's Parabellum went straight through his heart.

From 10,000 feet the little single-seater dived into the ground, engine full on.

Squadron mates who arrived at the site of the crash by auto found four gendarmes and a number of soldiers of the 117th Territorial Regiment on guard over the wreck, standing in a silent circle. The body of the first Ace was covered by a strip of fabric from a wing. Still recognizable was Pégoud's good luck charm which his friends took back with them—the penguin.

*       *       *

ONE OF NAVARRE's closest friends was a pilot named Georges Pelletier Doisy, a Gascon born at Auch May 9, 1892. His father came from a military family and had been a commander of cavalry, a profession he wanted his son to follow. Accordingly, Georges joined the Dragoons in 1910, but his real love was aeroplanes. In 1912 he succeeded in obtaining a posting for flight training to Bron, where he had as a boy spent Sunday afternoons hanging around the flying field to watch the aeroplanes.

Immediately on joining *escadrille* HF 19 he acquired a nickname that was to stay with him the rest of his life. A squadron mate rushed into the canteen one day waving a new copy of a weekly fiction magazine, *The Adventures of Sapper Pivolo, Aviator*. Everyone present agreed that there was the most perfect resemblance between Pelletier Doisy and Pivolo and the former was rechristened on the spot with the name of the latter. (And gouged a suitable amount of champagne that the occasion might be properly toasted.)

Before the war *escadrille* HF 19 had performed a mass flight—a 4000-mile circuit of France—without accident or casualty. The successful navigation, as well as the safety record, had caused the flight to be considered a remarkable accomplishment. Pivolo took part in the flight as a *brigadier-pilote,* a rank equivalent to corporal, and was awarded the *Médaille militaire*. Long range navigation was thereafter a rewarding challenge to Pivolo. In 1924 he became the first to fly non-stop from Paris to Tokyo, and in 1926 the first to fly non-stop Paris to Peking. In 1927 he was awarded the La Fayette Trophy—Champion of the World—by the International Aviators' League.

But in 1914 he was still a *brigadier-pilote*.

Upon the Mobilization *escadrille* HF 19 changed its equipment and was transformed into MF 8 (the machines being Maurice Farmans). On an observation mission during the Battle of the Marne, Pivolo spotted a motorcade near Nancy, in the region of the Grand Couronné, the quality of whose autos and the size of whose escort convinced him that no less a personage than the Kaiser must be aboard, waiting possibly for the moment to set foot in France. Pivolo hurried back to report his discovery, but his "extravagant assertions" were treated with disbelief at GQG. A confirmation came later, too late to do anything about it. It really had been the Kaiser.

Early in 1915 Pivolo was transferred to M-S 12 under *Capitaine* de Bernis, and there met and became friends with Navarre.

On April 2, 1915, Pivolo and his observer *sous-Lieutenant* René Chambe succeeded in forcing down an Albatros with only four bullets. The crew landed safely behind the French lines, but managed to set fire to their machine before they were taken prisoner by the *poilus*.

Pivolo and Navarre were sent to Brias, near Saint-Pol in the Arras sector, at about the time that the Campaign of Arras began.

Although it was dusk when they received their transfer orders they decided to start out immediately rather than wait till the following day. Pivolo said he knew the way and cited his vast navigational experience. They took off with their observers, Pivolo leading, and as soon as it grew dark they were lost. Navarre

*Pivolo.*

34

clung to within fifty feet of Pivolo's tail so as not to lose him. As much as possible, Pivolo had been following the railroad tracks, an almost universal method of navigation that worked well enough, given adequate visibility, for everyone but the British pilots on their hops across the Channel.

An agglomeration of lights below indicated a town and Pivolo buzzed the railroad station at a height of about ten feet trying to read its name on the sign-board. This went on until Pivolo ran out of gas and coasted to a landing in a dimly lit field, Navarre right behind him. Luckily, the field was a smooth one, and miraculously, both aeroplanes and all four aviators were intact.

"Wait here," said Navarre, a superfluous instruction, "I'll go find you some juice." Ascertaining the direction in which Brias lay by the excellently simple but not always practicable method of asking the local peasants, Navarre took off and located Brias. Thanks to a rough and ready flare system, he landed there safely. The usual improvised illumination for night landings consisted of oil and gasoline-soaked rags laid in parallel strips and lit on hearing an aeroplane approach. Navarre requested the gasoline for Pivolo's aeroplane, but was refused by the supply sergeant and a lengthy palaver ensued, the supply sergeant insisting that he had no authorization and Navarre telling him he knew what he could do with his authorization. In the end, with the aid of threats and bribery, Navarre pried twenty litres out of the sergeant. With the gasoline in cans piled in the front seat, Navarre took off and found the field where Pivolo was waiting and landed, Pivolo having contrived to outline the field with lanterns borrowed from the local people.

For the last leg of the trip, Pivolo had to cling to Navarre's tail.

On the morrow, both men wondered if it might have been not worth it, for they learned that all flying at Brias was to be done at scheduled times according to an elaborate system of rotation. For Navarre particularly, this was hard news; while he would gladly have done any amount of flying, he felt that one should be left some initiative.

One day while taking off on patrol one of the pilots crashed his machine accidentally and was killed. The squadron commander raged against the *parasol,* calling it a death trap, a flying coffin, and a hazard unfit to fly. While the crash hurt squadron morale, it was not so serious as the really deleterious effect of the

35

C.O. condemning the ship the men were expected to fly. Navarre innocently said that the *parasol* was a good aeroplane but that one had to know how to handle it, and he offered to put on a little demonstration to show how good it was. He was expressly forbidden to do any stunting in the *parasol*.

"They'll be telling me how to eat, pretty soon," grumbled Navarre.

In defiance of the no-stunting injunction, he took off and staged an exhibition right over the field, ending up with two meticulously controlled tailspins, one to the right and one to the left. He landed and was placed under arrest. He protested that he was only trying to give a boost to morale by showing what could be done with a Morane. He was sentenced to 15 days confinement to quarters and forbidden to fly.

During the 15 days arrest, his brother Pierre cycled into camp. Pierre was in the trenches near Arras and had obtained permission to visit Jean at Brias. When the time came for Pierre to return to his outfit, Jean asked for permission to accompany him, but was refused. He went anyway. Not only went, he flew him back. When he returned he was given 15 days for disobeying confining orders and 15 days after that for flying while grounded. At this rate the war would be over before he could exhaust the spite of his C.O.

His luck turned when fortune intervened in the person of *Colonel* Barès, director of aviation at GQG, who showed up one morning at Brias with an old Gras musket and incendiary ammunition for it. He wanted someone to have a crack at the German observation balloons—*Drachen*—against which no one had as yet enjoyed any particular success. As soon as Navarre got wind of it, he presented himself before *Colonel* Barès and requested permission to try the experiment. This, of course, hard on the heels of the rest of the squadron having declined the honor.

The commanding officer turned red and his eyes bulged but he didn't say anything because Barès promptly evinced an interest in Navarre and started a conversation with him, the upshot of which was that Navarre's remaining punishment days should be rescinded and he should try the experiment.

The next morning Navarre and *Lieutenant* Jean Moinier took off in the *parasol,* armed with the Gras musket and six rounds of the special ammunition. In those days the *Drachen* all operated at a standard height of 900 metres, or 3000 feet, so Navarre climbed to a comfortable height above that, crossed the lines, and spiraled down over the first balloon. *Lieutenant* Moinier blazed away with all six balls but the old musket was not made for accurate shooting and its unrifled bore spewed the slugs out every which way. Navarre held the spiral down past the balloon to give the *Lieutenant* as steady a platform as possible and when the ammunition was gone and he leveled out the aeroplane was only three hundred feet off the ground and the Germans were throwing up a curtain of lead. The Morane plowed through cannon, machine gun, rifle and pistol fire while Navarre and Moinier sat sweating, eyes closed, teeth clenched. The noise was terrific; when it stopped, they opened their eyes and saw that they were back over the French trenches—in an aeroplane that was shot full of holes.

*Colonel* Barès had a citation published for both of them.

One rainy day when no one else would have dreamed of flying, Navarre sought out an observer who was known as a sunny character and suggested they fly up to Amiens.

"How?" asked the observer.

"What the hell, in an *aeroplane!*"

"In this rain?"

"Why not? You afraid of water?"

"No, but a *parasol* in this weather . . . ?"

"Would you prefer a *parapluie?*"

"Well, no, but . . ."

"Don't worry. Stick with me. I won't break anything. I've flown in worse weather than this."

It was agreed that they would return that evening before the C.O. returned, for, needless to say, he just happened to be away at the time.

They landed in a field as close to the city as possible, and headed for civilized pleasures. A *patisserie* offered the first of these, after which followed a few restaurants and cafés. When the heroes gaily returned to their aeroplane they were loaded. Cavaliers down to their fingernails, they proposed to salute the great cathedral of Amiens by stunting over it then littering the streets with flowers purchased expressly for this magnificent gesture. Roaring over the roof tops to loose the flowers over the side, they were gratified to see a pretty girl blowing them kisses from a balcony. They marked well the location of the house, then landed again at their cow pasture outside town and walked back to a pleasant reception. Not surprisingly, it grew dark before anyone noticed. There was nothing to do but to telephone the aerodrome that they were detained because of engine trouble and would be back first thing in the morning.

It was still rainy the next day, but during a break in the morning they took off—and the engine conked out. By great good luck Navarre landed right side up but he had to trudge miles to the nearest telephone. Then for two nights he and his companion in misery slept under the wings of the *parasol* waiting for a repair crew to drive out from the aerodrome.

One can imagine their return. Navarre felt he was lucky to draw only eight days confinement.

When he was allowed to fly again there were no Germans to be seen in the air in this particular sector and he was beginning to think things were a complete mess. His brother Pierre came to visit him once more, one bright spot in the gloom. Again Jean flew Pierre back to his outfit, bicycle and all. The squadron commander concluded that Navarre was incorrigible and determined to have him transferred back to M-S 12.

Navarre and Pivolo were summoned to the C.O.'s office—for Navarre it was the first time he had been in it without receiving punishment. When they heard their orders to report back to M-S 12, they nearly broke their arms saluting.

It was mid-winter and the snow was deep on the ground but the runways had been kept clear enough for flying to continue at what was called a "normal seasonal rate." Impetuous as always, Navarre and Pivolo left immediately. They briefed their mechanics and packed their kit. On takeoff, Navarre espied the staff officers lined up at the end of the runway, waiting for the exhibition of stunting they were sure Navarre would put on. The temptation was overwhelming. He held his machine on the ground, heading straight for the group of officers. Apprehension, then terror flitted across their faces as he roared down on them. To a man they hit the dirt as Navarre zoomed over the end of the runway.

Reporting to *Capitaine* de Bernis on their arrival at Rheims and M-S 12, Navarre and Pivolo found him interested to know some details of their recent history and the conditions of their departure from Brias. Navarre blurted out the story. *Capitaine* de Bernis said that he had just been on the telephone with the C.O. at Brias who had told him of the too-sensational departure and had demanded that both lunatics be given 30 days. However, de Bernis added, the sentence need not be imposed if the two of them (and particularly one of them) would settle down and get with it.

To forestall an outburst of indignation from Navarre, de Bernis shooshed them out of his office.

An hour or so later, judging that Navarre had calmed down, de Bernis called him back. He had a special mission, he said, and if Navarre was fed up with the air service and wanted a transfer to the infantry, then he, de Bernis, didn't know who was going to fly the special mission.

"I'll go," said Navarre.

And he did. In fact he flew three special missions. These were usually very dicey operations, involving the landing of saboteurs, *agents provocateurs,* or spies behind the lines. The landings were particularly dangerous since they had to be carried out at night in unfamiliar territory on unlighted fields.

Navarre volunteered for the first to make up for some of the trouble he had caused at Brias. He volunteered for the second and third to make up somewhat for cracking up an aeroplane, injuring a comrade, while duck hunting. In May Navarre and *sous-Lieutenant* René Chambe had decided to have a go at the *canepétières,* a species of duck inhabiting the plains around Rheims. To be different, they thought it would be good sport to hunt from an aeroplane.

Returning from a routine patrol, they headed for the *plaine de Geux* where they soon flushed some game. As the duck skimmed along the ground, Navarre went after it and Chambe raised the rifle. The bird zig-zagged across the fields, Navarre following its movements, coming up close. Suddenly the bird turned, an abrupt turn, absolutely at right angles to his previous line of flight. Navarre turned too, instantly, forgetting in the heat of the chase that he was only a few feet off the ground. When he brought up his left wing, his right wing went into the ground. The aeroplane somersaulted several times with a terrific splintering noise and came to rest upside down, pieces fluttering down all around.

Navarre sat up and blinked. He was drenched with gasoline, the wreck lay some distance away, and an equal distance away in another direction lay Chambe.

It was quite a return to the aerodrome. "If only we'd had the duck, too," said Navarre.

38

At the hospital that night, Chambe sat in bed swathed in bandages. Navarre sat out in the corridor, feeling guilty about Chambe and the aeroplane. The chief of aviation for the Fifth Army, *Commandant* de Rose, came striding out, thunder seated upon his brow, his magnificent walrus moustache quivering with indignation. "Are you satisfied?" he asked. Navarre wilted so perceptibly under his glare that de Rose was inclined, for the moment, to let it go at that.

Tricornot de Rose held the first military aviator's commission issued in the French army. A former *lieutenant* of the Lunéville Dragoons, he had transferred to aviation in 1910, qualifying as a pilot in March 1911. In August 1914 he had given a demonstration of sangfroid that combined oldstyle cavalry dash with flying skill. Out of gas after a long reconnaissance, he was forced to land on the highway outside a frontier village. He obtained gasoline in the village, and as he was filling his tank, a spearhead of German cavalry came trotting down the road at the other end of the village. Impassive, de Rose continued his work, started up the motor with assistance from his observer, and took off over the heads of the surprised enemy troopers who had supposed him to be one of their own. He was an experienced, resourceful officer and a skilled aviator.

*Commandant* de Rose later said to *Capitaine* de Bernis that the antics of Navarre were insupportable and that he, de Rose, was going to ground him.

"I have an alternative to suggest," said *Capitaine* de Bernis, "give him the Legion of Honor."

*Commandant* de Rose regarded de Bernis as one regards a lunatic. While he was still too stunned to speak, de Bernis took a breath and plunged into his arguments: Navarre was the most accomplished pilot at the Front, he could do anything with an aeroplane, his skill and daring were beyond belief, his nerve incredible; he had just finished three special missions, each of which should have won a citation; not only that . . ."

"You believe I can propose this nut for the *Légion d'Honneur* after the stunts he has pulled? No! Impossible!"

The following morning de Rose called de Bernis. "The proposition for Navarre was accepted by GQG to whom I telephoned yesterday evening. Are you happy now?" He hung up. A few minutes later de Bernis called Navarre into his office.

"Navarre, the *Commandant* was furious at you yesterday evening. For a moment I really thought you were going to end up in the infantry."

"So much the better!"

"But the *Commandant* agreed to pass along to GQG a request from me which has been accepted."

"What request?"

"For the Legion of Honor."

He said nothing, but tears welled up in the eyes of Navarre the Incorrigible.

*      *      *

ALTHOUGH *Kriegszeitung* stated explicitly that Roland Garros set fire to his aeroplane, there was certainly enough salvaged for German technical experts to comprehend the importance of their lucky capture. They perceived that this was the very aeroplane with which Garros had shot down three German machines. If the French had successfully launched one such apparatus they might be planning to introduce any number of machines with a like equipment, and the consequences of such a move were unforseeable. And disagreeable to contemplate.

Since the principle and the mechanism were so simple, the Germans decided to assume the worst: namely, that the French were preparing every single-seater they had in a similar fashion so as to launch a sudden aerial offensive that would sweep the German observation machines from the sky.

Well, it was a two-edged sword. Since it was so simple, the Germans could arm every single-seater they had and meet the French on better than equal terms because the advantage of surprise would be on their side. The aeroplane was ready to hand: the Fokker M.5, the machine in which Tony Fokker had won the accolade of "master of the sky" from the German newspapers, and in which he had so impressed General von Falkenhayn, the Prussian Minister of War, just one year before.

Fokker was immediately ordered to produce a copy of the Garros/Morane deflector gear suitable for installation in his monoplane. The unique mechanical genius of the Flying Dutchman finally came into the game. The pendulum completed its first stroke.

A standard infantry machine gun was issued to Fokker, the first one he had ever seen up close, much less handled, but its workings were easy enough to understand. He instantly apprehended that the essential problem was how to shoot *between* the blades of the propeller. This business of deflecting bullets was not safe—the ricochets might go anywhere, they might damage the engine or even hit the pilot, and the hammering on the prop might throw it out of true eventually. That was particularly dangerous because a vibrating prop can tear the whole engine loose. Besides, the standard-issue machine gun cartridge for the French used a relatively soft copper-coated bullet, whereas the comparable German ammunition was jacketed with steel. A slug like that might smash the propeller, deflector plates and all. The trick was to shoot through the propeller by interrupting the flow of bullets whenever the blades passed before the muzzle of the gun. How to interrupt at the right time? By causing the propeller itself to fire the gun. A small knob judiciously located on the propeller hub would strike a cam, and by a simple, direct mechanical linkage the firing mechanism would be tripped and the gun would fire—600 rounds a minute as long as the pilot held his thumb down on the firing button on the control stick. When the pilot let up his pressure on the firing button the connection would be broken between cam and trigger and the gun would stop. Splendid. He came up with the idea and the finished mechanism within 48 hours.

Official demonstrations for the ordnance boards followed, Fokker himself doing some of the flying, and upon acceptance the new armament installed in

the M.5 monoplane was delivered to several *Fliegerabteilungen* for operational assessment. Two machines, now bearing the military designation Fokker E I (E for *Eindecker,* or monoplane), were issued to *Fl. Abt. 62* at Douai. Both machines were earmarked for Boelcke who flew them in alternation with two-seaters in which he continued to serve as a chauffeur for observers. The *Eindecker* was considered a military secret and special instructions were issued regarding its use, one such instruction being an injunction against flying it over the lines. It was hoped that specimens might thus be kept from falling into enemy hands. Boelcke's nature was to fight, however, when a fight could be forced, and since fighting at that time was mostly chasing, it followed that sooner or later he would chase somebody over the lines. Which he did. He shot down a Bristol Scout

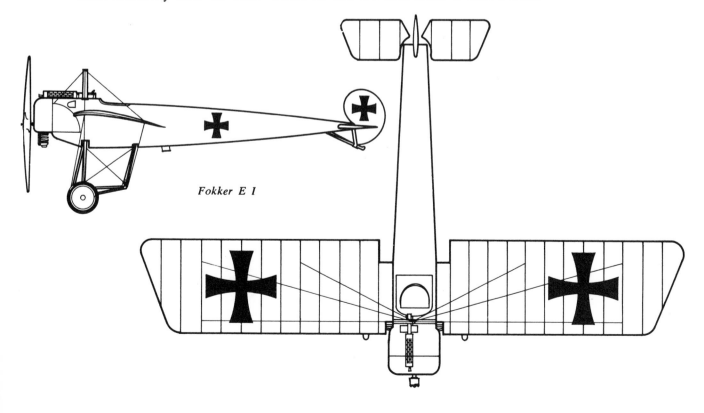

*Fokker E I*

behind the British lines near Arras in the summer of 1915, but since the event was not seen by any German observers it was never officially recorded.

The *Eindeckers* were issued singly or in pairs to the *Fliegerabteilungen* to be flown as escorts to the two-seaters, many of which were as yet unarmed. Several of the early Aces started their careers in *Eindeckers* during the summer and fall of 1915 and the damage done to Allied morale, to say nothing of the Allied air services, was considerable. There's an old saying that reflects the army's tradition of stoicism in the face of disaster, "The situation's not bad, it's downright serious." The situation was so serious for the RFC that the last half of 1915 was known as the period of the "Fokker Scourge."

On the first day of August 1915 the RFC bombed Douai, and Boelcke took off in pursuit in one of the *Eindeckers*. Immelmann dashed for his two-seater, but his comrade and regular observer, Ehrhardt von Teubern, felt that it would not be wise to take off since the weather was very uncertain. Immelmann, wasting no time, took up the other *Eindecker* and followed Boelcke after the British machines. They had a ten-minute start on him and Immelmann was still trying to catch up when he saw Boelcke ahead in the distance dive on the rearmost British machine, break away, and head for home. He learned later that Boelcke had had a gun stoppage after firing only a few rounds. That left Immelmann alone to take on ten enemy two-seaters. How to do it? He had flown the *Eindecker* only twice before, and he had never attacked an aeroplane. He was confident, as always, but obviously this was a business that exacted stiff penalties for blunders. He picked out a straggler and flew straight at it.

It was a pretty easy thing, after all. Immelmann didn't know it beforehand, but the pilot of the British two-seater was flying solo, having carried bombs instead of a gunner. After having made a rambling series of attacks from the side, below, behind, having sprayed a hundred rounds in all directions, Immelmann saw the British machine go into a steep glide. He followed it down. It landed in a field on the German side of the lines and Immelmann landed too. He climbed out of his *Eindecker* and called out *"Prisonniers!"* That part was bluff—he was unarmed and he expected two men to be in the machine.

The pilot, however, was ready to surrender because he was wounded in the left arm. He extended his right hand in token of surrender and Immelmann promptly shook it, then escorted his *prisonnier* into the hands of a doctor.

Boelcke was delighted with Immelmann's performance. It had been inept and amateurish, but he had done the job he set out to do, and few men could claim a victory the first time they went up as fighters. Both Boelcke and Immelmann began flying voluntary "hunting patrols" when they were free from chauffeuring or escort duties. Toward the end of August they teamed up to shoot down a French Caudron G.4 and the next day Immelmann scored a victory unaided. In September Immelmann scored his third victory, a British B.E.2c down in flames, and so equalled the score of the great Roland Garros. In October he shot down another machine and in November a fifth to become an Ace. He was still stationed at Douai, but now that he was an Ace people were

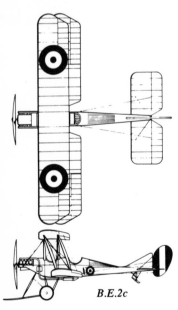

B.E.2c

42

bound to hang a title on him, and since Lille is five times as big a town as Douai, he was called the Eagle of Lille, *der Adler von Lille.*

At the beginning of October Boelcke and von Teubern were transferred to Metz to take part in the operations of the Metz Carrier Pigeons and Immelmann remained at Douai with *Fl. Abt. 62.* From a clumsy beginning, Immelmann quickly progressed to mastery. He and Boelcke may be said to have founded German fighter aviation. They discovered the advantage of height, and the necessity of surprise, co-ordination and good shooting. They evolved tactics and techniques. Boelcke was the organizer, the man who could put across his ideas, Immelmann was the originator of certain standard manoeuvres. Immelmann is generally considered to be the man who introduced the concept of tactical manoeuvre. Just flying rings around an opponent doesn't really get you anywhere. If you can put your ability to manoeuvre to work as a means of shooting down an enemy—that's tactics. The manoeuvre known as the "Immelmann turn" was only a graceful stunt when Pégoud performed it before the war. When Immelmann worked it into his repertoire it became a means of attacking swiftly, changing direction after attack, and gaining height to attack again.

*Boelcke with his Eindecker.*

At Metz, von Teubern was disappointed to learn that Boelcke was not to be his pilot, but had been transferred there as an *Eindecker* pilot to fly escort to the bombers. Over Metz, Boelcke scored a significant victory—he shot down a Voisin that was taking part in a bombing raid on the railway station just at the time that the Kaiser was scheduled to arrive. This brought him to the attention of that august personage and it seems hardly likely that this kind of recognition did him any harm.

In November the Chief of Army Field Aviation, Major Thomsen, called Boelcke to a conference at Supreme Headquarters (*Oberste Heeresleitung,* or OHL). This was the first of a series of conferences between Thomsen and the most experienced aviators in the field, chief among whom, as representative of fighters, was Boelcke. The purpose of these conferences was to fashion an air policy that would confer maximum efficiency by standardizing means and methods. To do this a realistic evaluation of the functions of the air service had to be prepared, and Boelcke was there to define the role of the fighters. Broadly speaking, the role of the fighters in all the air services was divided like Gaul in *partes tres:* preventing enemy aeroplanes from performing their missions, protecting friendly aeroplanes, and some specialized forms of ground attack such as shooting up enemy aerodromes and strafing enemy troops. Boelcke contributed many sound observations on organization and tactics and this helped lay the foundations of the future fighter force.

During the stay at Metz, Boelcke and von Teubern used to motor into town on duty-free afternoons and stroll through the streets. They would stop at a café for some coffee and take an evening meal at a restaurant. In each other's company it was not necessary to say much. They would return to the base and one would say to the other, "This was still a beautiful afternoon." What would tomorrow bring?

43

*Immelmann, February 1916.*
*His Pour le Mérite portrait.*

Ehrhardt von Teubern

Boelcke returned to Douai in December. Ehrhardt von Teubern was sent to Hamburg for a throat operation. After his convalescence, Ehrhardt served for a time in Champagne, Bulgaria, and Macedonia, finally was transferred to Berlin, where he served the rest of the war as personnel director for observers in the office of the Inspector General for Aviation.

Air-to-air victories were still rare enough to make newspaper headlines and Boelcke and Immelmann were celebrities. Immelmann received 30 or 40 fan mail letters a day. By the end of the year he had scored his sixth and seventh victories.

The New Year brought uncertain weather but the RFC took another crack at the aerodrome at Douai. At daybreak on January 12, 1916, word came through that several flights of enemy machines had crossed the line at various places. Immelmann took off in his *Eindecker* and climbed to 10,000 feet. Away to the east he spotted shell bursts at about 8500 feet. The smoke puffs from anti-aircraft fire could be seen from a greater distance than aeroplanes and were a sure indication that enemy machines were stooging around. Their color was fairly characteristic—black for German, white for Allied—so the aeroplanes whose presence they betrayed could be identified friend or foe before they could themselves be seen. Their altitude and direction could also be judged by watching the trails of smoke puffs walk across the sky.

Immelmann stalked his quarry for a time, but before he could launch his attack, one machine turned abruptly toward him. He dodged aside and fired from the flank. The machine, a British two-seater, turned toward him again and the process was repeated. This time a flash of fire streamed from the two-seater's engine and the pilot headed for the ground where he landed smoothly and scrambled out of the blazing aeroplane. The gunner was dead, but the pilot was unhurt, and once again Immelmann shook the hand of a defeated adversary.

Immelmann and Boelcke now had eight victories apiece. On January 13, 1916, both were awarded the Order *Pour le Mérite,* the first aviators to be so honored. The Order—literally "for merit"—was Germany's highest award, comparable to the *Légion d'Honneur* or the Congressional Medal of Honor. It was instituted by Frederick the Great and bore a French name because French had always been the language of European court etiquette.

Immelmann's fan mail rose to 50 letters a day and his orderly became his secretary. In the RFC it was supposed that the Eagle of Lille covered the entire Front from Ypres to Valenciennes and could somehow stay in the air for a week at a time.

In February Boelcke returned to Metz and received a promotion to *Ober-leutnant.* During the spring of 1916 he shot down ten enemy aeroplanes at Verdun. In May he was promoted to *Hauptmann,* one of the youngest men in the German Army to hold that rank and wear the *Pour le Mérite* as well.

\*        \*        \*

44

PAUL TARASCON became involved in aviation in 1911 at Miramas where he made his first flights in an Anzani-powered Blériot of the Channel-crossing type. In August 1911 a control broke and the aeroplane crashed heavily. Tarascon spent eight months in the hospital and suffered the amputation of his right foot.

In August 1914 he was in Casablanca. He presented himself at the mobilization center to sign up for the duration. The Major ignored the amputation, listened for a heart beat, found one, passed Tarascon for the infantry. He was whisked away to quartermaster, issued a rifle, a pack, and all the gear. This was not exactly the kind of service he had envisioned. He managed to get next to a medic and to convince him that while he, Tarascon, was healthy, sturdy, and willing, he couldn't be much use in the infantry with only one foot. The doctor got him a twenty-four-hour *permission*. He dashed to a hotel in Casablanca and composed a long, detailed letter to the military governor who arranged an interview with the General of the Territorial Army. The General arranged for a pass and the necessary transport to get him to Buc-St-Cyr where he was properly enrolled in the *Service d'Aéronautique* at the military aerodrome. Tarascon was an excellent pilot and was soon transferred to Pau as an instructor.

While serving as an instructor at Pau, Tarascon was approached by a Doctor Lostalot who sought his assistance on behalf of a skinny, gawky youngster, barely eighteen and puny, who had been rejected by the army and who dreamed of flying. Tarascon took the case to the commandant, *Capitaine* Thierry, and argued that there were many jobs, such as washing aeroplanes and sweeping out the hangars, that could be performed by even such poor physical specimens as this kid. The *capitaine* consented; after all, even Tarascon was a cripple, and "the Kid"— *le Gosse*—was given a job.

For a month the Kid did all the dirty jobs, until his father, who was a St-Cyr graduate, and Tarascon used their influence to get him enrolled as a student pilot. Tarascon was his instructor. The Kid's name was Georges Guynemer—a name that will be repeated many times.

On the 19th of July, 1915, two young French aviators were cruising above the lines near Coucy. They were annoyed with themselves for they had let a *Boche* get away. The pilot, a *caporal,* had just learned to fly; he had joined the squadron six weeks before; he had made his first flight over the lines five weeks earlier. Later, in 1917, a man who survived for five weeks was as experienced as a man could be. The casualty tables indicated that a man who had flown 150 hours was either on his own or in the hands of the gods because at that point he passed the limit of survival. In the summer of 1915, however, the war in the air was only just becoming serious.

Up until a few weeks previous to this sunny Monday in July, pilots and observers waved to each other, generally. Sometimes aeroplanes would pass each other unnoticed, the pilots and observers so engrossed in their photography or artillery-spotting that they didn't think to look around to see who else was sharing the air with them. Now it was different. Flyers who didn't look around constantly didn't last long.

The *caporal* pilot was a frail, weak-looking youth, whose obvious immaturity was offset by the astonishing fire in his eyes. He never looked at anything, he glared at it; he never walked, he ran; he never waited, he fretted; he never tried anything without overreaching. The *escadrille* to which he was posted was M-S 3, commanded by *Capitaine* Brocard, a sturdy, broad-shouldered son of France whom even the most reckless unconsciously deferred to because of his commanding aspect. Brocard was to make the name of his squadron—the Storks—a synonym for Ace. The *caporal* pilot, whose name was Georges Guynemer, was to make his own name legendary.

That, however, was in afteryears, when a generation of French school children were taught that the aviator who disappeared on September 11, 1917, had flown so high he could never come down. Between this July day of 1915 and the end in September 1917, was a struggle so arduous that it consumed him.

Guynemer and his gunner fussed over the machine gun that had jammed, and had thus allowed the *Boche* to get away. They cleared the gun and continued patrolling, hoping to get a second chance. Over Coucy, they spotted an Aviatik headed toward Soissons. They followed, gradually overtaking the two-seater. Guynemer put his *parasol* into a shallow dive to pick up speed and approached to within 150 feet, slightly above, behind, and to the left of the Aviatik. His gunner, a mechanic named Guerder, squeezed off the first salvo, the Aviatik lurched and pieces flew off of it. The observer in the Aviatik fired back with a rifle. One bullet whistled through the wing and one grazed the hand and head of Guerder. Guynemer held the shallow dive, placing his *parasol* directly under the Aviatik and Guerder fired another burst that went straight up into it from a distance of about 60 feet. The Aviatik fell in flames between the trenches.

Guynemer and Guerder landed immediately behind the lines to get a confirmation. The entire 238th Regiment had followed the fight and the Colonel wanted personally to interview the flyers.

"Well, really, the pilot did the whole thing," said Guerder, to whom *Colonel* Maillard had addressed his first questions.

At this point, Guynemer, skinny, gawky, entered the tent carrying his flying togs.

"Who's this?" asked the *Colonel*.

"My pilot."

"Really? How old are you?"

"Twenty," said Guynemer.

"And the gunner?"

"Twenty-two," replied Guerder.

*"Bon dieu,* don't we have anybody but children left to fight the war with?"

The following day, *Colonel* Maillard sent a message to *Commandant* Brocard, saying how much the regiment had enjoyed the fight.

The war in the air was still only a side-show for the infantry.

46

During the next four months Guynemer flew voluntary patrols as often as the weather permitted, hoping to get another crack at a *Boche*. He had a number of chances but did not succeed in bringing down an aeroplane. When uncertain weather set in, he spent much of his grounded time at his father's house in Compiègne.

Sunday, December 5, 1915, Guynemer was flying alone when he caught sight of two *Boches* over Chauny, near Compiègne. He attacked the nearer one, firing a short burst at about 150 feet, then firing again, a long burst at about 60 feet. The machine fell in a tailspin. He did not wait to see it crash but turned his attention to the other, which was now high-tailing for home. Guynemer gave up on the second and flew back to where he guessed the first should have hit, but could find no sign of it. Where did it go? It *had* to crash—that machine was out of control when it fell. He was running low on gas and he couldn't circle around indefinitely trying to spot the wreck. He glanced at his watch. Noon. His mother and father would be coming out of Mass now. He headed toward Compiègne and landed as close to town as he could, then climbed out of his aeroplane and ran.

"Father!" he yelled, "I've lost my *Boche*!"

"You've lost your *Boche*?"

"An aeroplane I shot down. I have to get back to the squadron, but I don't want to lose him."

"Of course not, but tell me, what do you want me to do?"

"Go find him for me! He should be out in the direction of Bailly, towards Bois Carré."

With that he dashed off and returned to the squadron. His father organized a search and the body of a German pilot was found but no wreck.

With the Storks—*les Cigognes*—Guynemer was transferred to Verdun in March 1916. Now he was no longer flying over his own front yard. He could not celebrate each victory with stunts over his father's house. He had served his apprenticeship, had, in fact, become an Ace, but the transfer to Verdun meant something more. Now he would have to grow up.

*        *        *

AN AMERICAN ACE who flew in British and American squadrons, George A. Vaughn, Jr., recounts an episode from the 'thirties. He was in Great Britain selling Link Trainers to the RAF. He heard that the Chief of the Technical Office of the new German *Luftwaffe* was interested in Link Trainers, and, since the General in question was a friend of his, Vaughn naturally decided to stop by Berlin on the way home and take an order for a few more.

In Berlin under the new regime flags were everywhere, soldiers were every-where, pictures of the new Leader were everywhere. At the Air Ministry ramrod soldiers slammed to attenion and the air was filled with the sound of clicking heels. The officious guards would never have let Vaughn in if he had not been a friend of the Chief of the Technical Office (whom he had met at the old Cleveland Air Races). Finally, the doors were thrown open, the visiting American was led down polished corridors and the guards withdrew.

There sat the Chief of the Technical Office sprawled in his chair, tunic unbuttoned, feet on his desk, bored to death, the perfect picture of that most miserable duck out of water, the aviator behind a desk. This was Udet.

Between the wars Ernst Udet was a well-known explorer, big-game hunter, and stunt pilot; during the early part of the Second World War he was one of the heads of the German *Luftwaffe,* a position for which he was selected partly because of his fame, partly because he was an excellent pilot, and partly because he was an easy-going chump. He was the scapegoat who eventually got the blame for the failure of the *Luftwaffe* after Hermann Goering's disastrous blunders. The machinations of Goering and Secretary Milch so distracted Udet that in June 1941 he committed suicide.

It was a contemptible end for Germany's second most successful fighter pilot of 1914–1918.

Udet first served in 1914 as a volunteer motorcycle dispatch rider at the age of 18. He was discharged from that service at the end of 1914, and immediately applied for admission to the Air Reserve—aeroplanes had interested him since his childhood. When his application was rejected on the grounds that he was too young, he took a civilian flying course at the Otto Flying School in Munich. His father paid for the lessons—2000 marks down and the refinishing of Herr Otto's bathroom.

On passing out of the school, Udet succeeded in wrangling admission to the Air Reserve and in the summer of 1915 he was posted to the aerodrome at Griesheimer Sand as an instructor. At this point he was an adequate pilot but not a brilliant one. That he was made an instructor almost as soon as he learned to fly himself is less an indication of his flying ability than of the informal methods of training that still existed at the beginning of the second decade of flight. The American Ace, Reed McKinley Chambers, for example, became an instructor with a total of 22 hours of flying time in his logbook.

The first squadron in which Udet flew operationally was *Fliegerabteilung 206* at Heiligenkreuz in the shadow of the Vosges Mountains. The equipment was Aviatik B machines and the work was principally artillery-spotting.

*Udet.*

*Heinz J. Nowarra*

48

Udet flew regularly with *Leutnant* Bruno Justinus. German aviation slang for a pilot was "Emil," and for an observer, "Franz."

They very narrowly escaped crashing in September 1915 while escorting a bombing raid on Belfort. A bracing wire for the outer end of the right wing snapped and the wing, with nothing to hold it steady, flexed dangerously in the wind. The Aviatik abruptly began a sliding fall to the left; the twisting of the right wing caused the wing to rise, forcing the left one down. Udet wrenched the control stick to the right to bring the left wing back up. Justinus turned about in the front seat and gave him a quizzical look. Udet throttled back, hoping that this might ease the strain on the wing and allow it to spring back to a more normal attitude. The aeroplane continued in its slip, however, so Justinus clambered out on the wing in order that his weight might restore the balance. Udet gaped at him as he sat nonchalantly with his arms and legs wrapped around the struts. Udet feared for Justinus out there for he wouldn't have a chance if the aeroplane suddenly took it into its head to cut any more capers. Besides, Udet had very little leverage in his favor to force the stick over to one side and hold it there—he was rapidly tiring and didn't think he could keep it up much longer. He shouted for Justinus to come back. The *Leutnant* returned to his front seat, climbed in and kicked out the plywood panel that separated the cockpits. Then he brought his own muscle to bear on the stick.

They limped over Switzerland losing height all the time and they made it back to Germany—barely—crossing the border at tree-top height, landing safely in a field.

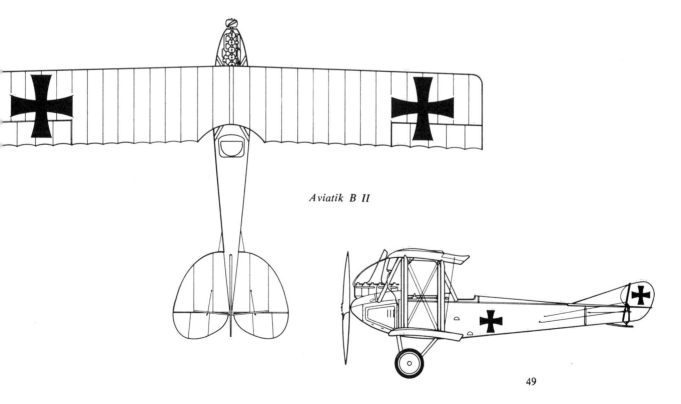

*Aviatik B II*

49

The same day two other men from the squadron were killed at Hartmanns-willerkopf when their aeroplane crashed, possibly as a result of the same defect.

"Emil" Udet and "Franz" Justinus were awarded the Iron Cross, Second and First Class respectively, for having saved their machine. They were satisfied to have saved their necks.

Before he managed to secure a transfer to single-seaters Udet survived two accidental crashes. Not surprisingly, he almost despaired of making it.

By late 1915, however, he made it, and was flying with a single-seater section at Habsheim, in what the German soldiers in Flanders and Champagne called "the sleeping army of the Vosges"—a pun in German deriving from the similarity between the words for "sleeping" and "battling."

The weather was clear and bright and cold, and at any altitude it was freezing. The pilots bundled themselves up till they looked like bears and greased their faces as protection against the bitter wind.

Udet came off second best the first time he met a French machine on patrol. It was a lumbering Caudron and Udet, flying a Fokker E I, should not have had any trouble sending it down—he was more experienced than most rookie fighter-pilots—but horror, fear, and a jumble of conflicting emotions deprived him of the ability to act or decide on any clear course of action. He sat in his machine, paralyzed, and stared at the two miniature human beings in the French birdcage. Why kill them? Why even shoot at them? They were *total strangers*. The French gunner suffered no such inhibitions. He loosed one accurate burst that peppered Udet's aeroplane and splintered his goggles, but miraculously did not either kill or blind him.

Udet came out of his trance and dived away, badly shaken and unwilling to try again for the Caudron. He called it quits for the day and was glad to get home. He had to get a grip on himself and make up his mind that he was really in the war now and playing for keeps.

He succeeded in creating in himself a will to fight. It was not so much fear he had to overcome—he was by nature a dare-devil—as simple reluctance to kill. He was an easy-going youth, and for any 19-year-old playing in man's oldest game the rules are hard.

His first victory came in March 1916, over a French Farman, one of a squadron of aeroplanes staging one of the first large-scale bombing raids of the war on Mulhouse. Udet dived steeply at the enemy formation, closing to about 100 feet before opening fire. He heard bullets from the French gunners hitting his machine as he opened fire on an aeroplane in the middle of the squadron. A cloud of white smoke suddenly poured from one of its engines, then he was through, continuing his dive to put distance between himself and the gunners in the French machines. He leveled out a thousand feet below them. The Farman he had hit, flaming now, tumbled toward the earth, one of its passengers falling free, turning over, arms outstretched.

*       *       *

THE FRONT-LINE infantry observers in the Château-Thierry sector signaled an L.V.G. two-seater over the French trenches early in the morning on October 25, 1915. Navarre, who like Pégoud was in the habit of sitting in his aeroplane waiting for an opportunity to fly, took off immediately and found the German machine within a few miles of where it had been sighted. It was headed roughly west so he followed it for a while hoping that it would fly close enough to Paris for him to have an excuse to land at Le Bourget and perhaps have a bit of a time in the capital. Unfortunately, the *Boche* didn't go that far. He turned abruptly about and the two aeroplanes were suddenly nose to nose. The German pilot ducked, the

*Navarre*

51

observer seized his Parabellum and threw a wild burst, and Navarre went over them on one wing, wrenching his Morane violently around to come in behind the L.V.G. The German pilot put his machine in a dive, Navarre fired, the propeller on the L.V.G. stopped dead and the machine glided down trailing a delicate wisp of white smoke.

Navarre followed and circled overhead, as the German pilot brought his aeroplane to a safe landing on the banks of the Marne.

Navarre continued circling, waiting to make sure the crew was taken prisoner, but no one showed up, not the infantry, not the *gendarmes,* not even farmers with pitchforks. He began to wonder what to do. He saw the observer ignite the fusee with which he obviously intended to fire the aeroplane. A brand new sparkling white machine? Oh, no. Navarre roared straight in at head-height and fired a few rounds over the two men. OK—no fire. The man threw the brand away and raised his hands.

Still nobody else down there to take charge of the prisoners. Navarre decided he had better do the job himself. He landed and taxied toward the L.V.G. and its crew.

"You wounded?" he called out.

"No."

He switched off and clambered out of the cockpit. They eyed each other.

"What were you doing?" he asked finally.

"Reconnaissance."

Navarre grunted, then stepped over to the two-seater. No bombs, or racks, anyway. Only the machine gun.

"Er," one of them said, "may one ask your name?"

"Navarre."

"Ah! It's you? We know you very well."

"How did I bring you down?"

"Your first shots went right over the pilot's head and struck the motor."

Navarre had fired only eight rounds from the clip of his Hotchkiss, and four of them had hit the motor.

"What's this?" asked Navarre pointing to a red and white streamer snagged on the tail of the L.V.G.

The two Germans looked at each other in astonishment. It was an accident, they explained. They had meant it to go into the French lines. There was a letter attached to the streamer containing news of two French flyers who had been brought down behind the German lines.

The *gendarmes* finally arrived and marched the prisoners off to headquarters in a café in town. Navarre followed. At the café he telephoned to *Capitaine* de Bernis to report. Knowing that Navarre had taken off while the rest of the pilots were having breakfast, de Bernis told Navarre he would bring him some lunch from the mess, which he did, and soon he and Navarre and the two Germans were sitting down to share it. They ordered a bottle of wine to wash it down and to drink to each other's health; then they chatted for a while, about aeroplanes mostly.

*        *        *

IN MAY 1915 *Fliegerersatzabteilung Nr. 7* at Cologne ran a class of about 30 officers through the standard four-week observers course. The rudiments of navigation and the greasy aspects of aviation, such as the internal combustion engine, were touched upon. Lectures on observation and photography were given, as well as map-reading, and the course included a few hours of actual flight time.

At neither the head nor the foot of the class was Manfred von Richthofen who, on completing the course, was posted to *Fl. Abt. 69* on the Russian Front.

As an observer von Richthofen flew almost daily over the traditional scorched earth of a Russian retreat. His pilot was a well-known pre-war automobile enthusiast and sportsman named Count von Holck. The Count, a former Uhlan like von Richthofen, had strolled onto the aerodrome on foot with his hunting dogs, looking less like a Prussian officer than a happy-go-lucky blue-blooded playboy, which he was.

By the familiar mystery of the attraction of opposites, which they were except for their youth and high birth, von Holck and von Richthofen soon teamed up as pilot and observer.

In August 1915 they were transferred to Ostend, in Belgium, where a squadron was formed under the name of the Ostend Carrier Pigeons—*Brieftauben Abteilung Ostend.* The B.A.O. was a "secret weapon"—a bombing squadron conceived and organized with the ultimate object of strategic raids on Britain. The plan did not pan out, however, and after a short period of duty in Ostend, von Richthofen was transferred from *B.A.O.* to *B.A.M.*—the Metz Carrier Pigeons. On the train to Metz, von Richthofen met Boelcke, who at that time had scored four victories, and introduced himself as an admirer and one who very seriously wanted to fight in the air. The unprepossessing Boelcke listened quietly to von Richthofen's expressions of growing dissatisfaction with the clumsy brutes he was riding around in, and explained to him how he had gotten his four victories by simply flying close, aiming well, and shooting. At Metz, von Richthofen continued to ride in big, lumbering barges while his friend von Holck switched to an *Eindecker,* and Boelcke and Immelmann continued to gain victories.

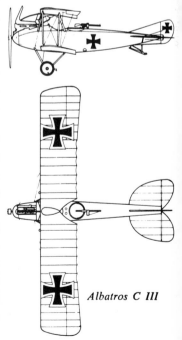

For the second time von Richthofen, the impetuous cavalryman, decided to step out of the war for a brief spell of training in the hope that this would enable him to come to closer grips with the enemy. He applied, and was accepted, for pilot training at Döberitz; he soloed on Christmas Day, 1915.

In March 1916 he rejoined *B.A.M.,* now labelled *K.G. 2 (Kampfgeschwader 2,* or Battle Group 2), at Verdun as pilot of an Albatros C III. Attached to the top wing of the Albatros was a machine gun on a rigid mount. Although it is officially unconfirmed, it is said that he managed to shoot down a French aeroplane with this machine on April 26.

On May first, while flying in the vicinity of Fort Douaumont, von Richthofen saw a fight between a Fokker *Eindecker* and three French two-seaters. The action was some distance off and up-wind from his position so he was unable to join the fight but he saw its end. The *Eindecker* suddenly dived straight down and disappeared in cloud. The pilot, von Richthofen later learned, had been killed outright by a bullet through the head. It was his old friend from the Russian Front, Count von Holck.

*Albatros C III*

## "THE INEVITABLE RESULT"

*"As I have said before, the whole business reminds me of duck shooting—there is just that same tendency to become overanxious which one must conquer . . . Quickness is essential, but there is a certain quick deliberation which I think must be acquired by practice. Just the difference again between the quick unaimed snap shot of the beginner in wing shooting and the equally quick aimed shot of the old hand. And when the bird shoots back it does make an awful difference . . ."*

CHARLES J. BIDDLE

VERDUN. There are a number of towns in France named Verdun, but only one Verdun in history—the one remembered in the phrase, "the hell of Verdun." The city of Verdun took its name from a Roman fortress, *Virodunum Castrum,* built in the century of Augustus, that had taken its name in turn from the name of the tribe inhabiting the pre-historic Gallic *oppidum.* There in 843 the three grandsons of Charlemagne signed the Oaths by which they divided up his empire. In 1792 the Prussians occupied Verdun for a few weeks, until the victory of the French at Valmy forced them to beat a retreat. In 1870 the Prussians again besieged and occupied Verdun, it being the last stronghold evacuated by the army of occupation in 1873.

From 1873 to 1914 the Citadel of Verdun and its ring of satellite fortlets were enlarged and strengthened until they formed, next to a similar complex at Toul, the most heavily fortified threshold in France. This system of fortresses stood athwart the valley of the Meuse, reinforcing the natural barrier of the river at a point where the German frontier approached to within 90 miles of one of the ancient paths to Paris, the valley of the Marne. On the night of February

21, 1916, the German Fifth Army began the bombardment that was the curtain-raiser to the Battle of Verdun.

Artillery was the characteristic feature of this battle: the guns massed for the opening represented the heaviest concentration of firepower in history. From February until June the earth was mauled along a constricted 15-mile front until it looked like the barren surface of the moon. Entire regiments were wiped out in the trenches. The trenches themselves were obliterated and soldiers were driven mad by the fearful pounding. Men were buried alive under the vast quantities of earth thrown up by the explosions, dug out and buried again. Both sides used the expression "the hell of Verdun" to describe the battle that for sheer horror is unsurpassed.

General Henri Phillipe Pétain took command of the defense of Verdun within a week of the start of the battle and declared in one of his first orders the absolute necessity of obtaining air parity.

At the start the Germans held the air. They had, in fact, aerial supremacy, although it wasn't called that yet. It was the high-water mark of the Fokker

*Eindecker* which had driven the French observation machines from the sky, and the German two-seaters flew their photography and artillery-spotting missions free from interference.

The success of the *Eindecker* is attributable to the fact that it was armed, of course, but there had also been a major advance in organization which was to have a considerable effect on the subsequent course of the war in the air. A year earlier, at the time of the spring offensive at Arras in 1915, the French had gained the upper hand in the air and it was only by sheer luck that the Germans were able to complete any long reconnaissance flights. This crisis continued on into the summer until a remedy was suggested by *Stofl. 6,* the Staff Officer for aviation troops of the German Sixth Army, a Bavarian Major named Stempel. Following Major Stempel's suggestion, all German single-seaters on the whole Western Front were combined into three units called Single-Seat Combat Detachments (*Kampfeinsitzer-Kommandos,* or *KEK*). By December 1915 there were 86 Fokker and 21 Pfalz *Eindeckers* at the Front. (The Pfalz was almost identical to the Fokker in layout, but was a trifle better in speed and climb.) The *Eindeckers* were sent up in small groups to patrol a beat along the German lines, forming a "barrage" which prevented the French machines from crossing over into German air. When aggressive pilots went hunting over the French lines, the Germans acquired, without having defined the concept, aerial supremacy.

For the French, the defense of Verdun depended on the flow of supplies from Bar-le-Duc, 35 miles south. Clearly, the *Voie sacrée,* the "Sacred Way" connecting Verdun and Bar-le-Duc, could not be kept open if the Germans could send over bombers and artillery-spotters at will.

The development of fighter aviation was thus thrust upon the French as a defensive necessity. General Pétain demanded, and got, a rapid concentration of all available machines, facilities for servicing them, and somebody to organize and lead them offensively, as fighters. No better choice could have been made than the choice that was made—the great walrus moustache, Tricornot de Rose.

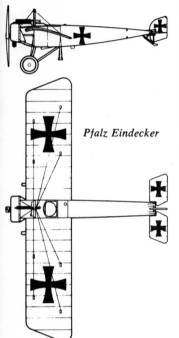

*Pfalz Eindecker*

*Tricornot de Rose*

SINCE THE GERMANS held the upper hand, the French were obliged to send work machines out with an escort. A half-dozen or a dozen aeroplanes would sometimes escort one photography or observation machine. The Germans would send up an entire *Eindecker* section of six machines to attack in unison, trying to down one two-seater in the middle of a gaggle of escorts. In this way the earliest "dogfights" came about. Since the aeroplanes still moved at a fairly slow turn of speed, a shade under 100 miles an hour, these fights occupied a relatively small piece of sky. In these crowded engagements the machines got in each other's way—*sous-Lieutenant* Guignand was astounded to see one *Eindecker* shoot another down in flames when the second blundered into the line of fire of the first.

Navarre was transferred to N 67 at Verdun at the beginning of the Battle. On February 26, he took off before dawn to patrol the lines alone. He spotted three German two-seaters and dived on them. All three broke for home. As he closed on the nearest one the gunner stood up in the seat and raised his hands. Navarre escorted the captive machine to Fort Rozières and flew home to breakfast. The telephone wire to the Front was temporarily out, so no immediate confirmation was forthcoming nor were any reports of spottings. The latter proved unnecessary when nine enemy aeroplanes appeared over the field. Navarre had had his Nieuport gassed up, and he promptly took off again. He approached the formation near Ancemont and the nearest machine accepted combat, turning hard to give the observer a clear shot. Navarre rolled away, came in again and fired a short burst. The two-seater turned on its back and started down, going steeper, tumbling wildly, crashing in a wood.

This was the first French double of the war, and it was the first time that the name of a *chasseur*—fighter pilot—was cited in an army communiqué.

The same day the squadron commander was transferred out of the unit—Navarre claimed a triple.

The new squadron commander, the *Marquis* de Saint-Sauveur, was an accomplished sportsman and a competent officer. He appreciated Navarre's qualities (as well as his spectacular inability to conform to discipline) and indulged him much as had *Capitaine* de Bernis—even to the extent of allowing him to paint his Nieuport red.

The Nieuport *Bébé* (Baby) that Navarre was flying at Verdun was the best single-seater of its time. It had been introduced in ones and twos to squadrons along the Front and was now being exploited in homogeneous squadrons by *Commandant* de Rose. It was far superior in speed, climb, ceiling, strength and manoeuvrability to the Fokker *Eindecker*. The *Bébé* had a distinctive wing plan: the top wing was swept-back and the bottom wing was so narrow it was called a half-wing. From this layout derived both strong points of performance and structural weakness. The sweepback of the top wing and the narrowness of the bottom wing were chiefly responsible for the manoeuvrability of the *Bébé;* the weakness arose from the fact that the narrow bottom wing was built around a single spar and was insufficiently rigid, so that it sometimes flexed and collapsed under the stress of diving or violent manoeuvring. The danger of wing collapse was not so great as to mean certain death, obviously, for Navarre scored most of his dozen victories at Verdun with diving attacks in a *Bébé,* and was, as we have seen, an inveterate stunter.

The *Bébé* was armed with a single Lewis gun fixed to the top wing in such a way as to fire straight ahead over the propeller. The gun was aimed by means of a ring-sight arrangement on the cowling in front of the cockpit. The lines of sight and fire were regulated at the target range on the ground to converge at 150 metres or about 500 feet. Most pilots, however, were not such good shots as to be able precisely to gauge distance in combat whilst the adversary and the *Bébé* were both moving in three-dimensional space, and so preferred to close in to point-blank range. Aside from the complex problems of co-ordination inherent in deflection shooting (any shooting in which the target is elsewhere than straight ahead), there was the problem of a severely limited supply of ammunition—the 47 rounds in the drum of a Lewis gun could be fired off in five seconds and the pilot of a *Bébé* could not afford to hose an area of sky in order to score a hit as could the observer of a German two-seater armed with a 500-round Parabellum.

Navarre was a virtuoso who could shoot as well as fly. He brought some of his victims down with only a half-dozen rounds.

On April 4, 1916, shortly after he was promoted to *sous-Lieutenant,* Navarre flew three patrols—one at dawn, one in the afternoon and one at sunset—in the course of which he shot down *four* enemy aeroplanes, an incredible performance for the time. Only one machine was officially credited since the other three had fallen behind the German lines.

\*　　　　　\*　　　　　\*

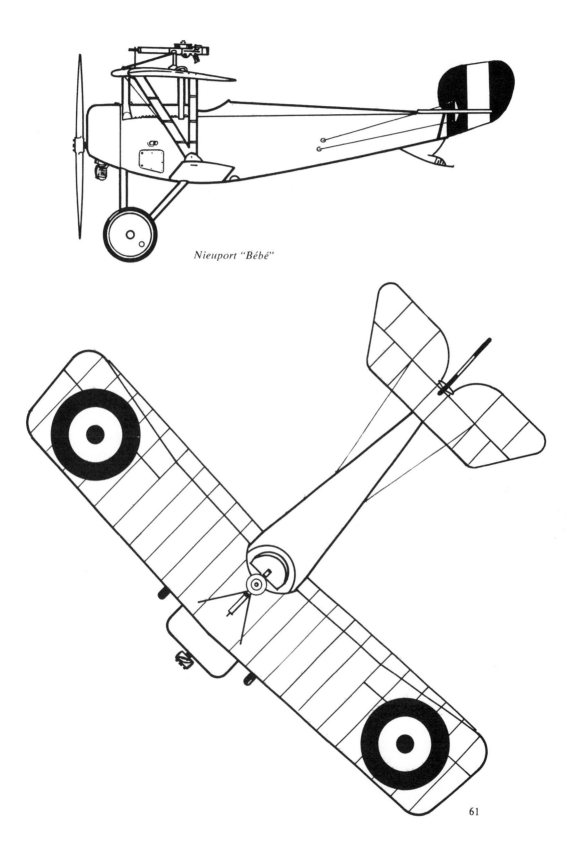

Nieuport "Bébé"

61

AMONG THE FLYING personnel assembled at Verdun as a result of General Pétain's directive was an ex-cavalryman named Jacques Leps, the son of a cavalryman, an old-time professional soldier who commanded the First Hussars. At the
beginning of 1915, Leps had been transferred at his father's request from his own
unit, the Ninth Hussars, to the First, as consolation for the loss of another son,
Guy, killed by a bullet through the heart.

By the summer of 1915 all cavalry had become obsolete and Jacques Leps
was in the trenches before the fortlet of Beauséjour. Perched upon the crest of a
crater he was surveying the German trenches when he perceived a party of German infantry working at repairing their lines at a distance of about 300 metres.
He called several Hussars and standing on the high ground directed their fire
on the working party. Ignoring the fire of snipers, Leps continued to call the
shots for his own men until he was finally shot through the chest. There were
often Jesuits to be found where the battle was raging and an Abbé de Ruble
appeared and gave Leps absolution—and was himself killed on the spot. A
medic took one look at Leps and said, "He's done for."

With amazing vitality, Leps held on, however, and the incident became
known, creating something of a stir. General Grossetti, commander of the XVI
Corps, came to see him on his stretcher and said, "You deserve to be punished;
I will award you instead the *Croix de Guerre* with palm . . ."

Removed to St. Etienne, he mended without complication in a short time,
and took advantage of his convalescence at the rear to obtain a transfer to the
air service.

When Leps arrived at Verdun, he was assigned to N 67 with Navarre, and
began serving as observer for long-range reconnaissance. One day Navarre approached Leps and asked him with a mysterious solemnity if he, Leps (who was
a good shot), would like to fly as gunner with him on board a new two-seat
fighter.

Leps accepted eagerly. Agreed: they would hunt together. Should they find
a *Boche* it would be easy. Navarre briefed Leps, "No matter what the aerobatics
of the German aeroplane may be, I will place you 15 metres below him and
you will have but to fire."

Leps has said since, "This was not mere boasting; he could really do it."

As it happened, Leps never had the chance to go hunting with Navarre, but
he did go out in the new two-seat fighter Navarre had been talking about.

This particular machine, a Spad product designed by Bécherau, who later
designed the Spad single-seaters, was so laid out that the pilot sat between the
wings and behind the engine while the gunner sat out in front of the engine. It was
a desperate solution to the problem of a front-firing gun. It was never popular
because it was not safe: if it came down too hard on the nose, the engine would
go through the gunner. Leps, however, was willing to try anything once—standing
up on the edge of no-man's-land and letting enemy snipers take pot shots at
him, or flying in the front seat of the Spad A.2.

Leps and his alternate pilot took off to try out the new machine. They were
soon over the lines where they were promptly attacked by an enemy aeroplane.

62

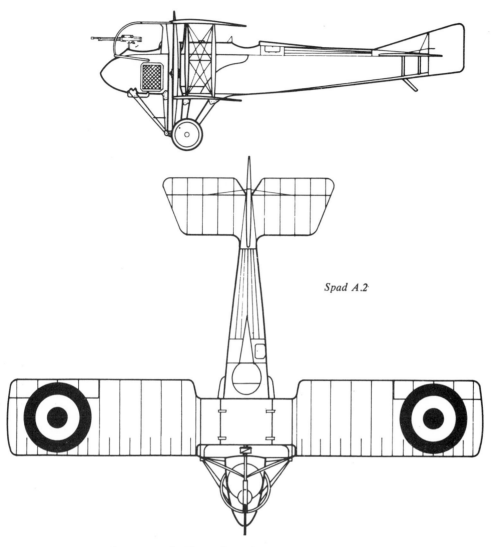

*Spad A.2*

A grotesque combat ensued. The pilot abruptly dived the Spad and Leps was ejected bodily out of his balcony, restrained at the extreme reach of his safety harness, which drew taut and flung him back into the bottom of his basket where he lay flat, unable to rise. The pilot cleared out and headed for home.

Leps tells the rest of the story in his own words: "My pilot returned to the field and approached the ground in front of the entire squadron which had assembled to watch our return and hear our report on the new aeroplane.

"The pilot overshot and the machine turned over—one can guess what remained of my pulpit, pulverized by the propeller and the engine.

"Everyone rushed forward, *Capitaine* de Saint-Sauveur at the head, to pick up the pieces. I was hanging head-down, but unhurt.

"I asked only that I be allowed to do my own flying from then on."

*　　　　　*　　　　　*

ON JUNE 17, 1916, Navarre, Pivolo, and *ajudant* (later *sous-Lieutenant*) Guignand on a patrol towards the Argonne espied a German two-seater spotting for an artillery shoot. They attacked in unison and shot it down. Since it fell behind the lines it was never credited to any of them. Continuing the patrol they came across a second two-seater at about 12,000 feet over Grand Pré, 3000 feet below them. Navarre waggled his wings and pointed to make sure his teammates had seen the target, then dived. As he led his men into a stern attack, Navarre swung wide to give Pivolo and Guignand first shots. Pivolo fired and broke away. Navarre looked around for Guignand, puzzled that he hadn't put in a burst too.

The German gunner caught him with a long burst. He felt a terrible blow in chest, arm, and side. Stunned, but still conscious, he dived hard as the best means of getting away. He was losing blood, he already felt weak and his vision was blurring. He blacked out and the Nieuport spun down to about 6000 feet before he regained consciousness. He switched off the ignition, brought the machine under control and, keeping the nose down, looked around for a place to put her down. Luckily, he was directly over a playing field. He came into it upwind after a beautifully executed bank ("just in case it should be the last"), touched down and rolled to a stop. He tried to climb out of the Nieuport and passed out.

When he came to, the first face he saw was Pivolo, who had followed him down and landed beside him.

One bullet had hit Navarre, breaking his left arm and entering his chest. On recovering consciousness and recognizing Pivolo he passed out again. In the hospital he was delirious for several days. He had lost a dangerous amount of blood and it seems likely that some brain damage resulted.

When he went on his first leave from the hospital he was incredibly emaciated and his constitutional debilitation was so great that he had no tolerance for alcohol whatever. One glass of wine made him blind drunk. He was depressed and moody. Returning to N 67 before he was fit, he tried a tailspin and passed out from a hemorrhage when his wound reopened. He came to and pulled out literally at ground level.

Clearly, he was not recovered and, worse, was not himself mentally. The cruel news, bluntly broken, that his beloved twin Pierre had been killed brought on a complete collapse. He was out of the war. Although he returned to active status in September 1918, he never flew operationally again.

*        *        *

IN THE FALL of 1915 the Germans began to realize that the Fokker victories they were enjoying were costly to them as well as to the Allies. While the Allies tied up four times as many aeroplanes for each reconnaissance flight as before the "Fokker Scourge," seeking safety in numbers but reducing results by that proportion, the Germans had lost something in the way of observation and artillery co-operation by providing pilots for Fokkers at the expense of the two-seater squadrons. Not every Fokker pilot was a Boelcke or an Immelmann, and so to give increased effectiveness to the *Eindecker,* it was re-engined from the fall of 1915 with a 160-horsepower Oberürsel rotary engine and armed with two guns. Only about 50 examples of this model, the E IV, were produced. By the spring of 1916 the *Eindecker* had had its day. For one thing, the Nieuport *Bébé* outclassed it on every count. For another, the British had introduced two new machines, both pushers with front-firing guns that required, obviously, no interrupter or synchronizing gear. One was the D.H.2, a single-seater, which had been designed specifically as a fighter and of which the first fighter squadron in the RFC was composed. Commanded by Major Lanoe G. Hawker, No. 24 Squadron had come to France in February 1916.

It had become apparent that if the air service was "eyes" for the army on one side in the war, it was "eyes" for the army on the other. If one side became "blind" with its aeroplanes shot down, so would the other. To protect British two-seaters on observation and photography flights, and chase away Germans on theirs, the British produced the D.H.2 as a fighter and sent it to France. It was slightly faster than, and climbed twice as fast as, the *Eindecker;* it was stronger and more manoeuvrable. The British pilots credited the D.H.2 with ending the "Fokker Scourge." (Since the Nieuport *Bébé* appeared eight months earlier than the D.H.2 it is easy to guess which aeroplane the French give the credit to.)

The other British machine was a two-seater, the F.E.2b, which went to France early in 1916 with No. 20, 22, 23, and 25 Squadrons, RFC. The original F.E. was a pre-war design, but the 2b model had been considerably revamped, and with a new powerplant, a 160-horsepower Beardmore, and a flexible Lewis gun in the front seat, it was able to hold its own against the Fokker.

*F.E.2b*

65

*Immelmann.*

*Imperial War Museum / London*

On June 18, 1916, observers on the ground at Lens saw a pair of *Eindeckers* attack a flight of three British F.E.2b's. The fight seemed to start over Loos, northwest of Lens, and end over Sallaumines, a few miles to the east. One F.E.2b was badly shot up and glided down with a dead engine. The other two were thrown about by their pilots to put the attackers off their aim. One *Eindecker* came in from the beam, fired into one of the F.E.'s, then zoomed up and over in a half-loop—it was Max Immelmann using his standard attack, the "Immelmann turn." When the machine slowed down at the top of the loop, the gunner in the F.E. had one clear shot. He fired. The Fokker rolled over, and those watching from the ground clearly saw it break up in the air. The fore part of the fuselage with the engine and the pilot came whining down and hit the ground with a muffled crunch.

The fight was over, but the war went on. The British gave credit for an aerial victory to the gunner of the F.E.2b. The Germans, shocked at the loss of Immelmann their young idol, talked about the disaster almost in tones of disbelief. Rumors of sabotage were more or less stopped by the findings of an official board of inquiry whose verdict was that the aeroplane had collapsed as a result of damage by antiaircraft fire. Tony Fokker had something to do with the official verdict because he was determined to protect his *Eindecker* against charges of structural weakness. There was considerable mistrust of the welded steel tube technique, although it was in fact stronger than the contemporary wood construction. There was also a mistrust of the Fokker interrupter gear. Many believed that it was not safe and that the machine's propeller had been shot off.

Actually, the propeller had been shot off, but not through any fault of Fokker's interrupter gear. The aeroplane in question had just had a propeller change and in the rush to intercept the three British F.E.'s it was taken up before the ground crew had had time to check the alignment of the propeller and the gun linkage. The propeller was bolted on in the wrong position and must inevitably have passed before the muzzle at the wrong instant.

It was no consolation to know that the loss was an accident rather than a defeat, for the result was the same either way—*der Adler von Lille* was gone.

*Ehrhardt von Teubern*

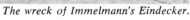

*The wreck of Immelmann's Eindecker.*

MID-SUMMER 1916. Time for a quick gasp for breath between the hell of Verdun and the Battle of the Somme. The armies were licking their wounds, exhausted. Then they would fly at each other's throats again. In the air the pioneers went down one by one. The new men, the young replacements, looked at the face of war and said that no one had told them it would be like this. The aviators looked down in fascination and horror as the infantry charged across no-man's-land and, with bloody losses, captured a trench 60 yards away. Then they (the aviators) looked up, looked ahead, and saw another trench 60 yards away, and another beyond that, and another and another and another. Then they looked around to see who else was in the air with them. No one—if they were lucky. But too often aviators would forget themselves in the torn and tortured scene below and a single-seater would come out of the sun to send them down into the ground in a burning aeroplane so that there was not even anything left to bury and if there had been there was no way of knowing whether it was French, British, German, American, Austrian, Italian, or Russian.

*         *         *

IN THE SUMMER of 1916 the Belgian Ace Edmond Thieffry engaged a German single-seater in an indecisive combat that lasted several minutes. Both pilots got off long bursts without effect. Thieffry, flying a Nieuport *Bébé,* exhausted the ammunition in the drum of his Lewis gun and extended his arm to pull back the gun for reloading. The German pilot, apparently seeing the outstretched arm and mistaking the gesture for a chivalrous salute, waved back, then flew away, leaving Thieffry astonished and alone.

*         *         *

MOMENTS OF CHIVALRY and humanity stand out against the background of the war like the poppies against the muddy fields of Flanders, but nothing in all the world will bring back one dead soldier.

*         *         *

THE GREAT walrus moustache was gone now, too. The man with the fierce regard and soft heart, *Commandant* Tricornot de Rose went down at Verdun leading the fighters he successfully organized for France.

Manfred von Richthofen secretly grieved for his friend, Count von Holck. They had celebrated von Richthofen's twenty-fourth birthday together only a few days before von Holck was killed. A few days after, von Richthofen expressed a familiar disbelief in a letter to his mother when he said it was impossible to imagine "that this strong, handsome, healthy man no longer exists."

The woodworkers in the squadrons used to make crosses out of broken propellers for the graves of airmen, friend or foe, whom they buried. One day the Belgian Ace Jan Olieslagers walked into the hangar shop and found a mechanic polishing a new propeller cross. There had been no recent losses, and Olieslagers asked in surprise, "Who's that for?"

The mechanic answered simply, "For the next one."

*         *         *

67

EN ROUTE TO VERDUN the end of February 1916 Georges Guynemer shot down his eighth victim, but was shot down himself shortly after his arrival. On March 13, after two inconclusive encounters with enemy machines, he came across two more and attacked the first head-on. He passed under the machine whose observer got in a good burst so that Guynemer's face was peppered with splinters. His goggles filled with blood and he reached up to tear them off, but his left arm wouldn't move—it had two bullets through it. He snatched off the goggles with his right hand, letting go of the stick, and the *Bébé* went into a spin. He brought the aeroplane under control and got worked over some more by a third enemy machine. He escaped further injury and the proximity of the French lines deterred further pursuit. He crash-landed behind his lines and was badly shaken up.

He was evacuated to Paris the next day, but spent the greater part of his recuperative leave at his father's house at Compiègne. As soon as he was able to be up and around he went to the air depot at Vauciennes to look over his new *Bébé*. As soon after that as he felt fit enough to fly he took it up to keep his hand in.

He began to wonder about his nerve. He was vaguely uneasy about how he might react to combat. He was afraid he might want to back out of a fight, or break off, unable to go through with it. He decided he would have to test his mettle before rejoining the squadron. Accordingly, he rose before dawn one morning, went to Vauciennes, checked out the *Bébé,* and took off. Cruising along the lines he spotted a German two-seater and launched a feint attack. He had decided the way to test himself was to keep making feint attacks without firing a shot until he had reached a point that was equivalent to psychological dominance over his adversary.

The German gunner opened fire, but the Nieuport flipped wildly out of the way and came in from the other side. He swung the Parabellum around and fired and the *Bébé* dropped out of sight, coming in from the blind spot under the tail. And so it went. After firing several bursts at the *Bébé,* the gunner ceased, and refused to fire. Guynemer waved and flew back to Vauciennes, satisfied that he had not lost his nerve or become otherwise unfit to be a *pilote de chasse.*

He had left the house early and he got back early. The rest of the family was still asleep and he let himself in quietly so as not to awaken anyone.

*         *         *

FROM THE AUTUMN of 1916 a new Spad single-seater was issued to the French *escadrilles de chasse* where it quickly made a name for itself. The Spad 7 was a variation of the Spad A.2, redesigned to take a stationary eight-cylinder engine. The word "Spad" was taken from the initials of the company that produced the aeroplane, the *Société pour Aviation et ses Dérives,* or Society for Aviation and

68

its Derivatives. The company had been founded by Armand Deperdussin and was originally named *Société pour Appareils Deperdussin* or, loosely, the Deperdussin Aeroplanes Society. Shortly before the war Deperdussin resigned as head of the firm, to be replaced by the famous aviator Louis Blériot. In 1909 Blériot had flown across the English Channel in a monoplane of his own design and in the five years before the war had won considerable celebrity piloting the speedy Deperdussin machines. Blériot had changed the name of the company but had kept the initials and hence the name of the product—a Spad is a Spad.

The first Spad single-seater was powered with the 140-horsepower Hispano Suiza engine. Hispano Suiza means, in Spanish, "Spanish-Swiss," and the phrase was chosen to convey the nature of the international collaboration of which it was the name. In 1899 Marc Birkigt of Geneva had gone to Barcelona at the age of 21 to accept a position with a Swiss engineer who was already established there. In May 1904 he set up his own company, the Hispano Suiza Motor Company, with the financial backing of Damien Mateu of Barcelona.

When the war broke out, Birkigt was working on a new aero engine, which, because of its novel features—concentric connecting rods and one-piece cylinder heads, for example—provoked considerable interest among the Allies. It was a superlative design and was produced in great numbers at the home factory at Barcelona and under license in France, Britain, Italy, and the U.S.A. Engines from the home factory were called Hispano Hispano; those from contract firms simply Hispano. So with the airframe—a Spad built by the parent firm was called a Spad Spad. A really lucky pilot flew a Hispano Hispano Spad Spad. (Pilot superstition and nothing else caused the parent firm products to be considered superior.)

The Spad 7 was a hot machine. Its thin wings gave it a high landing speed and the gliding angle of a brick. It was fast on the straightaway, having a top speed of 120 miles per hour (or 200 kilometres per hour, which sounds even better.) The armament was a single synchronized Vickers machine gun mounted on top of the engine cowling directly in front of the pilot. The synchronizing gear fitted to the early Spad fighters was a French variation on the mechanical linkage system used by Fokker. It was called the Alkan and was one of a series of similar synchronizers developed and used by the Allies.

As more powerful engines became available, they were fitted, and the horsepower crept up to 235 in the Spad 13. A score of 300-horsepower Spad 17's was delivered in the last weeks of the war.

The Spad was *the* fighter of the 1914-1918 war—nearly 8500 of all versions were built.

When *escadrille* N 3 of *Groupe de Combat XII* re-equipped with Spads in the autumn of 1916, the aeroplane with its Hispano Suiza engine made such an impression on the pilots that they adopted the Hispano Suiza trade mark, a stork, as the squadron insignia. Spa 3 was the lead squadron of the *Groupe,* the other squadrons being Spa 26, Spa 73, and Spa 103. All were known eventually as *les Cigognes,* the Storks, with stork insignias, but Spa 3 was the original.

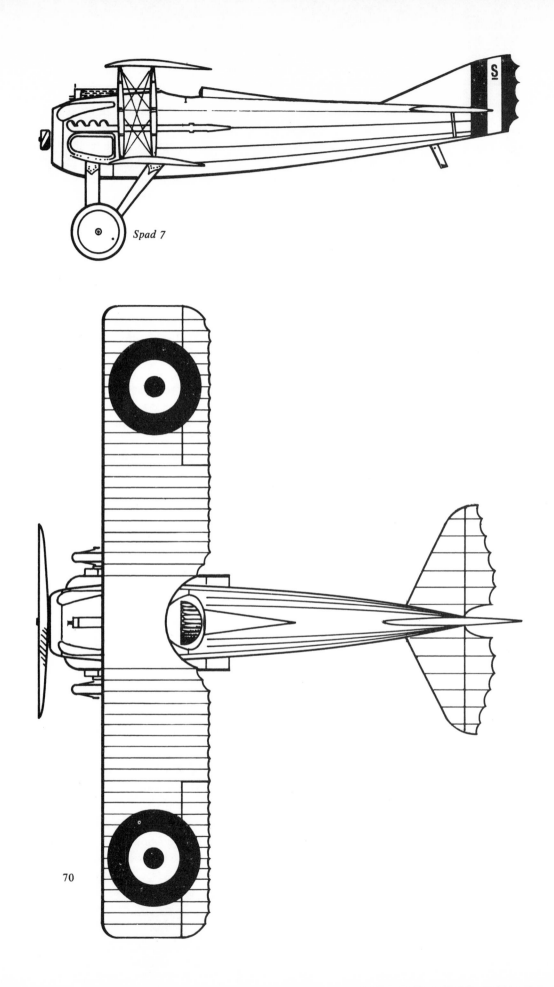

*Spad 7*

70

*Imperial War Museum / London*

A striking demonstration of the sturdiness of the Spad occurred in September 1916 when Guynemer was shot down for the sixth time—also thereby demonstrating his own sturdiness. (Once he had crashed in no-man's-land and had been rescued by the *poilus* who had spontaneously erupted out of the trenches and charged over the front to get him and bring him back.) On September 23, he shot down three German machines in five minutes—11:20 to 11:25. At 11:25½ (as he later wrote his father) the shell from a French 75 went through the water reservoir in front of the cockpit, spraying wreckage in all directions and starting the covering of his left top wing which promptly peeled bare in the slip stream. The Spad dropped in a tailspin from 9000 feet with Guynemer struggling to right the machine all the way down. He managed to level out but without being able to slow down much, hitting the ground at about 110 miles an hour, shearing off the landing gear while what was left of the wings folded up and tore off. The wreck caromed into the air again, coming to rest upside down about 120 feet away from where it first lit. Guynemer had actually crashed before his final victim of that morning hit the ground!

"The Spad is solid," he observed laconically to his father. "With another I would now be thinner than this sheet of paper. I landed within 300 feet of the battery that demolished me. They weren't shooting at me but they brought me down all the same . . ."

*                    *                    *

*Escadrille Lafayette—N 124.*

IN APRIL 1916 the French air service formally established N 124 on the roster of *escadrilles* on active duty. The name of the unit was *Escadrille Américaine,* and except for its French officers and ground crew it was composed of volunteer Americans. A number of American Francophiles had been in France when the war started and many of them joined the Foreign Legion in that first week of August. Norman Prince of Massachusetts wanted to form an all-American flying squadron but the idea at first met with a cool reception in French official *purlieux.* After a year of war, however, the French Government began to think that the American Government needed some prodding to take a more decisive part in assisting the Allies and that one good way to do it would be to permit the formation of an American unit to fight with the French.

The Americans at home would then see the example of their more spirited fellow countrymen and bring pressure to bear on their representatives in Washington to make a more affirmative commitment on behalf of the Allies. Whether or not the *Escadrille Américaine* speeded America's entry into the war, it got a few Americans into the war a little sooner than their draftboards would have. Norman Prince had enlisted some valuable support from the Vanderbilts and from Dr. Edmund Gros, one of the heads of the American Field Service. On April 20, at Luxeuil-les-bains, the *Escadrille Américaine,* N 124, received its charter.

Almost immediately the German ambassador in the United States lodged a protest against neutrals taking part in the war, so the name was changed as a cover-up. GQG suggested *Escadrille des Volontaires,* but the Americans didn't like it because it was too vague—anybody could volunteer—and because it had no style, no class. It was the most anonymous name imaginable. Dr. Gros suggested *Escadrille Lafayette,* after the great French statesman and general who fought in the American Revolutionary War. The idea of repaying France a favor after a century and a quarter pleased the Americans and the name was submitted to the French Government and accepted.

A total of 42 men—four French and 38 American—make up the entire roster of the *Escadrille Lafayette.* Not all Americans who volunteered for flying could be absorbed by the *Lafayette;* if there were no opening at the time a man completed his training he might be posted to any French unit. Such was the case with Charles Biddle who was sent to one of the Stork squadrons, Spa 73. Whatever unit a man served in, his status as an American volunteer was recognized by his being designated a member of the Lafayette Flying Corps. Some two hundred men in all served with the Lafayette Flying Corps and the *Escadrille Lafayette.* Many members of the Lafayette Flying Corps preferred to remain with their friends in French squadrons rather than transfer to American squadrons when the U.S. Air Service finally arrived on the scene. On February 18, 1918, the *Escadrille Lafayette* became the 103rd Pursuit Squadron, U.S.A.S.

*Student pilots of the Lafayette Flying Corps, March 1917. In the group are two future members of the Escadrille Lafayette, James Norman Hall (8) and Charles H. Dolan, Jr. (12). Some of the other famous Americans are Leland L. Rounds (1), George E. Turnure, Jr. (10), Oliver M. Chadwick (13), Walter D. Rheno (15), and Paul F. Baer (19).*

LATE IN 1915 the Halberstadt Aeroplane Works, of Halberstadt near Magdeburg, had produced a single-seat scout biplane powered by the 100-horsepower Mercedes engine. This aeroplane was given the official army designation of Halberstadt D I, the "D" standing for *Doppeldecker,* or two-winger. The D I was developed from the B II, an unarmed two-seater which had served purely as a fast reconnaissance machine. The first models to reach the Front, in June 1916, were the D II powered by the 120-horsepower Mercedes and the D III with a 120-horsepower Argus engine. The D II and the D III were equipped with the Fokker interrupter gear and armed with a single fixed Spandau machine gun. They were issued, like the Fokker *Eindecker,* in twos and threes to the *Fliegerabteilungen,* first as scouts and then as escorts for the two-seaters. The Halberstadt machines were fairly strong, and this was their chief value to the pilots since their performance was only a little better than that of the *Eindecker.*

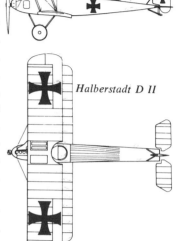

*Halberstadt D II*

During the summer of 1916 it became clear that the *Eindecker* was no longer able to meet the new Allied fighters and it was gradually withdrawn. It was replaced, however, with machines that were only a little better, while the British and the French were flying aeroplanes that were a lot better.

Thus the German air service almost lost the advantage so handily won by the *Eindecker* in 1915, and morale in some units began to sag again. It happened, however, that at precisely this point in the game a truly revolutionary aeroplane made its appearance.

The Albatros Works of Johannisthal, Berlin, had accumulated considerable experience in plywood construction. The Daimler Motor Company of Stuttgart-Untertürkheim had developed a superb engine, the Mercedes D III, a water-cooled six-cylinder engine of 160 horsepower. The Albatros D I was designed specifically to take advantage of the Albatros company's plywood technique and the Mercedes engine.

The Albatros D I was a revolutionary aeroplane in several respects and merits a close examination. The wings were of conventional wood frame construction covered with fabric, but the fuselage was semi-monocoque. In a true monocoque form the outer shell is so rigid it requires no internal bracing, like a mailing tube or the bodies of some modern racing cars the wheels of which are attached directly to the body, the weight of a chassis thus being eliminated. The semi-monocoque fuselage of the Albatros D I, and all succeeding Albatros fighters, was formed of thin transverse plywood partitions connected by six lengthwise strips of spruce called longerons. To this skeleton were screwed preformed slabs of plywood. The strength and robustness of this construction made it possible for the Albatros to absorb heavy punishment, a significant virtue in a combat machine. The power margin of the Mercedes conferred two tactical advantages: the aeroplane could regularly be armed with two fixed machine guns instead of one as was standard usage, and its pilots had at their command sufficient speed to start and break off fights when they chose.

In the summer of 1916 the Germans might have lost the edge they had won with the *Eindecker.* They didn't, because they had the Albatros D I, a superb new weapon, and because they had Oswald Boelcke to wield that new weapon.

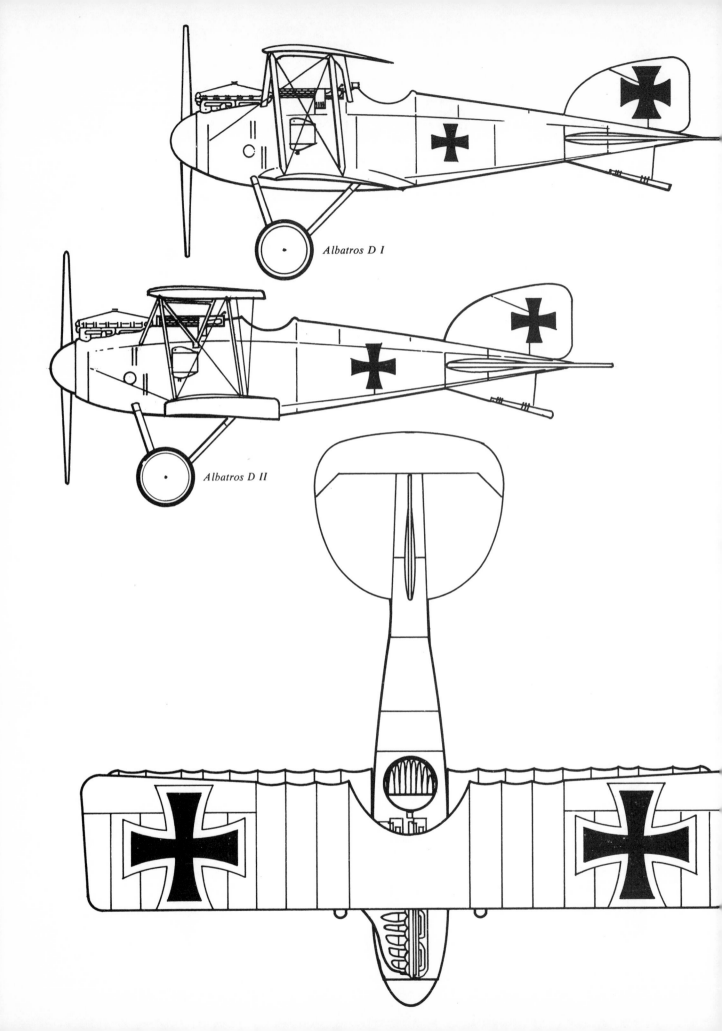

*Albatros D I*

*Albatros D II*

# ON
## THE ESTABLISHING OF
## THE GERMAN FIGHTER FORCES,
### OR
### HOW THE CIRCUS CAME TO TOWN

TO BEGIN at the top: the Chief of the Imperial German General Staff from the beginning of the war until the summer of 1916 was General von Falkenhayn, the former Prussian Minister of War, the same von Falkenhayn who had been so impressed by Fokker's stunt flying in the spring of 1914. He was blamed for the German "failure" at Verdun and replaced by General von Hindenburg.

Paul Ludwig Hans Anton von Beneckendorff und von Hindenburg was an old-time officer. He had won the Iron Cross at the Siege of Paris in 1871 and had commanded the IV Army Corps from 1903 to 1911 when he had retired at the age of 65. Recalled in 1914, he had showed up wearing a beautiful old-fashioned Prussian blue uniform because he had not had time to have one of the new German field gray uniforms made. He was appointed to command the Eighth Army on the Russian Front. His chief of staff was General Erich F. W. Ludendorff, the "Hero of Liège." The Hindenburg/Ludendorff combination promptly made its presence felt by handing the Russians a crushing defeat at Tannenburg. Hindenburg was made a Field Marshal and awarded the *Pour le Mérite*. When in 1916 he succeeded von Falkenhayn as Chief of the General Staff, Ludendorff went with him, still his right hand man. The H/L combination directed all German strategy for the remainder of the war.

It was Ludendorff who obtained the Kaiser's approval for the establishing of an independent air service. Until the summer of 1916 all air units had been under the control of the Director of Railways and Transport, their operation dictated by army corps commanders. (The United States did not establish a Division of Military Aeronautics directly responsible to the Secretary of War until May of 1918; up to then the air service had been a branch of the Signal Corps.)

General Ernst von Hoeppner, a 56-year-old infantryman, was appointed to command the new organization, which was given the name *Luftstreitkräfte,* or Air Combat Force. (The World War II name—*Luftwaffe,* which means simply Air Arm—was not used in World War I.) The Air Chief of Staff was a professional soldier named Major (later Colonel) Hermann von der Lieth-Thomsen. In the summer of 1916 Oswald Boelcke was Germany's premier *Jagdflieger,* with 18 confirmed victories, and was her most experienced air tactician. He and Major Thomsen, after a series of conferences, produced an air policy which contemplated, among other things, the creation of homogeneous and permanent fighter squadrons. The success of the *Kampfeinsitzerkommando* derived from the fact that sections of Fokkers had been allowed to go out and stooge around by themselves hunting for enemy observation ships without having to worry about protecting their own two-seaters. Although the *Eindecker* could no longer cut the competition, the Albatros certainly could, and it was therefore conceived that the time had come to spread all-fighter squadrons along the Front.

Seven such units were initially projected; by 1918 there were 81, numbered consecutively from *1* to *81,* plus 3 naval squadrons for fighting over land. The basic unit was the *Jagdstaffel,* literally "hunting echelon," which had a composition on paper of 18 aeroplanes, 24 pilots, and about 130 ground personnel. In practice, the effective strength of the *Jagdstaffeln* was nearer 12 or even 10 machines owing to combat attrition and depending on replacement difficulties in both personnel and matériel. In pilot slang *Jagdstaffel* was invariably shortened to *Jasta.* The first two *Jastas* were commanded by Martin Zander and Oswald Boelcke.

*          *          *

TOWARD THE END of the Battle of Verdun, Manfred von Richthofen was transferred back to the Russian Front. There he had his second meeting with Boelcke.

*Albatros D I*

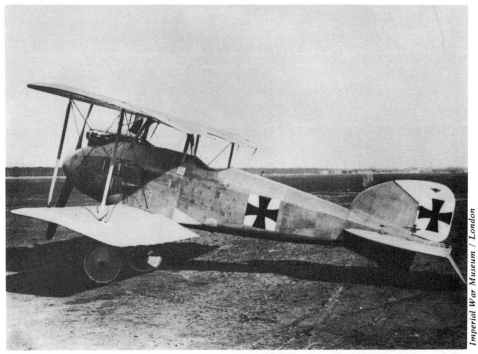

*Imperial War Museum / London*

At the behest of Major Thomsen, Boelcke had undertaken a tour of inspection of the German air service on all fronts and was at the same time, and with full backing of Thomsen, hand picking men for his own *Jasta.* He remembered von Richthofen and asked him if he still wanted to be a fighter pilot. "Yes!" answered Richthofen. "Sir."

The home aerodrome of Boelcke's *Jasta 2* was at Lagnicourt in the ancient province of Artois in northern France, two leagues exactly northeast of Bapaume. There von Richthofen reported on the first of September. Until the middle of the month Boelcke drilled his "cubs" in the methods and techniques of air-fighting. When the new Albatros fighters arrived, the training began in earnest, Boelcke and his pupils flying every day, practicing formation flying, team tactics and aerial gunnery.

76

Sunday, September 17, 1916, the *Jasta* made its operational debut. The aeroplanes were checked out and lined up on the turf in front of the canvas tent hangars where the mechanics started the engines and ran them up. The pilots, looking like teddy bears in their goggles and bulky flying togs, gathered around Boelcke for final instructions and a last pep talk. They climbed into their machines and took off. It was a bright clear morning and Boelcke soon spotted a formation of British machines crossing the lines. Two flights—obviously bombers with escort—B.E.2c's and F.E.2b's. Boelcke immediately began to climb to put himself and his squadron above them and in the glare of the sun. They were heading into German territory, so he would be able to pick his own time to jump them. He shrewdly guessed that when they reached their target they would all be looking down—the time to attack.

*Boelcke.*

It worked just that way. When Boelcke waggled his wings and gave the hand signal, every man had picked his target. The *Jasta* knifed down and cut the enemy formation to ribbons.

Those British pilots who survived the fight reported that it was indeed a tough lot of Huns that had beaten them up.

Early in 1916 Paul Tarascon, the one-footed pilot who had been Guynemer's instructor, succeeded in getting himself posted to an operational squadron, N 31 at Toul. In May he was transferred to N 3 to take part in the Battle of the Somme. The squadron was then located in the forest of Cachy, near Villers-Bretonneux. In August he brought down his first enemy aeroplane. He was, by the end of summer, one of the most skillful and experienced pilots at the Front. He was an excellent strategist and leader. More of a leader, in fact, than a fighter, he shared the quality of disinterestedness with Boelcke, and preferred to help a new man get a victory rather than to increase his own score.

In September 1916 Tarascon engaged a red Albatros in a duel over the Somme. The fight lasted seven or eight minutes—an incredibly long time, suggesting an even match. Both pilots exhausted their ammunition.

*Tarascon.*

Paul Tarascon

Each time one was set up for a killing burst, the other managed to whip away with some astonishing manoeuvre. "I can still see the black leather helmet of Boelcke"—Tarascon's favorite recollection—"as I crossed him like a flash and he tossed me a sporting salute."

With ammunition gone, there was nothing to do but wave. Tarascon and Boelcke, calling it a draw, headed home.

"It is with a great pleasure that, in a sense of sportsmanship, I render hommage to the great aviator that was Boelcke.

"Our combat was without mercy, for Honor, but of such a dignity, such a knightliness, that, if our combat had been favorable to me, I would have solicited for him, for this knight of the air, privileged treatment."

Thus Tarascon, after 48 years, returns Boelcke's salute.

By the end of October, Boelcke's *Jasta 2* was well blooded. There had been losses, but Boelcke was satisfied with his team. He himself had 40 victories; no other pilot of the time had anything like such a phenomenal score. He had been the leading fighter pilot of the war for so long that both sides had come to think him invincible. His number came up all the same.

During the morning and afternoon of October 28, 1916, Boelcke had led *Jasta 2* on four separate patrols. Between 3 and 4 o'clock in the afternoon he led again and came across a pair of D.H.2's from No. 24 Squadron RFC, Major Hawker's squadron. A short fight ensued over Pozières. At one point Boelcke dived on one of the D.H.2's whose pilot, a Canadian named Lieutenant Knight, turned hard to the left to avoid his fire, and Boelcke broke away to his right. As he turned away, Boelcke slammed his top wing against the landing gear of one of his comrade's machines. The collision was not violent, but it damaged the wing and burst the fabric, which then tore loose in the wind. He went down in wide circles while his men watched. He seemed to have his machine under control—it looked as if he might be able to set it down safely. Then the damaged wing collapsed and the Albatros dropped like a stone.

On November 3, 1916, von Richthofen shot down an F.E.2b in the morning for his seventh confirmed victory and attended Boelcke's funeral in the afternoon. Six days later, he had achieved his eighth confirmed victory. Immelmann and Boelcke had both been awarded the *Pour le Mérite* after eight and Manfred confidently expected to receive the Order himself; he was chagrined to learn that the General Staff had, after much deliberation, decided to establish sweeping reforms in the awarding of decorations. What was called the "tempo" of the air fighting was picking up in such a way that any number of men might qualify for the *Pour le Mérite* in a short time; so to avoid embarrassment the required number of victories for fighter pilots was set officially at 16.

*　　　　　*　　　　　*

ONE OF THE DYNAMIC figures of the Royal Flying Corps was Major Lanoe George Hawker who was born on December 31, 1890, the son of Lieutenant H. C. Hawker of the Royal Navy. As a boy, Lanoe was much interested in things mechanical and electrical, he had an active, inquiring mind and considerable ingenuity.

He became fascinated by aeroplanes almost as soon as aeroplanes made their appearance in the world. A visit to a movie theatre where a film of a Wright Flyer was shown, and a visit to an air meet at Bournemouth in the summer of 1910 were the sparks that lighted his young imagination. The flyer's way was his way and he built and flew kites and model aeroplanes with the same intense concentration that was later to win for him the Victoria Cross as the first of the immortal company of Britain's fighter pilots.

Hawker entered the Royal Military Academy at Woolwich in 1910 and while this was a most significant step professionally, it was not of any greater significance than the fact in 1910 he also joined the Royal Aero Club. He began taking private lessons with the hope of acquiring a pilot's license so that he might join the air service, but even the enthusiastic and ingenious Lanoe found enough complications in his path to delay his winning his "ticket" until March 1913. By that time he had graduated from the Woolwich Academy, and in October 1913 he was promoted to Lieutenant. He applied for the RFC and was ordered to report to the Central Flying School at Upavon on the day that "some fool thing in the Balkans" inaugurated the new Dark Ages.

No. 6 Squadron RFC was formed on January 31, 1914, at Farnborough, its scrambled equipment consisting of such pterodactyls as the B.E.2a, B.E.2b, Farman Longhorn, Blériot XI, B.E.8, R.E.5, and Martinsyde Scout to name a few. Squadrons at that time were not so much unities as conglomerations.

Lieutenant L. G. Hawker was posted to No. 6 Squadron on October 5, 1914, and on October 7 the squadron flew across the Channel to Bruges. The first days of active service for the squadron were a catch-as-catch-can operation, for there was no transport, no ground crew, no supplies, no anything. Not even a field—the squadron flew from the race track at Bruges. A few days later it moved to the race track at Ostend. After a week or so of popping around from place to place the squadron settled down at Poperinghe, but was on the move again shortly with a transfer to St-Omer.

The irrepressible Hawker always took his revolver along on his reconnaissance flights and pegged a shot at any German machine he chanced to meet.

The results were uniformly nil, but it was nice to know that one could take a shot at an enemy aeroplane.

The squadron finally set up a "permanent" station at Bailleul late in the year and received some new machines—B.E.2c's—in which Hawker perfected his skill as a pilot. In March the squadron moved back to Poperinghe in accordance with an ancient army tradition which inflexibly decrees that a unit must move to some dingy, foul and depressing spot as soon as the spot at which it is stationed has been made comfortable.

Hawker flew constantly—even after having received a painful wound in the leg from ground fire. (For a time he had to be lifted into the cockpit.) He was sent on sick leave during May 1915. When he returned to the squadron he was delighted to learn that he was to be issued "a beautiful little toy," a Bristol Scout.

The Bristol Baby Biplane was a pre-war sport design of which grand things had been expected in the racing season of the summer of 1914. The war intervened and the Bristol Baby went to war as a fast single-seater scout. No squadron was equipped with more than one or two at a time, but nearly every squadron in the RFC had one. It was a handy and manoeuvrable aeroplane and fairly advanced for its time.

Hawker designed a machine gun mounting for his Scout within a few days of having flown it to the aerodrome. (The squadron had been moved to Abeele.) He had been flying all manner of army co-operation missions—observation, photography, artillery spotting—and now he was going to fight. The Scout was not a bad aeroplane to fight with. Fast, manoeuvrable, with a good rate of climb, it was a fine machine by the standards of 1915. All it needed was a gun. He considered the qualities of the aeroplane. It was responsive and light on the controls. He considered his own qualities. He was a first-rate pilot and a good shot. Very well, the obvious thing to do was to fix a Lewis gun to the left side of the aeroplane just ahead of the cockpit pointing down a few degrees and out to the side to clear the propeller. The Lewis gun was light and would not seriously affect the machine's performance, and it would be within easy reach of his left hand (he would be holding the stick with his right) for firing and reloading. It would be no great trick for a pilot like himself to slip or crab into position to fire a burst from the diagonally aligned gun.

On July 25, 1915, Hawker was flying a high evening patrol between Passchendaele and Ypres. At about six o'clock he spotted a German two-seater just the other side of the German lines at Passchendaele. He dived on the machine and fired off a drum at it while its pilot turned and dived away. Hawker broke off and resumed patrolling. Twenty minutes later the show was repeated over Houthulst Forest, but this time a British antiaircraft section reported that the German aeroplane was forced down by Hawker's fire. Hawker resumed his patrol at 11,000 feet and toward seven o'clock spotted a third machine. His combat report (quoted in a new biography*) reads in part: "The Bristol climbed to

---

* *Hawker, V. C.*, by Lieut. Col. Tyrrel Mann Hawker, The Mitre Press, London, 1965.

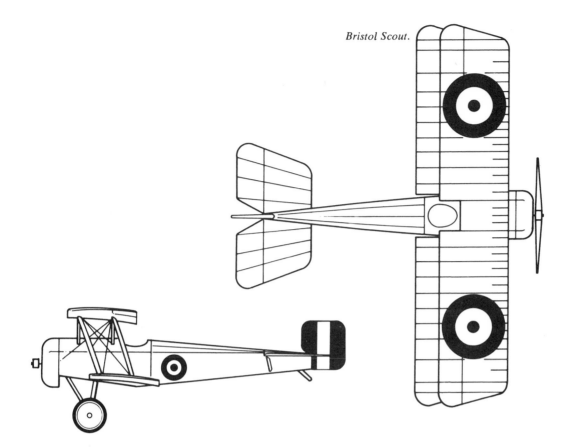

Bristol Scout.

Bristol Scouts of a naval unit
in France, October 1914.
The Union Jack anteceded the
roundel as national
marking on the
first British machines
at the Front.

81

11,000 and about 7 p.m. saw a hostile machine being fired at by antiaircraft guns at about 10,000 over Hooge. The Bristol approached downsun and opened fire at about 100 yards range. The hostile machine burst into flames, turned upside down, and crashed E. of Zillebeke." The fall of the burning machine was witnessed by thousands of British troops.

One week later, Hawker wrote to his brother (Lt. Col. T. M. Hawker, an artillerist and Lanoe's biographer): "I strafed a Hun last Sunday, over Ypres on the Bristol.

"Opened fire at about 100 yards—I had come on him from behind unawares —and he burst into flames and crashed in our lines.

"I felt very sorry for him when he fell in flames, but war is war and they have been very troublesome of late."

By August 24, 1915, when his Victoria Cross was gazetted, Hawker had become an Ace. When he returned to England in September he had completed just under a year of active service and was long overdue for a breather. From October 1914 to September 1915 he had flown every kind of mission in every kind of aeroplane in every kind of weather. He was one of the most experienced men in the RFC, and that in addition to his value as an inventor. He had devised new ground-air co-operation schemes, gun sights and brackets, he had designed hangars and all manner of ground installations. On his return to England in September the help and encouragement he gave to his dentist, a man named Prideaux, materially assisted the invention of the Prideaux disintegrating-link machine-gun belt. It was Hawker who devised the protective fabric cover for the tips of wooden propellers, and with the help of an engineer named French he developed the double drum for the Lewis gun. His improvements and refinements of equipment permeated the Royal Flying Corps and the inspiration of his example was ubiquitous. Easy to see that he had become a celebrity then in spite of official British policy which discouraged the focusing of attention on individuals. After all, not even the British can make a secret of the Victoria Cross.

On returning to England, Hawker reported to Hounslow near London, a once-desolate stretch of heath where stood a forest of gibbets for the highwaymen who resorted there. In January 1916 the first deliveries of the D.H.2 were received and Hawker called the machine "a beauty." It had indeed a kind of primitive charm, with its box kite wings and tail booms, but it had some serious drawbacks, two of which were inherent. In the first place it was cold. The large open cockpit was so drafty that McCudden was once moved to remark that he didn't care whether he was shot down or not, he was so cold. Hawker designed fleece-lined hip boots specifically for D.H.2 pilots. Secondly, the aeroplane was not aerodynamically stable because the motor was located in the center of the structure rather than in the nose and this imparted a fore-and-aft sensitivity that required alert and careful handling. In itself, the absence of stability is no serious problem in a fighter, but at the time that the D.H.2 came into service, aerobatics was not fully understood, and students were more often told to avoid spins and stalls than taught how to control them. The 100-horsepower Gnôme monosoupape rotary engine that powered the D.H.2 was obtained in large part from secondhand

French surplus, since the British war industry was developing about as slowly as Allied co-operation. These balky engines were prone to going dud in the air and when that happened the D.H.2 would usually drop into a spin. Inexperienced pilots might automatically try to recover from a spin by pulling the stick back to raise the nose. But this would only make the spin worse, and unless the controls were neutralized before the stick was pulled back the machine would spin into the ground. There were fatal accidents with the D.H.2 and it acquired an unenviable reputation and a ghastly nickname, "The Spinning Incinerator." Hawker tried every stunt he could think of, including right- and left-hand spins, and made sure his chaps knew the D.H.2 inside and out—everything it could and could not do. As for the engines, however, there was no answer but prayer. For besides their tired balkiness, they sometimes just simply came apart. There were many accidents caused by the departure of one or more cylinders from the whirling engine, and when these in their passage sundered the tail booms, the whole aeroplane broke up in the air. With better engines and a better state of flying instruction, the D.H.2 would have been much less of a pain in the neck.

Hawker was commissioned a Major and sent to France by boat a few days before the squadron flew the Channel early in February 1916. The squadron set up shop at Bertangles just north of Amiens and began flying regular solo patrols and escort missions for photographic two-seaters.

One of the men who flew with No. 24 Squadron from the beginning was Lieutenant John Oliver Andrews, now Air Vice Marshal Andrews, who had transferred to the RFC from the Royal Scots and had served at the Front in No. 5 Squadron. (At the time of the Second World War, Andrews was director of armament development for the Air Ministry.)

Andrews, like Hawker and most of the men in the squadron, as well as the D.H.2 itself, was hand picked for a specific job—putting a stop to the first period of German air supremacy, the Fokker Scourge. Things had come a long way since Hawker observed that the Germans were becoming "very troublesome," and in the spring of 1916 the *Eindecker* was a problem of the first magnitude on the British Front. Since the French had few Nieuport *Bébés* to spare for the British— *Commandant* de Rose was just putting together the Nieuport *escadrilles* at Verdun—it was up to Hawker and his squadron of D.H.2's to insure the protection of the RFC two-seaters on photography and observation missions.

For a time No. 24 Squadron sent up a regular escort for two-seaters of neighboring squadrons, but no particular action developed because the roving *Eindeckers* had avoided attacking close formations. Late in April the first real test came when a four-man escort led by Andrews crossed into German territory near Bapaume with an observation mission of five B.E.2d's from No. 15 Squadron. Instead of allowing one or two *Eindeckers* to chip away at British two-seater formations, a technique adequate up until now, the Germans decided to accept the challenge of the fighter escort and show that by a mass attack the two-seaters could still be destroyed. As the B.E.'s droned eastward and the D.H.'s buzzed around them, a flock of *Eindeckers* appeared and circled to place themselves between the British and the lines. They climbed for height. When the

*J. O. Andrews.*

83

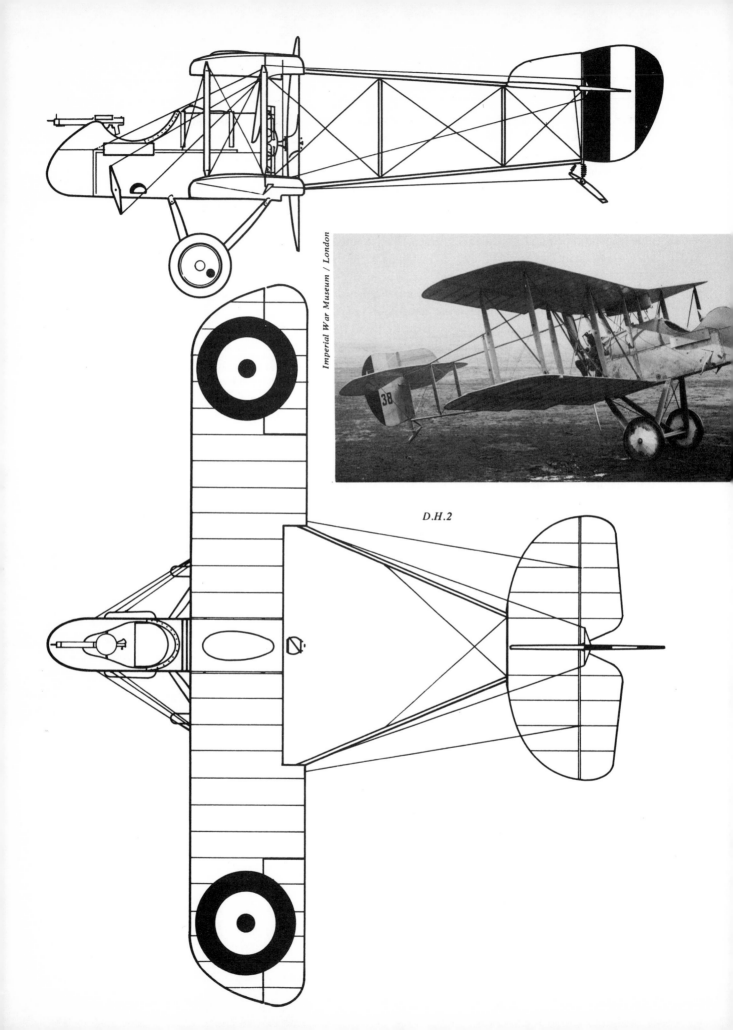

D.H.2

British machines reached their objective, the *Eindeckers* came down on them. Andrews had kept his men close to the two-seaters. When the Fokkers attacked he turned and led the D.H.2's into them head-on. The Fokkers scattered. For several moments there was a series of ill-defined chases taking place about the sky. A few *Eindeckers* cleared out altogether, the rest withdrew, and the D.H.2's returned to the two-seaters who were carrying on with the mission. There were no losses to either side, and of course no victories, so the fight could be called indecisive except that, from that moment, the grip of the *Eindecker* was broken.

From the first of July, Hawker instituted daily offensive patrols, or patrols whose function was "to destroy German aeroplanes on the German side of the front lines," in the words of J. O. Andrews who was by this time a Captain. Hawker himself flew on these offensive patrols as often as his administrative duties would permit, but he flew as a member rather than as the leader so as not to displace the regular leader. Whoever led the patrol was acting C.O. in the air regardless of his rank on the ground.

The offensive policy of the RFC was based on the premise that the German air service would be rendered ineffectual if all British flying were done on the German side of the lines. Given a parity in quality and quantity of men and machines, this was a fair elucidation. There was, however, a catch. The Germans had introduced the Fokker D III, the Albatros D II, and the Halberstadt D III, while the British were still flying the D.H.2. The Fokker D III and the Halberstadt D III were not brilliant machines, but they were a match for the D.H.2; the Albatros was the equal of any machine at the Front (not excluding the Spad whose ceiling and manoeuvrability it matched and whose superior speed it offset by carrying two guns instead of one.)

*Hawker.*

Boelcke's *Jasta 2* took a heavy toll in the RFC in the fall of 1916. The death of Boelcke, while a blow to the morale of his comrades and the Germans generally, occurred after he had successfully launched his unit on its combat career. In November, the month after Boelcke's death, *Jasta 2* was led to 25 victories in as many days by *Leutnant* Stephan Kirmaier who had succeeded to Boelcke's command.

Fighting seemed daily to grow more intense, and on November 22, Captain Andrews, by this time the only survivor besides Hawker of the original squadron, shot down Kirmaier.

The next day, November 23, 1916, broke clear and cold. Three men of No. 24 Squadron were flying an offensive patrol over Bapaume at about 11,000 feet. Andrews was leading, Hawker was number two, Lieutenant R. H. M. S. Saundby was number three. It was just before two o'clock in the afternoon when Andrews spotted two German two-seaters northeast of Bapaume at about 6000 feet. He led the patrol down on them and the two-seaters turned and fled. Andrews has given this account of the action of the next few seconds: "We were soon dived on by a number of German single-seaters, and almost immediately my engine's tanks, which are behind the pilot in a D.H.2, were shot up. Major Hawker was then perhaps a couple of hundred feet below me and in pursuit of the German two-seaters. With my engine knocked out and being only at a medium height of perhaps some 5000 feet, I was obliged to turn at once for the lines and try to glide over them." Andrews and Saundby had turned away after the first attack on the two-seaters, but Hawker had pressed on. Andrews turned again to rejoin him when he saw the enemy fighters coming down on Hawker. He got in one burst at the lead machine and then was hit from behind himself. He turned once more for the Allied lines and went down pursued by one of the German fighters that put several bursts into his machine from dead astern. The engine stopped the bullets and Andrews was not hit. Saundby caught up with the two aeroplanes and drove off the enemy attacker. Andrews landed safely behind the lines.

The three D.H.2's had been attacked by von Richthofen and his comrades of *Jasta 2*. Hawker and von Richthofen quickly squared off and began chasing tails, each trying to get in line behind the other. None of the other German pilots sought to interfere. All circled above, letting the two settle the affair man to man. Perhaps because of the memory of the Boelcke tragedy, or a sense of fair play, or Manfred's jealousy—whatever their reasons, they stood clear.

Hawker and von Richthofen turned 20 times one way, then 20 times the other. They lost height, whirling around like the cups of an anemometer, dropping down to perhaps 2000 feet, and drifting, because of the wind, into German territory. The aeroplanes were banked all the way over on their sides, wings straight up and down; the men looked at each other across the diameter of a circle that at times measured no more than a few hundred feet. Once, Hawker waved. They were getting down low and it was up to Hawker to make the move to get away or get it over with. He broke abruptly and went into a loop—the D.H. had the edge in manoeuvrability. He got in a quick un-aimed burst. He couldn't hit that way but he put von Richthofen off for a moment. Hawker was going straight down when he came out of the loop and fired. He kept on going straight down to pick up speed, then pulled out at barely 100 feet and hedge-hopped for the British lines. He had a little over a half-mile to go. The Albatros had the edge in speed and von Richthofen was quickly on Hawker's tail and gaining on him. Hawker began to zigzag, but that slowed him down. At a range of 50 yards von Richthofen opened fire. Another burst and his guns jammed. He nearly went wild. He gave the cocking lever a yank and cleared the jam. He fired again from 100 feet and shot Hawker through the head. The D.H.2 dropped and tore into the water-filled shell holes just beyond the German lines. The machine cartwheeled and broke up.

BY JANUARY 1917 von Richthofen had accumulated a total of 16 victories and was one of Germany's most successful living Aces. He received his *Pour le Mérite* and was appointed to the command of a squadron, *Jasta 11*. He was also promoted to Captain, the rank name being *Rittmeister,* or Riding Master, since he was an Uhlan. He was coming to the notice of the powers—including the German newspapers—and knew from interviews with prisoners that he had a name on the British side of the line as well. He had all the prompting he needed to begin asserting himself, and an excellent way to do this was to have his aeroplane painted up in some nice bright color. That way his presence would never go unnoticed or his personal challenge ignored. Navarre had flown an all-red Nieuport at Verdun. The *Rittmeister* would fly a red machine, too.

It was evident that there was a decided tactical advantage in having the machine of the squadron leader identified by a distinctive color scheme. Like the orchestra conductor who works best if he is standing up on a podium where everybody can see him, the squadron leader would handle his men best if they could see him easily. For if they had to waste time to look for him they wouldn't do so, not when they might get shot down while peering around trying to pick his out of a dozen similar machines. If, on the other hand, the men could spot the commander's machine instantly because it is painted bright red, they could always keep an eye on it and follow his lead.

Moreover, it became apparent that the personal color of the leader should be the color of his *Jasta*. The Albatros machines of von Richthofen's squadron were therefore ticked out with various decorations in red—a tail, a wing, a stripe around the fuselage, and so on. This had the added advantage of making it easier for ground and air observers to confirm victories.

The practice was quickly adopted by the rest of the German air service. Yellow, for example, became the color of *Jasta 2*. As a variation, *Jastas 3* and *6* used patterns—black and white checkerboard for the former, black and white stripes for the latter. Actually, von Richthofen's own machines were never *all* red. He flew a number of aeroplanes in his career, and may have had more than one at his disposal at one time or another. The mechanics attended to the servicing and maintenance of the aeroplanes first and decorated them when there was time. The standard factory finish of the early Albatros machines was varnished plywood for the fuselage and a streaky dark green on the wings and those parts of the tail that were covered with fabric. As aeroplanes were wrecked, worn out, or withdrawn for repair, new ones were issued to take their places, and the new ones were decorated as the opportunity to do so offered itself. When von Richthofen's aeroplanes were painted red, the Maltese crosses on the wings were usually set off by being placed in the center of large white squares.

IT HAD BEEN a long time coming, but the idea of "aerial supremacy" was finally put into words on both sides of the line and the words framed a definite tactical concept. During the Battle of the Somme, July to November 1916, the Royal Flying Corps put in long hours.

In order for the reconnaissance, observation, photography, and artillery-spotting aeroplanes to be able effectively to perform their various functions, the British sent up fighters in increasing numbers to patrol on the German side of the lines, forming a screen behind which the RFC two-seaters could operate safely and through which the German fighters could not pass. Continual fighter escort might have been provided for the two-seaters, but this method, while it might have been more economical, was judged less effective. Fighter squadrons were therefore collected into wings, then groups, until eventually great swarms of aeroplanes crossed the line, stacked up on several levels.

It was assumed that German fighters would attack British fighters, if there were any around, before they would attack two-seaters for the simple reason that the fighters were the more dangerous, and until they were out of the way the two-seaters could not safely be attacked.

Aerial supremacy implied, therefore, not only establishing dominion over a given stretch of air, but holding it regardless of cost. Remember that the prevailing wind over most of the Front was westerly so that British aeroplanes returning home bucked a headwind and fights naturally tended to drift toward German territory rather than British; also, that a firm rule of aerial supremacy is that all patrols be over the enemy's lines; and lastly, that the British did not, at this period, have the best equipment. In fact, Guynemer said that if the Germans had been flying such poor machines as the British he would have guaranteed to shoot down one a day.

The RFC established aerial supremacy and held it regardless of cost—but the cost was frightful.

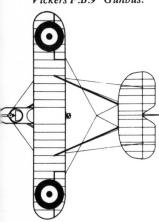

*Vickers F.B.9 "Gunbus."*

No. 11 Squadron was a British fighter, reconnaissance, and photographic unit in Flanders equipped with F.E.2b's, Vickers "Gunbus" two-seaters, Bristol Scouts, and French Nieuports. During the Battle of the Somme which began on July 1, 1916, the squadron's single-seaters provided fighter escort for bombers. On May 7, 1916, a 19-year-old Lieutenant named Albert Ball joined the squadron. On May 7 one year later, he had won 44 confirmed victories, the Victoria Cross, the *Legion d'Honneur,* the Russian Order of St. George—and he was dead.

Ball had come to France in February 1916, assigned to No. 13 Squadron to fly B.E.2c's on observation missions. He had on numerous occasions flown a Bristol Scout belonging to the squadron and had shown promise as a single-seater pilot. No. 11 Squadron had come to France in July 1915 equipped with 12 Vickers F.B.5's and F.B.9's, the first two-seater fighter squadron at the Front. In 1916, No. 11 had varied its equipment to assume the duties of an army co-operation squadron, and from May to August 1916 Ball served with this squadron as pilot of one of the Nieuport fighters.

88

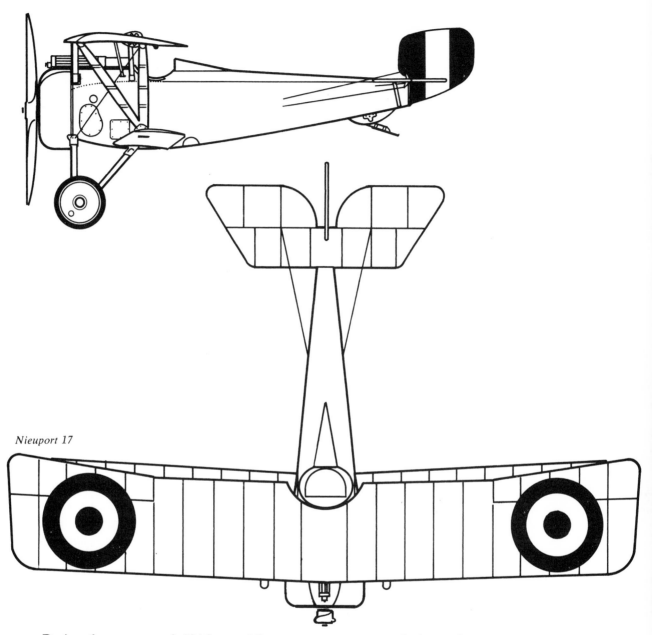

*Nieuport 17*

During the summer of 1916, two Nieuports were concurrently in service, the old *Bébé* and a new version of it, the Nieuport 17, powered with a 110-horsepower Le Rhône rotary engine. The 17 was faster than the *Bébé,* having a top speed of about 110 miles per hour, and it climbed nearly twice as fast, but its chief distinction over the *Bébé,* at least with the French, lay in the fact that it was armed with a synchronized Vickers gun in addition to the Lewis on the top wing. The British Nieuports retained the top-wing Lewis gun as the only standard armament.

Albert Ball had been born in Nottingham on August 21, 1896. As a child he had been a crack pistol shot. This, like many of his other accomplishments and preoccupations, was vital to his eventual success as a fighter pilot. He was mechanically inclined, always "messing about," as he put it, with mechanical and electrical devices. Later, in the RFC, he spent a great deal of time souping up the engines of his aeroplanes, and doing all of the maintenance work on his own machine guns. He also knew how to relax—he played the violin and cultivated neat, tiny vegetable patches wherever he was stationed.

Ball flew ceaselessly with No. 13 Squadron in the obsolete B.E.2c's, which were easy meat even for the *Eindecker*. In No. 11 Squadron he flew without interruption from May to the end of July. With No. 11 he evolved his unique tactics. He felt there was safety in numbers—enemy numbers. The larger the formation of German aeroplanes, the safer he felt in attacking them. His method was to plunge straight in without any jockeying for position, for he believed once he was in the midst of the enemy machines their pilots and gunners would be unable to shoot at him for fear of hitting their squadron mates. As for him, he couldn't miss, since targets were all around him. As a result of these tactics he brought his Nieuport home full of holes on many occasions and crashed on many others, yet he always got away with a whole skin.

He was still the marksman he had been as a boy, and another of his tactics he evolved from a combination of that and his good reflexes. He would begin his attack on an enemy machine by diving. As he passed his victim and went on down he would pivot back the Lewis gun on the top wing and squeeze off a short burst during the instant that the enemy machine was in his line of fire—aiming either at the engine or at the spot in the under side of the fuselage where he had to hit to put his shots up into the pilot's cockpit. He rarely missed.

90

Ball was awarded the M.C. for his efforts just prior to the Battle of the Somme; and during July 1916, the first month of the battle, he flew so arduously that he was forced to ask for a rest around the beginning of August. Instead of being given a leave he was reassigned to a two-seater squadron to fly B.E.'s again on artillery-spotting missions. This was no rest, certainly, and he preferred to fly a Nieuport, if he had to fly operationally, rather than a B.E. where he was nothing but an Aunt Sally for the German Archie.

Back he went to No. 11 Squadron—at least it was better than being a sitting duck. One day in August he lit into a formation of five German two-seaters and forced three of them to the ground. A few days later, the day after his twentieth

Ball.

birthday, he was out prowling the lines alone, looking for trouble when he sighted a flight of seven two-seaters in a V-formation, like a flock of wild geese. He sailed into them and shot one of them down with a burst of about 20 rounds. The two-seaters scattered in all directions. He spotted another formation of five and repeated the performance with the same results up to a point. After a short burst one of the planes went down, but the rest of the formation, instead of scattering, pounced on Ball. He headed straight for the nearest one and blazed away. The machine dropped abruptly, but Ball was too busy to see if it crashed. The whirling fight worked lower and lower and Ball fired his last five or ten rounds into another machine which tore into a house and exploded. He was out of ammunition and the fight was over. He headed home hedgehopping, but nobody felt like chasing him.

He flew almost every day during the remainder of August and the following month. He had a more or less permanent roving commission and he accumulated an extraordinary number of hours in the air. His flying was not so dashing as that of some pilots—he was called a "careful" flyer—but his marksmanship was unerring, his reflexes fast and his eyesight keen. His nerves remained steady in spite of the exhausting pace he kept and the strain of feeling "utterly rotten," as he put it in letters, every time he scored a victory.

The nervous strain of combat flying in the Great War was terrible at times, and little has been said about it, but much has been implied. The aviators of those years were the first professionals in a new profession. Powered flight was 10 years old, and until the war came along there had been little change in aeroplane design or performance. Only a handful of flyers had dared anything more than getting up and getting down: Garros flying across the Mediterranean; Blériot

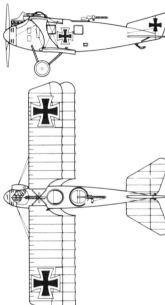

Roland CL II.
The two-seater type Ball encountered frequently on the Somme in August 1916.

91

flying across the Channel; Pégoud looping the loop. Among the pioneers there was none who was not devoted to flying itself. The war brought the first disinterested professionals.

In the first year or so the romantics were killed off. Next came the adventurers. Unless these could become professionals they too went down. At the Front a new kind of aviator began to appear, a man whose primary interest was doing a job—winning the war—and who just happened to be making his contribution by flying. Such a one was the humorless youth that was Albert Ball. Such a one also was Manfred, Baron von Richthofen. These were the tough ones. They were killed as easily as any man, for they were only human, but they accomplished more, could carry on longer, before the strain betrayed them into a fatal error. With a few exceptions none had much imagination. Flying, in war or peace, is a deadly serious job, and the man who lets his mind wander usually doesn't last long. In the squadron mess, places were not left empty at the table, nothing was sacred. The civilian luxuries of grief and a funeral for a close friend were rarely indulged in. Hairbreadth escapes were dismissed, forgotten. They had no meaning once the danger was past. Future danger was not worth considering since it, like peace, did not exist. An inflexible self-discipline had to be imposed lest normal feelings become fatal weaknesses.

Albert Ball was considered a loner in the air and on the ground. He preferred the solo roving patrol to team flying and had many acquaintances but few friends. He may have avoided making friends for fear of losing them. It wouldn't be the first time that a soldier chose to protect himself by isolation.

In October he returned to England where he was assigned to a training school, a job he accepted reluctantly and found boring.

In February 1917 he received a posting to a combat squadron, No. 56, newly formed at London Colney. He was promoted to Flight Commander and went to France with the squadron in April. No. 56 Squadron flew its first patrol on April 23, in the course of which Ball scored the first victory for the squadron. In the two weeks before his death Ball scored 13 victories, an average of almost one a day.

On May 7, the squadron sent up an 11-machine patrol late in the day, with Ball leading his own flight. The patrol leader spotted six Albatros about 3000 feet below. He promptly led his men down to attack, and von Richthofen's *Jasta 11* came down on top of them. Another German patrol stumbled upon the fight and waded in. Then No. 8 Squadron of the Royal Naval Air Service joined in. A frantic and disordered fight spread out among the cold and towering masses of cloud. During the fight, one of Ball's squadron mates followed him into a cloud and came out the other side alone. That's all there was to it, as if the cloud had swallowed him up.

Only five of the machines from No. 56 Squadron straggled back to the aerodrome at Vert Galand that evening and none of the pilots knew what had happened to Albert Ball. He had simply vanished. The only thing known for certain was that he was gone for good at a time when the RFC needed him badly.

FROM THE BEGINNING of 1917 a warning system had gone into effect for the benefit of the German fighter squadrons. Called the *Flugmeldedienst,* or Flight Report Service, it had been evolved from the suggestions of many experienced squadron leaders. Its organization was perfectly simple: all aeroplane sightings along the Front were reported by telephone to a central station at Corps headquarters. The telephone duty officer there contacted the telephone duty officer at the appropriate *Jasta,* and the *Jastaführer,* or Squadron Leader, decided what action was necessary. It was thus impossible, in principle, for Allied machines to cross the lines without being intercepted.

By the spring of 1917 over 30 *Jastas* had been formed and more were on the way. The Albatros fighters dominated the scene, replacing Fokkers and Halberstadts in many squadrons. The newest version of the Albatros, the D III, was available now in considerable numbers and, as it represented a considerable improvement over the D I and D II, it was a dangerous adversary. The wings had been thoroughly redesigned and now appeared in a sesquiplane or half-wing arrangement, the lower wing being the "half-wing." As with the Nieuport, the lower wing was so narrow it could be connected to the upper wing only by a "V-strut" arrangement. The upper wing was given a marked rake at the tips and relocated closer to the fuselage to improve manoeuvrability and view, respectively. The Mercedes engine was souped up by increasing the compression ratio and an extra 10 horsepower was obtained. The D III weighed a trifle less than the D I and D II and, while it was no faster, its rate of climb was much better.

With the *Flugmeldedienst,* superior equipment, and a rapidly growing fighter force, the Germans decidedly held the upper hand in the spring of 1917. They had one other factor working in their favor, although it was not an advantage that they had consciously contrived. With the exception of Nieuports and Spads borrowed from the French, the British were flying aeroplanes that had been obsolete since the autumn of the year before.

*Albatros D III*

Peter Grosz

93

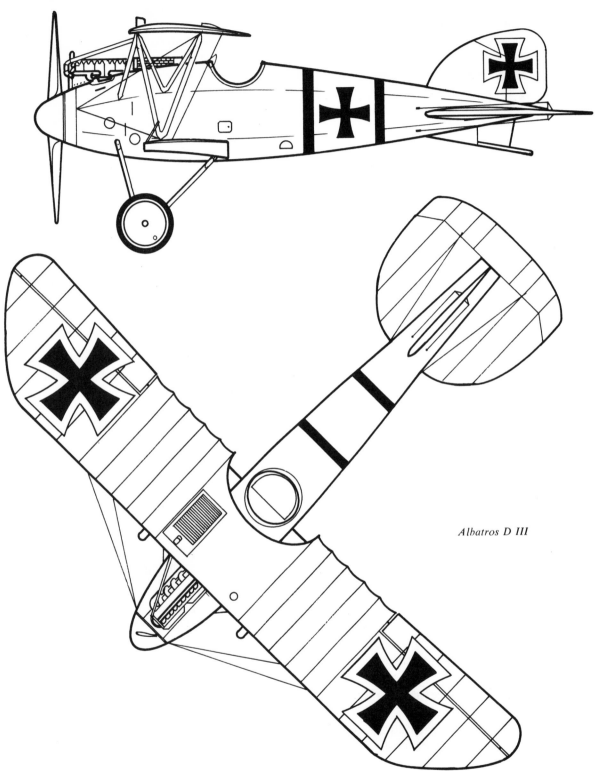

Albatros D III

94

The F.E.8, for example, was a single-seat pusher that came to France six months after the D.H.2. It might have made a good showing against the *Eindecker,* but it was helpless against the Albatros. At the beginning of March 1917 five Albatros D III's of *Jasta 11,* led by Manfred von Richthofen, nearly wiped out No. 40 Squadron RFC, shooting down an entire patrol of nine F.E.8's without loss to themselves.

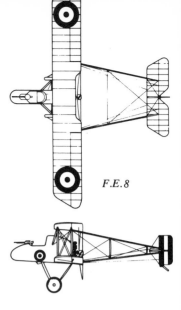

*F.E.8*

On March 24, 1917, von Richthofen shot down his first Spad. After a lengthy round of sparring, he worked into position and shot the Spad's motor into junk. The pilot tried to make the British lines but von Richthofen fired a warning burst over his head and he turned back to land inside the German lines. Having been brought down by the *Rittmeister* he was lucky to be a prisoner.

On April 29, 1917, three Spad 7's of No. 19 Squadron RFC, plus six Sopwith Triplanes, attacked a flight of eleven Albatros D III's, five of which belonged to *Jasta 11* led by von Richthofen. In the ensuing scrap one Albatros was destroyed, two were damaged and all three Spads were shot down. One of the Spad pilots was the leader of No. 19 Squadron, Major H. D. Harvey-Kelly. On August 12, 1914, Harvey-Kelly, then a Lieutenant of No. 2 Squadron, had been the first pilot to land in France on the occasion of the RFC fly-over.

*        *        *

IN APRIL 1917 the United States entered the war. It made little difference at the time; April 1917 is not known as "the Month the United States Entered the War." The war went on as it had been going. RFC losses continued on the increase. In April the climax was reached and the situation became truly desperate. That month is known with bitter simplicity as "Bloody April."

*        *        *

ON APRIL 2, 1917, the effective strength of *Jasta 11* was eight men: Baron von Richthofen and his younger brother Lothar, *Leutnants* Krefft, Kleinhenz, Wolff, Allmenröder and Schaefer, and *Vizefeldwebel* Festner. At one time or another during that day all of them were up. They scored five victories, Manfred von Richthofen being credited with two of them.

The *Flugmeldedienst* reported a flight of British two-seaters very early in the morning. Lothar von Richthofen, Wolff and Allmenröder—all of whom were to win the *Pour le Mérite*—took off to intercept. As they flew away from the aerodrome, Lothar, looking back, could see his brother's red Albatros parked in front of its hangar. The three pilots found the six British machines and attacked them, but the engagement was inconclusive and they returned to the field after about an hour. As they approached, Lothar could see his brother's red machine still sitting in front of the hangar.

Landing, Lothar asked where his brother was, and was told he had gone back to bed. Gone *back* to bed? It was true, Manfred had been in bed when the first flight left, had been awakened when more British planes had been spotted, had taken off, shot one down, returned, and gone back to bed.

The aeroplane he had destroyed was a B.E.2d of No. 13 Squadron RFC. He had harried the machine down to tree-top height firing short bursts, and the pilot, instead of surrendering and landing, had tried to make a run for it. Unfortunately, he hadn't the air space to manoeuvre, since he was almost on the ground and von Richthofen was right on top of him. It was over abruptly when von Richthofen literally ran him into a wall in the ruins of the village of Farbus.

*　　　　　　*　　　　　　*

THE TERMS *escadrille* and *Jasta* have been used throughout this text as if they were synonymous with squadron. As basic units of organization they were identical in function, but there was rarely a precise correspondence between the units of the various nations. Most fighter squadrons had a strength of 15 to 18 machines by definition, but the actual number of aeroplanes and pilots available at any time varied considerably, even from day to day.

In the RFC, squadrons were grouped into Wings and Wings into Groups. A squadron was commanded by a Major, a Wing by a Lieutenant Colonel, and a Group by a full Colonel. In the French *Armée de l'Air* an *escadrille* might be commanded by a *Capitaine* or a *Commandant,* the latter rank being the equivalent of Major. A body of squadrons was a *Groupe,* comparable to a British Wing. Usage in the U. S. Air Service was similar to that of the RFC, except that a unification of squadrons was a Group rather than a Wing.

In the *Luftstreitkräfte* from June 1917, *Jastas 4, 6, 10* and *11* were permanently amalgamated as an autonomous body called a *Geschwader* and placed under the command of *Rittmeister* von Richthofen. As a naval term *Geschwader* means squadron, but in the German air service it meant the equivalent of a Wing in the RFC, and was further qualified by *Jagd*—for "hunting." The von Richthofen *Jagdgeschwader* was *J.G. 1* since it was the first of its kind; others were soon formed: *J.G. 2* under von Tutschek; *J.G. 3* under Bruno Loerzer; *J.G. 4* (Bavarian) under Eduard *Ritter* von Schleich. These large combinations were shifted en masse by rail up and down the Front according to needs arising from the tactical situation. Because whole trains were required to move a *Geschwader* and because the aeroplanes were painted in lively colors, the *Geschwaders* came to be known collectively as "Circuses."

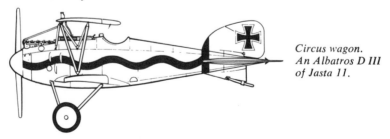

*Circus wagon.*
*An Albatros D III*
*of Jasta 11.*

FROM THE SPRING of 1917, Russia was more and more out of the war. All this meant to the Allies at the time was that Germany would be correspondingly stronger in the West.

96

THREE FORMIDABLE British aeroplanes made their debuts in April 1917, too late to save the situation for the RFC during "Bloody April."

The first was the Bristol F.2 Fighter, known from its birth as the "Brisfit." One of the outstanding machines of the war, it was so soundly designed that it remained in service with the RFC and the RAF for almost 20 years. It was fast and strong, amenable to any number of adaptations, alterations and refinements, and it had the sterling virtue of adjacent cockpits for pilot and gunner, making communication easy. Its chief distinction was none of these, but rather its manoeuvrability. It was by far the most agile two-seater in the RFC. That this quality was not appreciated is evident in the fact that in its first contact with enemy fighters, a flight of Albatros from *Jasta 11* led by the *Rittmeister,* four out of six Brisfits were shot down. The fault lay with the commanders, as usual, who had sent out inexperienced men in an unfamiliar aeroplane.

The leader of the Brisfit patrol was a young man named Leefe-Robinson who had had the great good fortune to shoot down a zeppelin and the wicked bad luck to be awarded the Victoria Cross for it. It seemed obvious, apparently, that a man who could shoot down such a terrifying bag of wind as a zeppelin would brush aside the German fighters like reeds. Accordingly, he was promoted to Major, placed in command of No. 48 Squadron and sent to France with his Brisfits. He knew nothing of the war in the air, and could only assume that all two-seaters were the same—that to have any chance against fighters, they had to stick together so as to be able to concentrate their fire. When *Jasta 11* fell on Leefe-Robinson and his men, he was the first to go. He had lasted half an hour at the Front.

Experienced pilots, however, soon realized that the Brisfit was no ordinary two-seater, that in competent hands it could hold its own against the German fighters if it were used as a fighter. The thing to do was not to hold formation, but to break and mix it up, using fighter tactics. One of the most successful of the Brisfit pilots, Captain A. E. McKeever, a Canadian of No. 11 Squadron, scored most of his 30 victories flying his Brisfit like a fighter.

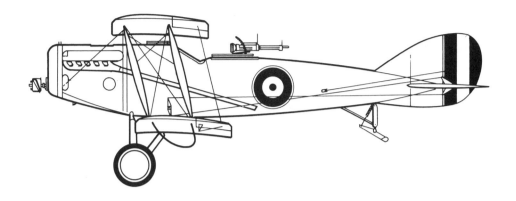

*Bristol F.2 "Brisfit."*

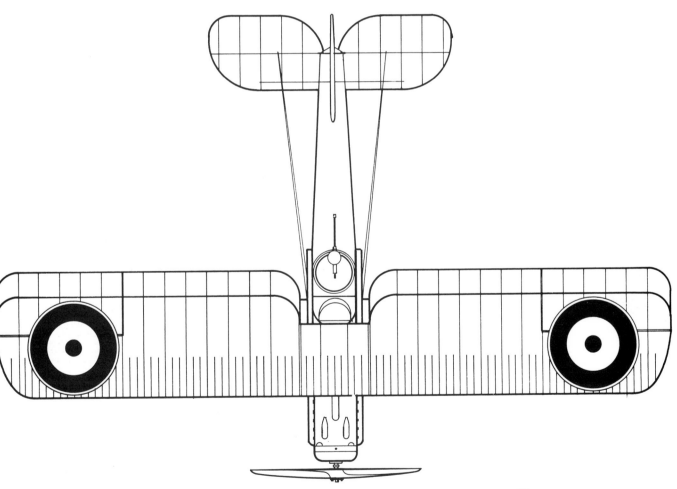

99

The S.E.5 was the product of a British government establishment, the Royal Aircraft Factory. Some 5000 machines in various models were built by the Factory and its sub-contractors. The S.E. was all wood, the basic skeleton being shaped by plywood formers and spruce stringers covered with fabric. In the nose, plywood panels and an aluminum cowling enclosed the Hispano Suiza engine and the radiator respectively. The 150-horsepower Hispano Suiza was the standard engine in the S.E.5. From the beginning of 1918 an improved model, the S.E.5a, began to reach the Front. The engine for the S.E.5a was the Wolseley Viper, a 200-horsepower British version of the Hispano Suiza with a souped-up compression ratio. With the Viper engine the S.E.5a was far and away the fastest of the major single-seaters at the Front, its top speed at ground level being just shy of 140 miles an hour.

The S.E., like all Factory aeroplanes, was stable, sturdy, and extraordinarily angular. It was steady in a dive and responsive on the controls. In a fight the S.E. could be dived very steeply either to attack or to get away, and in a zoom climb after a sharp recovery it would pull away fast for the first few seconds.

Besides its speed and strength, the S.E.5 had one other significant feature that was not the least of its virtues. It was the first British single-seater to be equipped with two guns—a Lewis on the top wing firing over the propeller and a synchronized Vickers mounted on the top left side of the fuselage midway between the engine and the cockpit. Both guns fired upward at an angle of five degrees.

The American Ace George Vaughn survived an accident to testify to the solidity of the S.E. He had learned to fly in a Jenny in the Princeton Aero Club, and had enlisted as a private in the Signal Corps, Flying Section. He was sent to England (a chilly disappointment—he had thought he was going to Italy) and after a brief single-seater course in Sopwith Pups at Hounslow Heath, went on to the combat training school at Ayr in Scotland. There he experienced a spectacular forced landing in an S.E.5 that might have proved fatal even in a Spad.

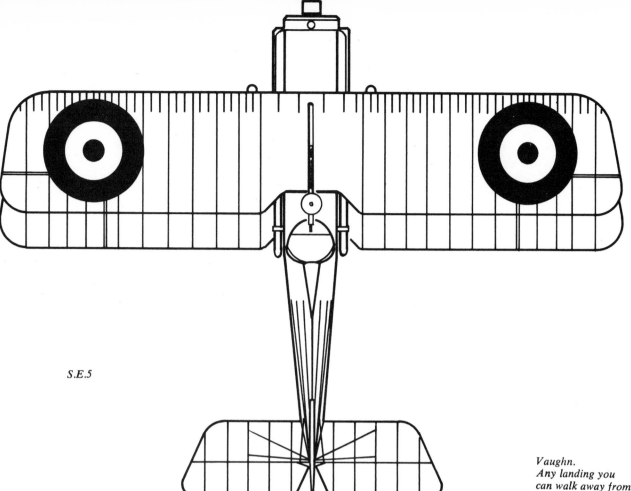

S.E.5

*Vaughn.*
*Any landing you*
*can walk away from is*
*a good landing.*

On this day he had just taken off when his engine conked out. He was too low to turn back, too low to try to pick a spot to land. He instantly put her nose down to maintain flying speed, but since he had just taken off he was dangerously low, and since he had put her nose down he was getting lower. An orchard lay ahead; there was no sound but the whistling of the wind in the wires. The S.E. went through some telephone lines bordering the orchard, shredding them like spider webs, effectively severing all telephonic contact between Ayr and the rest of the world, knocked the chimney pots off a farm house and went on down into the orchard, tearing the wings off and shearing the branches from the trees.

At the up-wind end of a trail of splinters sat the only two parts left intact, that part of the fuselage in which Vaughn was sitting, and Vaughn, who climbed out without a scratch. "The S.E. had that great big long nose sticking out in front to take the shock," he recalls. "You could run it into almost anything and get away with it."

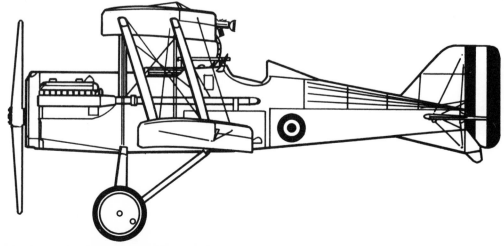

Grease monkeys. A modest salute to the devoted artificers of all the Air Services who did the dirty jobs, worked far longer hours than any pilots, and sweated out every mission just as anxiously. Their only reward for work well done was more work.

The Sopwith Triplane appeared in smaller numbers than just about any first-line fighter; only 150 were built. The Triplane's layout was novel and imaginative compared to other fighters that had been thus far produced by the British. Until the spring of 1917 the British were a half year behind everybody except the Americans, and the Sopwith Triplane was an amazing innovation.

By breaking up the necessary minimum of wing area into three parts instead of two, the Sopwith designers expected to produce an aeroplane whose shortened span and chord would impart a high order of manoeuvrability. That is exactly what was achieved. The Triplane was not particularly fast, its climb was adequate rather than brilliant, and it was armed with only one gun; but to a large degree its handiness offset these limitations.

The "Tripehound" could outclimb and turn inside the Albatros. It could also "split-S" beautifully. In this excellent evasive manoeuvre, the pilot rolled his ship on her back and pulled briskly back on the stick. The nose would snap down and the machine would fall away like a shot. It was more or less the opposite of the Immelmann turn, and a dazzling way to dive.

The Sopwith Triplane was flown by No. 1 and No. 8 (Naval) Squadrons from April 1917 and by No. 10 (Naval) Squadron from May. Naval Ten had had some Triplanes on strength since February, but was not fully equipped until May. The type was flown by Royal Naval Air Service squadrons only, whose pilots were among the most fiery at the Front.

*"Tripehounds" of Naval One.*

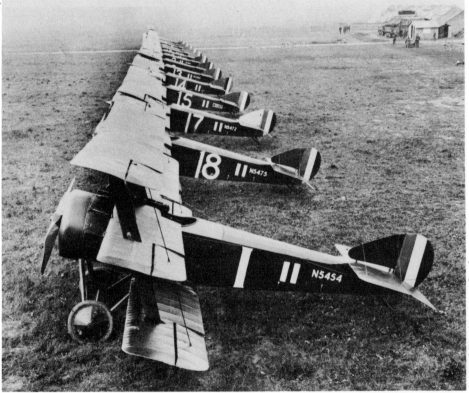

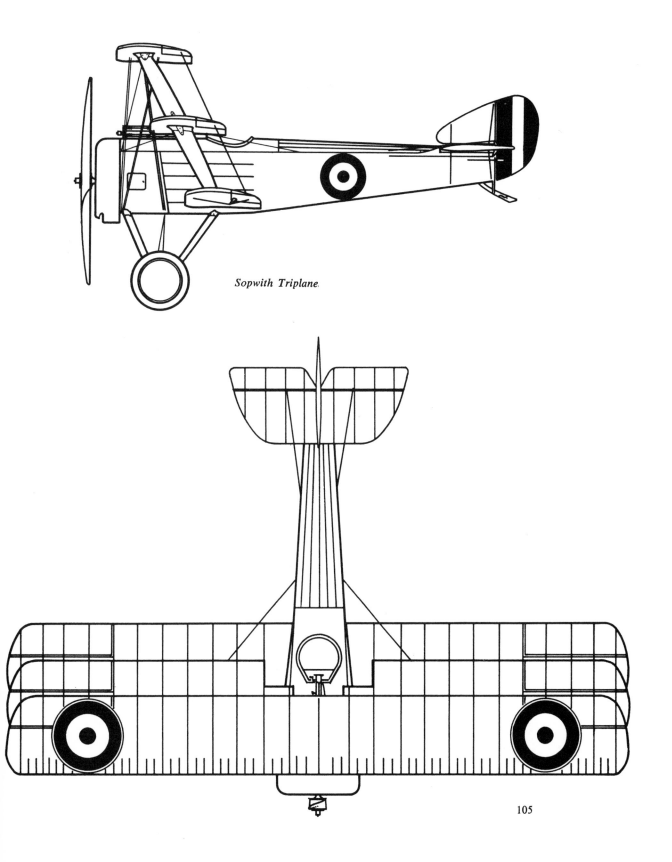

*Sopwith Triplane*

105

Naval Ten was formed in February 1917 and went to the Front in March, operating from a field near Furnes on the Belgian coast.

On April 1, 1917, Flight Lieutenant Raymond Collishaw, a Canadian, joined Naval Ten as the leader of "B" Flight. Collishaw, now a retired Air Vice Marshal of the Royal Canadian Air Force, had been born in Nanaimo, British Columbia, on November 22, 1893. He had gone to sea at 16, sailing in Canada's coasting trade and as a member of Captain Scott's Antarctic expedition of 1912. At the outbreak of the war he had entered the Department of the Naval Service of Canada, whence he had transferred to the RNAS in January 1916.

On August 2, 1916, he had been posted to No. 3 Wing RNAS where he had flown fighter escort on Franco-British bombing raids.

Collishaw had scored several victories by the time he joined Naval Ten, the first of them during the raid on the Mauser factory at Oberndorf.

The attack on Oberndorf was the anticlimax in a chain of events the meaning of which was not clearly appreciated until a later war. In 1915 the French had formed special Bombing Groups which operated under the direct control of GQG. At first these units had been nothing more than a feeble supplement to the artillery—they attacked front-line targets and used artillery shells for bombs. Slowly the scope of certain bombing squadrons was broadened and targets beyond the range of the artillery were selected by a few imaginative officers, one of whom was *Capitaine* Félix Happe. When some success was experienced by squadrons attacking supply depots, and rail and road junctions, the principle of strategic bombing was evolved. The difference between tactical and strategic bombing is roughly this: that while tactical bombing in support of or in preparation for an attack might put enemy units out of action on a particular spot of the Front, successful strategic raids against industry and transport might paralyze or starve an entire army.

*Groupe de Bombardement IV* under *Capitaine* Happe and No. 3 Wing RNAS under Wing Commander Richard Bell Davies, V. C., were based at Luxeuil-les-Bains, northwest of Belfort and 60 miles from the Rhine. At Oberndorf on the Neckar, just 50 miles the other side of the Rhine, was located a works known as the Mauser Weapons Factory. Here the standard German Army rifle, the 1898 Model K, was being produced at the rate of 4000 a day. It was decided that the Mauser works could be profitably hit by an Allied force under Happe. His own *Groupe de Bombardement IV* was to supply three squadrons of bombers, a total of 20 machines, with 12 French-built Sopwith 1½ Strutters as escort fighters. The *Escadrille Lafayette,* also stationed at Luxeuil, was to provide four Nieuport 17's as additional fighter escort.

No. 3 Wing under Wing Commander Davies was to provide 19 single-seat 1½ Strutters as bombers, and seven standard two-seaters as escort.

Between 1 and 2 o'clock in the afternoon on October 12, 1916, the raiding force of 62 aeroplanes took off and headed somewhat north of east, toward Oberndorf on the Neckar.

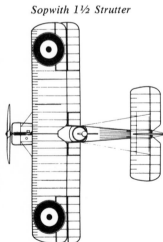

*Sopwith 1½ Strutter*

106

Of the 39 machines that took off to bomb, 24 made it, the rest having turned back, gotten lost, force-landed, or been shot down.

First reports by returning crews indicated that the factory had been virtually demolished. In addition, the French and British escort fighters claimed seven German aeroplanes shot down. One was credited to Collishaw, who flew one of the 1½ Strutter escorts; one each was credited to the four *Escadrille Lafayette* pilots; and two were credited to an escort pilot in one of the French 1½ Strutters.

For Raoul Lufbery of the *Lafayette,* the victory credited was his fifth and he became an Ace.

After the first hasty conclusions about the success of the raid, the debit side of the ledger began to fill in. In all, 21 Allied air personnel were lost, including Norman Prince of the *Lafayette,* who crashed on landing after the raid. The *Lafayette* pilots had escorted the bombers to the limit of fuel range, had returned to Luxeuil to refuel, and then had gone out to meet the bombers coming home. So it happened that Prince was coming in to land at dusk at an unfamiliar field and failed to see telephone wires strung along the boundary. He snagged his undercarriage on the wires, the Nieuport flipped over, and Prince was hurled to the ground.

The official German statement on the raid stated unequivocally that no military damage was done nor was work at the factory interrupted. Even the Oberndorf newspaper didn't bother to mention the raid until nearly a week later, and then only to announce that three civilians had been killed and seven injured, and that these had been standing out in the open and nowhere near the factory. Further, official German records list no losses to aviation personnel for that time and place, although it is possible that some German fighter pilots may have been shot down without being killed.

*Collishaw (right). Photograph taken at No. 3 Wing aerodrome, Luxeuil, in summer of 1916.*

Raymond Collishaw

It would appear that the raid was an unmitigated failure. *Capitaine* Happe was relieved of his command, humiliated, and sent into the trenches, his ideas on strategic bombing dismissed as "visionary." *Capitaine* Happe was a very unlucky man, but he was also right, and nothing will change that. His doctrines were finally accepted after bitter experience proved their validity.

On March 5, 1917, Raymond Collishaw was cited by *Commandant* du Peuty of the French Air Staff and awarded the *Croix de Guerre* with Palm for his work as escort pilot on this and other Allied raids.

When he took over command of "B" Flight of Naval Ten, Collishaw had scored several confirmed victories and was an experienced, capable leader. Like Collishaw himself, the personnel of "B" Flight were Canadians. The original members were Flight Sub-Lieutenants W. M. Alexander, E. V. Reid, J. E. Sharman, and G. E. Nash. The Flight was known as "Black Flight" because the engine cowlings and wheel covers were painted black to facilitate recognition. Similarly, "A" and "C" Flights were "Red Flight" and "Blue Flight."

These color markings were largely for the benefit of the ground crews who were expected to run out to meet the squadron when it returned from patrol and hold down the wings of the aeroplanes so that the pilots could taxi the machines in to the hangars. The rotary engines of the First World War period generally had no throttle and had to be run full on or else switched off. A cut-off button on the control stick could be used to cut the ignition to certain cylinders, but then raw gasoline was exhausted and this presented a fire hazard on the ground. It was much simpler to have a couple of men hanging on the wings to restrain the aeroplane. To make "Black Flight" more recognizable, the entire forward section of sheet-metal panel was eventually doped black. Outside of the black areas, however, the aeroplanes were painted a standard dark greenish-khaki.

On June 4, 1917, Naval Ten moved to Droglandt where it flew under the operational control of No. 11 Wing RFC, and during the months of June and July, Collishaw and his Canadians literally ran wild.

On June 5 he dived on an Albatros two-seater between Wervicq and Poelcappelle. He fired 50 rounds into the enemy machine and it dropped out of control, bursting into flames on the way down. Northwest of Poelcappelle he and Reid both fired on a second machine which fell erratically until lost from view.

On June 6 he led an offensive patrol over Polygon Wood and tangled with 15 Albatros scouts. Collishaw shot down two machines in flames, a third one out of control. The following day he sent another scout down out of control while leading a patrol in the neighborhood of Lille. On June 14, while leading a patrol in the vicinity of Menin, he attacked six Albatros scouts and again drove one of them down in a spin. On June 15 he led an offensive patrol north of St-Julien where a flight of five German scouts was encountered. He attacked one of them from close quarters and it dived straight down, the pilot or motor hit. After Collishaw shot his man down he saw Reid also shoot down one of the enemy. On the same day he led another offensive patrol with two more Canadians, Fitzgibbon and Page (who later commanded "C" Flight), and Nash, Alexander, and

Reid. Near Moorslede he attacked an Albatros scout out of the sun and fired at close range. The machine stalled and fell out of control. Collishaw then drove off one of the enemy who was attacking Reid, and, after that, shot down one of the enemy who was attacking Alexander. The right-hand wings of this machine carried away and it fell in pieces. On June 17 he led an offensive patrol near Roulers, where he attacked a formation of eight enemy scouts and shot one of them down. On June 18, in the vicinity of Ypres, Collishaw and Reid each shot down an enemy machine.

On the same day, Collishaw's Distinguished Service Cross was gazetted, and on June 24 he and Alexander were cited by General Sir Herbert Charles Plumer, Commander of the British Second Army and holder of the Ypres Salient.

The fighting went on day after day in the beautiful summer weather.

On June 25 Collishaw led the original Black Flight—himself, Reid, Sharman, Alexander and Nash—on an offensive patrol over Quesnoy where they ran into the red machines of *Jasta 11*. In the fight that ensued, action was too fast for most of the men to be sure afterward what had happened. When the Black Flight reformed, Nash was missing. He had been wounded and forced down by *Leutnant* Karl Allmenröder, the deputy commander of *Jasta 11*.

Allmenröder was born on May 3, 1896, at Wald, near Solingen in the Rhineland, the son of a Pastor. He had wanted to be a doctor and had commenced his studies at Marburg when the war broke out. He was sent with Field Artillery Regiment Nr. 62 to the Eastern Front, but contrived a transfer to the air service and was sent to the Halberstadt Flying School. On passing out of the school he was posted to *Fl. Abt.* 227, where he flew chiefly artillery co-operation missions. The career of Boelcke stirred his imagination and he once more sought a transfer, this time to fighters. In November 1916 he was posted to *Jasta 11*; on February 16, 1917, he scored his first victory. On April 2 he scored his sixth, and was appointed deputy squadron leader by von Richthofen. Allmenröder often went out on voluntary patrols with von Richthofen and the two of them hunted well together. At one time, Allmenröder flew an Albatros D III with a white tail and red fuselage. He was awarded the *Pour le Mérite* on June 14, 1917.

On June 25 he raised his score to 30 when he brought down Gerald Nash and an artillery-spotting R.E.8 while hunting with von Richthofen.

A few days after having been taken prisoner, Nash heard the church bell tolling in the town where he was being held in temporary quarters. He asked his captors what was going on and was told it was *Jasta 11's* funeral ceremony for Allmenröder, who was to be taken home to Solingen-Wald for burial. Nash was surprised by the news and asked what had happened. He was told that Allmenröder had been shot down by one of the Black Flight Triplanes.

The *Record of Combats* of the Air Historical Branch of the Air Ministry gives the following account of the actions of Black Flight for June 27, 1917: "Collishaw and Flight Sub-Lieutenant Alexander engaged a two-seater aircraft north of Armentières. Although the two-seater was observed to dive very steeply, it was probably under control.

"Collishaw led a (second) offensive patrol and led his formation down to assault a formation of three red-coloured Albatros believed to belong to No. 11 Jasta. Another hostile formation of three red Albatros had taken up a threatening attitude above and so Collishaw decided to open fire at long range on the targets below. (This was the flight led by Allmenröder.) He did so, and while he was firing, the uppermost hostile fighters assaulted him and his pilots. There was no time to see what happened to the lower targets, as Collishaw and his pilots had to take immediate avoiding action. Collishaw had six indecisive combats during this patrol.

"On the same patrol, Collishaw's flight became involved in a general engagement with a flight of Albatros near Courtrai and Menin. Collishaw destroyed one in pieces in the air and he shot the pilot in a second Albatros. Confirmed by the pilots in his flight."

A hard day's work. In regard to the specific encounter in which Allmenröder was shot down, Collishaw has this to say: "There was nothing at all spectacular about my adventure with Allmenröder. I was flying with two other Triplanes and I saw three Albatros scouts below and to a flank and on looking around I saw a second three Albatros well above and to a flank in the opposite direction. It was rather an awkward position for the Triplanes, as we could easily become the meat in the sandwich. However, the upper formation did nothing untoward and I thought that they had not seen the Triplanes. I therefore decided to make a rapid attack on the Albatros below and then leave the scene quickly. I made the signal for the assault to my pilots. We went down in a steep dive and I opened fire on the central leading Albatros, while my two pilots opened on the adjoining targets. I had fired from long range, as I intended to do a "tip and run" raid, and had expended perhaps 100 rounds, when suddenly I felt my aircraft hit by bullets. At the same instant I saw my target go out of control. I immediately took violent avoiding action and so did my pilots and we rejoined at the lines. At the time, I paid no attention to this brief, what I thought of as indecisive, action. Experienced pilots, when suddenly attacked, always took such violent avoiding action, which momentarily placed their aircraft out of control. As I had fired at long range, I simply thought that the German pilot was acting normally and that there was nothing more to the affair. It was not until Gerald Nash returned from P.O.W. and told me about Allmenröder's death that I knew what had happened.

"The pilots in Allmenröder's formation could scarcely believe that he had been shot down because the firing had been done from such long range. A German officer observer on the ground watched Allmenröder's fall. His aircraft went momentarily out of control and then proceeded to glide, what appeared to be normally, to the eastward; but after a brief interval, the Albatros went into an uncontrolled dive and crashed."*

* The material relevant to Collishaw's successful attack on Allmenröder was loaned to the author by Mr. O. A. Sater of Jamaica, L.I., N.Y.

∗                              ∗                              ∗

110

UNSHAKEN by the calamitous experiment in the Spad A.2, in the wreck of which he was last seen hanging by his heels, the indestructible Jacques Leps came back for more. He applied for pilot training. Because of his service record, his request was approved immediately and he was sent to Amberieu for instruction.

At the beginning of 1917 Leps had flown with Spa 81, stationed near Belfort. As an observer/gunner he had been over the lines many times before and the war in the air was nothing new to him. He had, therefore, less to learn than other *chasseurs débutants,* in addition to which he was a natural pilot. His talents manifested themselves in such a way that he broke, without any conscious effort to do so, the field record for quick learning. The commandant of the school informed him of his success, of which he was unaware, by telling him he could pick his own specialty.

"Fighters," said Leps without hesitation.

In March 1917 on the occasion of his second encounter with an enemy formation, he scored a double, one of the enemy machines being an Albatros two-seater. Word of his feat was telephoned to the aerodrome from the infantry in the trenches who had followed the show with delight. Returning to the field, Leps was informed that he was to be cited by his squadron commander for the *Légion d'Honneur.*

The citation reads: "A courageous and ardent young officer. Already wounded and cited for the Order of the Army, conducted himself brilliantly on March 16, 1917, shooting down in the course of a single flight two enemy aeroplanes, one of which fell into our lines."

*"Une victoire."*

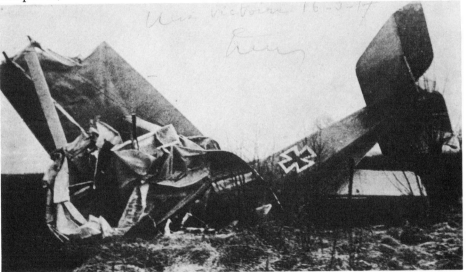

Jacques Leps

One of his hardest fights and narrowest escapes occurred on April 30, 1917, when he tangled with two German fighters in the course of a solo patrol. The pilots were well-matched. Leps was unable to get into position for decisive shooting because one or the other of his adversaries was always on his tail, while he himself managed to keep out of the way of their shots. The action was short but

111

fast as the three machines spun around each other, each looking for an opening. It couldn't last long, of course, and it didn't. One of the German pilots got in a burst that smashed half of his controls and wounded Leps in the chin. His Spad tumbled down in a wild spin. Stunned and unable to co-ordinate, Leps was on his way out.

*"Une défaite."*
*Any landing you*
*can walk away*
*from is*
*a good landing.*

Jacques Leps

A few hundred feet from the ground, he regained enough control to avoid a fatal crash, but he was still over enemy territory. He had very little control over his crippled ship and less height, but he decided to try for the French lines rather than land behind the German lines and spend the rest of the war a prisoner. At tree-top height he crossed no-man's-land, having weathered the parting salutes from the rifles and small arms of the troops in the German trenches. He piled up on Mont Cornillet, a devastated hillside between the first and second French lines, his Spad a splintered and jumbled wreck.

*Leps*

The commanding officer wanted to have him evacuated, but Leps refused to leave the squadron, for which he was awarded the Voluntary Combattants' Medal.

Leps the indestructible. He was back in action in a few weeks, cited for the fourth time on July 23, 1917, for a victory he had achieved in June when he had literally shot an Albatros to pieces in the air. In all, he was cited ten times for his service in the Great War. His eleventh citation acknowledges the fact that this distinguished officer, a squadron commander of *Groupe de Chasse XXI* was grievously wounded on June 6, 1940—one war later.

Leps the indestructible.

Once, Leps let himself be attacked by two Albatros, calculating their moves to a nicety and judging, correctly, that if he let them make the first move, it would be easy to catch them off guard. He was alone when he caught a glimpse of the two enemy fighters in the sun about 2000 feet above him. He held his course and waited for them to commit themselves. In a moment they were coming down together, supposing, probably, that they had not been seen. Leps knew exactly how much room was needed to loop a Spad and how long the manoeuvre took, and at the right moment he gunned the engine and yanked the stick all the way back. He came down on the rear Albatros and sent a burst into it. It disintegrated. He lost two or three seconds avoiding the debris and the other Albatros pilot managed to get away by diving to the safety of his own lines.

About this time Leps found occasion to experiment with a variation on the Immelmann turn which Guynemer had enunciated before him. The manoeuvre was essentially a loop. The power of the Spad made it possible to loop her fast without much slowing down near the top. That slow-down could be fatal. Leps was out alone again on a voluntary patrol when he spotted a big two-seater climbing over the German lines. After having identified it as an enemy artillery-spotter, he dived hard on it. A burst, a zoom into a loop to regain height, taking full advantage of the speed built up in the dive. Completing the loop and coming down again, he was in position to fire another burst. In his own words: "I returned to the attack to finish it off. Unspeakable horror! I perceived the blue-white-red cockades of France! This was one of the first Dorand machines at the Front, an unfamiliar type. Although badly damaged, the aeroplane was brought to a safe landing by its admirable crew. A glass of champagne set things right between us.

". . . but Guynemer's technique did work."

✳        ✳        ✳

HERMANN BECKER was born in Trebus near Rothenburg on September 10, 1887, the son of a goods dispatcher. He studied at the Oberrealschule and the Technical College at Gorlitz where he specialized in machine construction. At the outbreak of the war he was a practising engineer at Schweidnitz. Although he was declared indispensable to the engineering firm for which he worked, Becker declined to be exempt from service and volunteered for aviation duty. He entered the *Fliegertruppen* at the beginning of 1915 and was sent for training to *F.E.A. 2* at Adlershof, Berlin.

In April 1915 he was sent to Galicia as Technical Officer of *Fl.Abt.57*. The position of Technical Officer (Werkmeister) was equal in rank to that of Warrant Officer and the job entailed full responsibility for the serviceability of the squadron's aeroplanes. All mechanics assigned to individual aeroplanes were under him. That Becker was assigned to such an important job after a relatively short service was due in large part to his civilian engineering training, by which he profited again in the summer of 1915 when he reported to *F.E.A. 8* at Graudenz for pilot training. Qualifying for both Army and Navy certificates, he remained at Graudenz as an instructor until December. In January 1916 he was posted as a bomber pilot to *Kagohl 5* (*Kampfgeschwader der Oberste Heeresleitung 5.*) The early tactical units of the German air service came directly under the control of Supreme Headquarters (OHL), as opposed to the *Fliegerabteilungen,* which were under the control of Chiefs of Aviation for the individual Army Corps. In December 1915 the old B.A.M. and B.A.O. were renamed "Battle Groups"—*Kagohl 1* and *Kagohl 2*. At the same time three more *Kagohls* were commissioned, a sixth in April 1916 and a seventh in June. Each of these seven Groups had six *Staffeln* equipped with six aeroplanes.

With *Kagohl 5* Becker took part in the Battle of Verdun and the Battle of the Somme. In November 1916 he was commissioned *Leutnant*. On January 12, 1917, he was awarded the Iron Cross First Class in recognition of his devotion and extraordinary record of intensive flying on both day and night missions.

During his flying with *Kagohl 5,* Becker was merely a chauffeur for officers who flew as observers, bombardiers, and gunners, and he was dependent on their marksmanship and fighting spirit when enemy scouts attacked. By the end of 1916 Becker had had enough of that, and besides, the images of Boelcke and Immelmann were grown large in the minds of young pilots throughout the German air service. These were giants worthy of emulation, and Becker eagerly accepted the opportunity to convert to single-seaters when *Kagohl 5* was broken up. After a brief conversion course at the *Kampfeinsitzerschule* at Paderborn, he was sent to the *Jagdfliegerschule Nr. 1* at Valenciennes.

At Valenciennes Becker came to the attention of the *Führer* of *Jasta 12*, *Oberleutnant* von Tutschek. It was customary (but not invariable) in the German air service for Front-line squadron leaders to visit reserve centers such as those connected with *Jagdfliegerschulen* and pick their own replacements from among the more likely-looking recruits. Adolf *Ritter* von Tutschek couldn't know it, but when he picked Becker as a replacement he was also picking a man to succeed him as *Staffelführer*.

When Becker reported to *Jasta 12* the squadron was stationed at Epinoy, on the road between Cambrai and Douai, where the opposition was mostly the dashing British pilots of the RFC. In his first days as a fighter pilot at the Front, Becker learned the lessons that were to bring him later success.

One day in May 1917 Becker was alone over the Front, trying to find a familiar landmark by which he might orient himself. He was alone because he had become separated from the rest of the patrol, a common experience for new men (even veterans of another branch of the air service). Absorbed in scanning the earth below, and accustomed to having an observer guard his tail, he left himself wide open to an enemy pilot who came up behind him and put a burst into his machine. The British pilot must have been close, for Becker heard the crackling and felt the blow at the same time. The blow, on his right side, caused him involuntarily to fall against the stick which was driven forward, and the Albatros dived into a violent half-loop which took it out of the attacker's field of fire. Becker was upside down in an instant and when he recovered control and righted his ship the enemy aeroplane was nowhere in sight.

Keeping a sharp watch out, Becker found his way home and landed smoothly at Epinoy. He found that he had suffered a trifling graze on the ribs and that only one bullet had hit him. It had passed between his arm and his body, putting holes in the sleeves of his flying togs and the uniform jacket underneath. It couldn't have been closer. But for that shove his career as a fighter pilot would have come to an untimely end. Rule number one was evolved forthwith: NEVER show your back to the enemy.

For Becker, the rest of the rules were soon educed, albeit without such drastic lessons. Attack is the best defense, speedy, surprise attack. Always close to within 20 or even 10 metres of your opponent (regardless of whether he fires or not). These were the rules by which he fought—and lived. When he commanded his own squadron he continually exhorted his men to follow them.

"Target-sure," he would say, "so close that every burst becomes target-sure. That this may happen to one's own self must not deter one. Whoever has the stronger nerves is the victor."

Manfred von Richthofen expressed the conquering of fear thus: "One must overcome the inner *Schweinehund*." John Kirbach, a veteran of the German Army in the First World War and of the American Army in World War II, was asked how "overcoming the inner *Schweinehund*" might be translated. "The best American equivalent is possibly 'to overcome turning yellow,'" he answered. "The German word means anything from coward to turncoat to being just a mangy dog good enough only to keep company with swine."

So much for the inner *Schweinehund*. Did this really work? Can it be said that success required only that one have the guts to bore into point-blank range to fire? It worked for Hermann Becker: "I achieved my 24 victories only by adhering strictly to these rules, and was never in serious trouble."

\*　　　　　　\*　　　　　　\*

GILBERT SARDIER of Clermont-Ferrand, the present Representative of the French National Association of Aces, was born in Riom (Puy-de-Dôme) on May 5, 1897. (A graduate of the Faculté de Droit of Paris, he has for many years been associated with the La Nationale assurance company, and is the author of a number of books on aviation and space travel.)

With the Mobilization in August 1914, Sardier entered the *Chasseurs d'Afrique*. Like the rest of the cavalry troops he was unhorsed by the stagnation of the trench war and began to consider aviation as a means of getting back into the war and out of the mud. Toward the end of 1915, he was accepted for flying training and was sent to Pau to begin the standard "Blériot school" instruction. At Buc-St-Cyr he won his military pilot's brevet in a Caudron G.3 in April 1916.

*Sardier.*

*Gilbert Sardier*

116

No successful pilot went through all the stages of training and apprenticeship without something going wrong and Monsieur Sardier is no exception. On the cross-country check-out flight from Buc to Chartres, a sensational error of navigation found him at St-Cyr after one hour of flying time—a little over a half mile from his point of departure!

To Pau again for aerobatics, he celebrated his graduation in August 1916 by an impromptu exhibition of stunting for the benefit of General Girod. For the benefit of discipline, General Girod gave him 15 days close arrest.

In the fall of 1916 Sardier received his posting to N 77, then in process of formation under the command of *Capitaine* de L'Hermite. The squadron was composed mostly of sport celebrities—Maurice Boyau, an international rugby champion, killed in action after 36 victories; Georges Boillot, an automobile racing champion; Henri Decoin, a swimming and boxing champion; Mouronval, another rugbyman; Strolh; Felloneau—the unit was named *"les Sportifs"* with good reason, but *Capitaine* de L'Hermite regarded his command and the squadron's mission as holy, like a crusade. He chose their insignia—the Cross of Jerusalem.

The first victory for Sardier, in November 1916, was also the first victory for the *escadrille*. It was not an easy victory—Sardier came back with 36 holes in his Nieuport.

Among his numerous combats of the next two years, two stand out with particular vividness. One of them, in the spring of 1918, was a single-handed encounter with a flight of four German single-seaters, three of which he shot down. The action earned him the *Légion d'Honneur* and the American Distinguished Service Cross since it took place above the American lines at Montdidier.

Eventually, Sardier was appointed to the command of Spa 48, *"Les Coqs"*, and that in spite of his own objections, for he was barely 21 and it was a heavy charge, particularly since he assumed command of officers older than himself.

*Spa 48.*

One other combat that is especially memorable is one over Pagny-sur-Moselle on March 16, 1917. Sardier and Boyau struggled inconclusively with an Albatros whose pilot was defending himself with magnificent skill and courage . . .

On the morning of March 16, 1917, Georges Guynemer shot down two Albatros two-seaters in flames. In the afternoon he was out hunting along the lines again in his Spad, *"Vieux Charles,"* when he came upon a fight between two Nieuports and an Albatros D II. He watched for a few seconds, then came in like a whirlwind and with ten shots put the Albatros out of action, pilot wounded, engine dead. The machine went down, Guynemer escorting it all the way to the ground, almost before Sardier and Boyau knew what had happened. One look at the stork and the blue-white-red riband on the fuselage made everything clear.

The German prisoner was *Leutnant* von Hausen, nephew of General von Hausen, commander of the German Second Army; his Albatros, almost undamaged, was subsequently displayed in the Place Leczinski in Nancy.

On landing, Sardier was informed that there was a call for him. It was Guynemer, who gave him a long lecture on tactics over the telephone.

\*　　　　　　\*　　　　　　\*

THE STORKS—*Groupe de Combat XII*—shifted up and down the Front in much the same way as a German fighter Circus, the main difference being that they were not completely self-sufficient and had to move to an established base rather than just any cow pasture. They arrived in Lorraine in February 1917, settling down in a field near Nancy.

On May 25, Georges Guynemer shot down four enemy aeroplanes in one day—his best day yet. On June 11, he was named an officer of the Legion of Honor, his victory score standing at 45.

By the end of August he was being acclaimed as Ace of Aces with over 50 confirmed victories.

He was at the top, the height of his success, but there's only one way to go from the top.

He had been wounded too many times, he had lost too many friends in combat. He was of a frail constitution and precarious health to begin with and had sustained himself on nothing but nerve for a year.

In July les Cigognes transferred to St-Pol-sur-Mer near Dunkerque to partake in another muddy, bloody, dreary, futile battle in Flanders.

Guynemer spent a few days at home where his father broached the subject of Guynemer retiring from combat, since he was more valuable as an instructor and technical adviser than as a pilot, even if he got 50 more victories.

"And it will be said that I have ceased to fight because I have won all the awards," said Georges.

"Let them say it, for when you reappear stronger and more ardent, they will understand . . . there is a limit to human strength."

"Yes, a limit! A limit to be passed. If one has not given everything, one has given nothing."

*Guynemer.*

Guynemer returned to *les Cigognes* on September 4, to learn that Heurtaux, one of his best friends, had been critically wounded the day before. The news seriously upset him and it seemed as if the wheel of fortune had carried him past the zenith, for now everything seemed to go wrong. His favorite aeroplane was out of action and he was forced to fly an old one. His guns jammed at the critical moment; forced landings and bad weather kept him grounded. When he couldn't fly he paced up and down, fuming. He was irritable; he would flare up, eyes blazing, even at his old comrades. As frustrating as anything was to spend a day flying—four or five patrols of an hour and a half to two hours and a half—and not spot any *Boches*. This would put him in a black depression. He had the incredible bad luck to suffer three forced landings in three different aeroplanes on September 10.

The following day, a Tuesday, dawned on uncertain weather. The morning mists eventually began to clear, but not before the unfortunate start to the day had put *Capitaine* Guynemer, who had not slept well, in a pretty bad state. He was nervous and irritable.

*Commandant* du Peuty, one of the Staff Chiefs for Aviation at GQG, and *Commandant* Brocard, former C.O. of the *Groupe des Cigognes* and now *Chef de Cabinet* for the Air Ministry, were both due in at nine or ten o'clock from

118

Paris. They would be anxious to see him, perhaps they would have important new plans for *les Cigognes*. And that evening, without fail, he could go to the factory at Buc to see about his special Spad. He couldn't wait. He paced nervously back and forth from the barracks to the hangars.

Finally, he could stand it no longer. There were holes in the overcast, the sky would clear, *sous-Lieutenant* Bozon-Verduraz would accompany him on a patrol over towards Poelcapelle. The machines were rolled out and checked over. Everybody tried to think of a way to hold him. "*Commandants* du Peuty and Brocard will be here any minute. They'll want to see you."

Guynemer pointed at the sky—a patch of blue showed, giving promise of a clear day.

*Commandants* du Peuty and Brocard arrived at 9:00 and promptly asked for him. The two Spads had taken off at 8:30.

Climbing towards the southeast, the two sturdy, box-like Spads piloted by Guynemer and Bozon-Verduraz approached the lines near Bixschoote. They passed along the Front towards Langemarck, taken by the British on August 16. No *Boches*. They crossed the enemy lines at Poelcapelle and Guynemer spotted a target, one aeroplane, low down. He waved a conventional signal to Bozon-Verduraz and turned to climb towards the sun. The weather, which had been such a source of torment lately, frustrated his plan, for the sun at that moment was obscured by clouds and there would be no blinding glare out of which to attack. Guynemer then altered his tactics: he signaled to Bozon-Verduraz, who had been glued to his tail, to attack from below, to come up underneath the enemy two-seater in the gunner's blind spot, while he, Guynemer, would bore straight in from the side. It was a standard two-man attack, but the pilot of the German machine must have been an old campaigner, for he threw Guynemer off by a neat stunt: a flat, abrupt spin, and the observer got in a shot at Bozon-Verduraz on the way down. As Guynemer dived after the two-seater, Bozon-Verduraz spotted a flight of Albatros D III's approaching. He turned toward them himself to lure them away from Guynemer who, he feared, might be so intent on the chase of the two-seater that he would not see them come up behind him. Bozon-Verduraz headed his Spad directly into the formation of Albatros, and opening his throttle, closed with them at a startling speed. He went through the enemy formation and scattered it, then dived hard to get away. He came back up over the spot where he and Guynemer had begun the attack on the two-seater and circled around patiently, waiting for Guynemer to rejoin him, but the sky was empty.

Low on fuel, Bozon-Verduraz finally headed home. He had waited for an hour and his neck muscles were cramped from continuous swiveling. For the last ten minutes he had been telling himself that each circuit would be the last, that he had to return. He landed at St-Pol-sur-Mer with his tanks dry.

"Is Guynemer here?" were his first words.

"No, not yet," was the answer.

They all knew then, regardless of what they said, that it was the end.

*       *       *

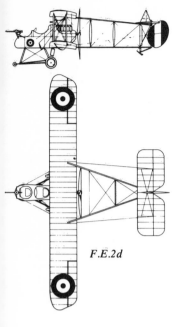

*F.E.2d*

NO. 20 SQUADRON RFC was a two-seater fighter squadron stationed at Ste-Marie-Cappel. It had come to France in January 1916, the first squadron equipped with the F.E.2b. In 1917 the squadron was flying the F.E.2d, the "Fee," that great wooden birdcage whose gunner had to stand on his seat in order to fire back over the top wing and the pusher engine.

About ten o'clock in the morning on July 6, 1917, six Fees took off for an offensive patrol between Ypres and Armentières. The job was simple: look for trouble, pick a fight. Offensive patrol.

At about the same time, Collishaw took off from Droglandt leading Reid, Page, Alexander, Sharman, and Fitzgibbon on an offensive patrol. The six triplanes shaped up over the field and headed east to the Ypres-Armentières line.

At *Jasta 11* near Courtrai a report came in from the *Flugmeldedienst* shortly after 10 o'clock. The *Rittmeister* noted the co-ordinates and took off with seven of his men to intercept the Fees. About 10:30 they spotted the big two-seaters and circled around to get into a position between them and the British lines. At a spot over the Lys at Deulemont, south-southeast of Ypres, they attacked. As they did so, another *Jasta* appeared and joined in the attack. The Fees formed a defensive circle as best they could and tried to work toward their lines. One, then another, went down to forced-landings in German-held territory.

The six Triplanes led by Collishaw tore into the scrap.

The *Record of Combats* of the Air Historical Branch of the Air Ministry supplies the following extract: "Collishaw shot down one red Albatros whose pilot appeared to be hit. In the general engagement . . . Collishaw attacked many other Albatros (scouts) and he succeeded in shooting down five of them out of control, but he could not watch for any final results because of counterattacks made on him. Flight Sub-Lieutenants Fitzgibbon and Alexander fired on aircraft attacking Collishaw, and Collishaw saw an Albatros fall as the result of an assault by one of his Flight."

The fight lasted for the extraordinary length of time of 40 minutes.

One Fee, piloted by Captain D. C. Cunnell (who was killed a few days later) with gunner Lieutenant A. E. Woodbridge (who survived the war and was killed in a civil flying accident), was attacked head-on by a red Albatros. The red machine came on at top speed, opening fire at close range, while Woodbridge, in his own words, fired "a steady stream of lead" at it. At the last second the red Albatros nosed down and passed under the Fee, not breaking away, but seeming to fall out of control.

It *was* out of control, and it fell a long way before the wounded pilot, temporarily blinded and paralyzed, regained his faculties and the control of his machine. Only the "thick von Richthofen skull," the *Rittmeister* later wrote his mother, saved him from winning the last award, the Wooden Cross. He had landed right-side up, tearing down a few telephone wires, but not minding that at such a time. Then he had passed out.

For the next three weeks, von Richthofen led the circus from Saint Nicholas Hospital in Courtrai.

120

General Sir Herbert Plumer, Commander of the British Second Army holding the Ypres salient, cited Collishaw to their Lordships in the following terms: "An excellent day's fighting—results remarkable. Lieutenant Collishaw of Naval Squadron No. 10 did splendidly, as he always does."

*    *    *

IT WAS IRONIC that the *Rittmeister* should have been brought down by the gunner of an obsolete Fee when one of the best British fighters of the war was entering the arena.

The Camel, next descendant of Sopwith lineage after the Triplane, was the first British machine to be equipped with twin synchronized machine guns—a year after the Albatros. The guns, Vickers, were mounted atop the fuselage in front of the cockpit, their breeches enclosed in a faired metal cowling, the "hump" that gave the Camel its name.

Nearly 5500 of these hornets were built, and between July 1917 and the Armistice, Camel pilots scored 1300 victories.

Although it carried a generous spread of plane surface—top and bottom wings were equal in span and chord—the Camel was extraordinarily manoeuvrable. This quality was chiefly the result of the combination of rotary engine and short fuselage.

The short fuselage made for a short "moment"; the machine could turn or loop on a small radius. The rotary engine imparted considerable torque, or twisting action. A rotary is an engine that literally rotates—the propeller is bolted to the engine and the crankshaft is bolted to the airframe. With the engine and propeller turning together a considerable twisting force is developed. In the Camel, this force expressed itself in the tendency of the aeroplane, in a right-hand turn, to drop its nose abruptly and go into a spin. Conversely, in a left-hand turn, the tendency was for the nose to rise. If the engine stalled on take-off the results were usually serious, for the loss of power meant loss of flying speed with a consequent loss of control effectiveness. Unless the pilot wrenched the controls hard the other way to counteract the torque, the dead but still spinning engine would pull the aeroplane around into a spin, and at take-off, there is no height in which to recover from a spin.

This is not to say that the Camel was tricky or dangerous. It certainly was no aeroplane to be treated casually. It had to be *flown* every minute in the air, and no daydreaming. In the hands of any pilot of average competence, the Camel was a first-rate fighter; in the hands of an expert, it could out-manoeuvre anything except the Fokker Triplane.

*Rotary engine—this one being an 80 horsepower Le Rhône installed in a Sopwith Pup.*

The standard synchronizing gear for Allied machines from the spring of 1917 to the end of the war was the Constantinesco gear or a variation of it. Constantinesco was an industrial designer of Roumanian birth and British citizenship whose specialty was hydraulic drills. Working with various armament experts he had developed an excellent hydraulic system that could be fitted to any engine and was simple enough as to be easy to maintain or repair. The engine itself

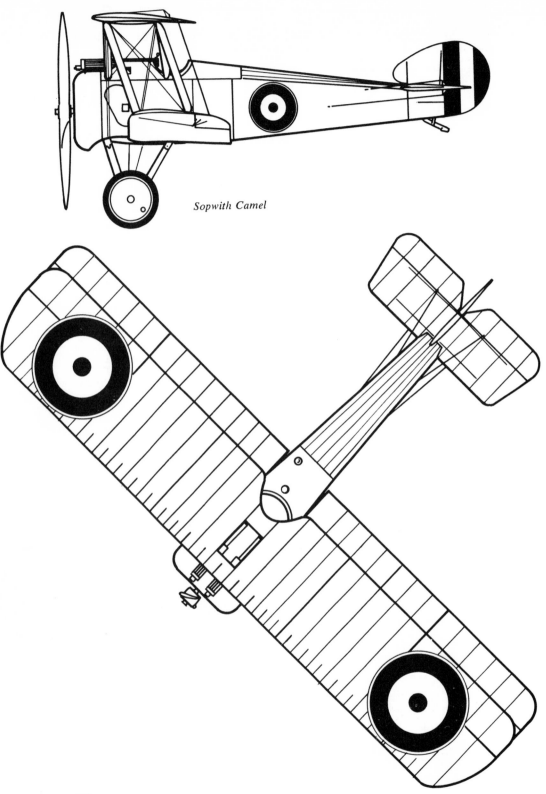

*Sopwith Camel*

122

provided the timing and the firing impulse was transmitted hydraulically. The pressure in the oil cylinder had to be maintained by means of a hand pump beside the pilot's seat, and once pumped up, the system would function through ten or twelve short bursts, the fluid being bled back into the reservoir. Then it had to be pumped up again or the guns wouldn't fire, since there would be no transmission of impulse. In the middle of a scrap this might prove a serious omission, but remembering to keep the gear pumped up was only a small matter of discipline and it gave the pilots something to think about.

\*                    \*                    \*

ON THE LAST DAY of July 1917, the Third Battle of Ypres began, and the RFC, like the BEF, began another maximum effort. Two-seater squadrons on contact patrol and observation missions, and single-seater squadrons on ground attack sorties and high offensive patrols swarmed over the lines.

On the same day, *Kogenluft* (*Kommandierende General der Luftstreitkräfte*—the Commanding General of the German air service) authorized the transfer of *Leutnant* Werner Voss to *Jasta 10* as *Führer* at the request of *Rittmeister* Manfred von Richthofen. It was a good choice by the Circus Leader, who made very few bad ones, for Werner Voss was a good man—or boy, rather. He was only 20 years old. (At that, he was not the only boy under 21 to command his own squadron). He had learned to fly at 19, had turned 20 during "Bloody April." He would never be twenty-one.

Werner Voss was born on April 13, 1897, in Krefeld, on the left bank of the Lower Rhine, not far from Essen. A member of the local militia company, the Krefeld Hussars, he was sent with his unit to Lorraine on Mobilization where, like many other dismounted cavalrymen, he found the trenches more unpleasant than the war. He applied for flying service and was accepted in August 1915, by which time he had won the Iron Cross First Class—at 17 years of age.

His first flying duty was as an observer, after some months of which he became a pilot, being assigned in May 1916 to *Kagohl 1,* the old Ostend Carrier Pigeons. He flew through the Battle of the Somme and saw every single man he had known on coming into the unit killed. In July 1916 he had gone on leave,

*Voss.*

124

with orders to report to Grossenhain, the ancient Grossen Hayn in Saxony, where he had converted to single-seaters.

Werner Voss was assigned to *Jasta 3* and commissioned *Leutnant* on September 1, 1916. The squadron, stationed at the time on the Somme, was equipped mostly with Halberstadt D scout machines. Voss, scoring two victories on November 27, showed himself to be a daring and resourceful pilot, obviously a man to be watched.

In *Jasta 2* a new leader had been appointed to succeed Oswald Boelcke who had died as a result of the collision with one of his men. The new *Jastaführer* was *Leutnant* Stephan Kirmaier, who led his men to 25 victories in as many days, and then was shot down himself by J. O. Andrews of Hawker's old squadron. Appointed to succeed him was *Hauptmann* Franz Walz, who arrived at *Jasta 2* the first of December, Werner Voss being transferred into the squadron at the same time to take a place in von Richthofen's flight. When von Richthofen left to assume command of *Jasta 11,* Voss moved up to take his place as flight leader.

By Imperial decree, *Jasta 2* was renamed *Jasta Boelcke* to perpetuate the name and example of its first leader, the father of the German fighter service.

Werner Voss was by all accounts a natural pilot. He was mechanically inclined and used to enjoy tinkering with his motorcycle and the engines of his aeroplanes. He was something of a "loner" as Ball was, and *Hauptmann* Walz permitted him to fly solo patrols contrary to the official policy of the *Luftstreitkräfte*. He survived several close calls in December and January and then hit his stride. Between January 15 and February 15, 1917, he shot down ten British machines; in the following six weeks he shot down ten more. He had suddenly become more than an Ace, for with twenty-two victories he was von Richthofen's nearest rival. The rest of the air service was interested in him professionally, and the civil population of Germany fastened on him as a new hero. He was ribbed by his squadron-mates about the *Pour le Mérite* which he would be getting any day. That meant little to Voss who preferred flying to parading.

Because he had been a two-seater pilot once ("poor devils," he called them) he planned his attacks on observation machines carefully with the aim of downing the machine rather than killing the crew. One burst into the engine after taking the British by surprise would do the trick, and because he was a superlative marksman, he could do it. He brought down one just that way on April 3, 1917, the machine going down in no-man's-land, but close enough to the British lines for the crew to run for it and make it. He was happy about that—he had shot an adversary down, but hadn't had to kill anybody to do it.

With fighters it was different. Voss was a terrific pilot, his reflexes were fast, and his shooting was deadly accurate. He combined all these attributes in a special attack he evolved and used several times. Patrolling high and alone, he could catch British scout formations by surprise as they approached or returned from the Front. He would come in broadside and high. To the enemy pilots, if they saw him at all, it probably looked as if he were going to pass over them. At the last instant he would tilt his wings and drop in a sideslip, nailing his victim with a short burst in the instant during which the machines were lined up. From the sideslip he would ease into a dive to pick up speed, either to get away, or to zoom for a return to the attack.

In March 1917 the Germans became aware, through a combination of security leaks and captured documents obtained by trench raids, that the new French Commander-in-Chief, General Nivelle, was planning another offensive in Champagne. Accordingly, German Supreme Headquarters began planning to meet it. Reinforcements flooded the area back of the Front where the threat was heaviest, and hundreds of new batteries were dug in and secured with barbed wire entanglements. The nine-division field strength was quadrupled and the number of *Fliegerabteilungen* proportionately increased. Last, but not least, a number of new Circuses pitched their tents in Champagne to prevent the French two-seaters from getting a look at the reception being prepared and to protect the German two-seaters who were keeping an eye on the French.

Werner Voss was one of the men moved into Champagne and he promptly proved to be as much a thorn in the side to the French as he had been to the British. Although the Spad was in many ways superior to the Albatros, few pilots were superior to Voss, and in May he shot down an aeroplane every three days.

In June, he went on leave. He returned to the Front the last day of July to assume command of *Jasta 10* as requested by von Richthofen. Voss's squadron, like all four squadrons of *Jagdgeschwader Nr. 1,* was stationed in Flanders near Courtrai. His return coincided with the first deliveries and introduction of a spectacular new fighter, the Fokker Triplane.

Tony Fokker had been languishing in the shade of his *Eindecker,* eclipsed by the Albatros on one hand and by the new Allied fighters on the other. The powerful Albatros concern had monopolized the Mercedes engine, for one thing; Fokker had produced only a few mediocre biplanes that were little more than variations of the *Eindecker.* In the summer of 1916 Reinhold Platz had become chief of the Fokker design staff. The Fokker Triplane was his first original design.

The startling success of the Sopwith Triplane had inspired a good deal of thought at the Fokker works. The Flying Dutchman, as usual, decided that the job could be done better.

As a matter of fact, the Sopwith Triplane was not really as good as it seemed. Its success was due more to the extraordinary skill of the pilots of the Royal Naval Air Service who flew it—Collishaw, Dallas, Little, others—than to any qualities of the aeroplane itself.

Be that as it may, the three-wing layout, *Dreidecker* in German, was the solution to Tony Fokker's problems. The engine would be the 110-horsepower Oberürsel rotary, a German version of the French Le Rhône, produced at the Motorenfabrik Oberürsel, A. G., a company Tony Fokker happened to own. The Oberürsel was available in considerable numbers, needless to say, so there was no headache about supply as there was with the Mercedes. True, the engine was not

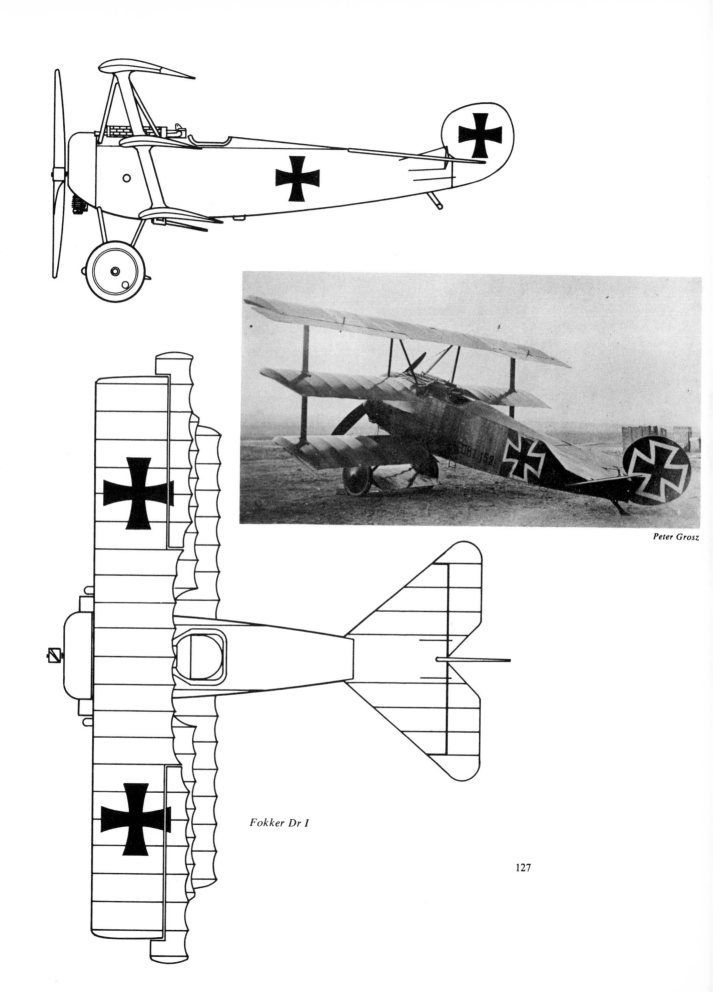

Peter Grosz

Fokker Dr I

127

a powerful one, but that hardly mattered—the goals for which Fokker and Platz were shooting were manoeuvrability and a good rate of climb, rather than speed and high ceiling.

Except for the first three production models which were labeled F I, the Fokker Triplane bore the standard army designation Fok Dr I, meaning the first Fokker Triplane design.

The Dr I, even with three wings, had far less wing area than its biplane contemporaries—200 square feet, as compared to 229 for the Albatros D V, 238 for the Pfalz D III, or 227 for the Spad 13. Its design balanced this reduction of supporting surface with a thick aerofoil section which gave relatively greater lift (and drag too, but the goal was manoeuvrability, not speed.) Its wings were short and narrow, giving little lateral resistance, and its fuselage was short—18 feet, even shorter than that of the Camel. The Dr I, moreover, was of the standard Fokker steel-tube construction with hollow box-spar wings, and was therefore light, a featherweight, in fact. Its weight was 1200 pounds, while the Spad, S.E.5, Albatros and Pfalz all weighed in at about a ton.

The Dr. I could fly rings around any machine at the Front. Its rate of climb was remarkable—it could shoot up a mile in two and a half minutes, nearly twice as fast as the Sopwith Triplane. Its manoeuvrability was fantastic—it could turn on a dime. Fokker conceded that it was slow, but he said Allied pilots never had a chance to find out how slow it was because of the way it stunted.

Hermann Becker, the German Ace, recently recounted how he scored a victory with the Triplane early in 1918 by taking advantage of its agility.

A French pilot in a Spad met Becker head-on in a challenge of nerves. Both flew straight at the other, both held their fire. At the last instant they broke, swerved, each rolling away to his right. They passed so close Becker could feel the wind of the other's passing, could look the Frenchman in the eye. Each now had one object, to get around behind the other man. The Triplane was so handy that Becker was around and on the Spad's tail almost before the Spad had begun to turn. He was right on it when he triggered a killing burst straight into the cockpit, *"er oder ich."* The Frenchman had had one chance, to dive, but he hadn't taken it, so he was done for. No machine could turn inside the Fokker Triplane. It was a winner; so was Werner Voss. The two of them together made what was perhaps the outstanding combination of pilot and aeroplane of the war.

Within a few weeks of having returned to the Front and having, along with the *Rittmeister,* introduced the new machine, Voss had run his score up to 48, shooting down an enemy aeroplane nearly every day.

In the early evening hours of September 23, 1917, Voss was out alone scouting the lines near Poelcappelle. The air was clear below 9000 feet except for the beginnings of a ground haze, while above 9000 feet a dense layer of cloud spread wide across the sky. As the sun dropped lower it occasionally managed to cast a few dull gleams through rifts in the ceiling. A patrol of S.E.5's from No. 56 Squadron RFC had just shot down a German two-seater and was climbing in formation back up toward the cloud layer when the pilots spotted

128

Voss ahead of them in the act of putting down another S.E.5. He was diving after it, on a course that brought him almost under the British patrol. The leader dived, followed by his men. The leader was Captain (later Major) James Thomas Byford McCudden, V. C. With him were Captain R. T. C. Hoidge, and Lieutenants A. P. F. Rhys-Davids, R. A. Mayberry, V. P. Cronyn, and K. K. Muspratt. Together, these six men achieved a final score of some 140 confirmed victories.

Against these six opponents, Voss put up a ten-minute fight that is still remembered when Kaisers and Kings are dust.

As they dived, McCudden went to the right, Rhys-Davids to the left, and they got behind the Triplane together. As they approached, Voss suddenly snapped it around and threw a burst at them before any of the British pilots had fired a shot. They scattered and closed in on him immediately, but his manoeuvres were so fast none could draw a bead. He seemed to be shooting at all of them at once. McCudden got behind him a second time and was thrown off instantly, unable to match the dazzling movements of the Triplane. They had him literally boxed in, yet he was shooting holes into all of them. Hoidge said that Voss was doing things that were beyond comprehension. He could turn flat around without banking, being headed the other direction in seconds. In that case there was nothing to do but duck and let him flash by. McCudden, above, began to fire and instantly the nose of the Triplane came up at him, both guns crackling. He saw the flashes at the muzzles and heard the bullets going through his wings.

*McCudden.*

A British officer in a two-seater watched the fight from above and to him it seemed the Triplane was moving like lightning. The S.E. pilots emptied the drums of their Lewis guns and had to change them. They hit the empty air nearly every time they fired because the Triplane inexplicably danced out of the way and came back shooting at them.

Voss was hit, however, and he was killed because he wasn't immortal. Sometime during the fierce and compacted tangle he must have been wounded, for when Rhys-Davids put the last burst into the Triplane it was flying straight and level and Rhys-Davids almost ran into it, so unexpected was the steadiness of the target. He passed the machine within inches and promptly lost sight of it because it was hidden in the blind spot under the S.E. The only man who saw the Triplane go down was McCudden, who was off to one side to change drums on the Lewis. After Rhys-Davids passed, the Triplane wobbled unsteadily then fell in a steep dive, going steeper and hitting the ground inside the British lines where it disintegrated, appearing to burst into thousands of pieces.

*Rhys-Davids.*

One day almost a year before, in November 1916, McCudden and Voss had met over the Somme. McCudden, in a D.H.2, had taken a position between a Halberstadt D II and the German lines while four other British D.H.2's had boxed it in. The Halberstadt had broken away and McCudden had tried to cut off its retreat. He had got on its tail, but it had turned quickly to put him off and the machine had passed at right angles at no more than 50 feet. McCudden had got a good look at the pilot's face in this pass and later swore that the pilot was grinning . . .

*Hoidge.*

IN AUGUST 1917 Naval Ten switched from Sopwith Triplanes to Sopwith Camels; in October the squadron moved to a new field near Teteghem, east of Dunkirk on the Belgian coast; and a young Canadian named Wilfred Austin Curtis joined "A" Flight, which he subsequently commanded. Curtis is one of Canada's great aviators, a retired Air Marshal today and former Chief of Staff of the RCAF. A native of Toronto, he is the founder of the Toronto Flying Club and an active representative of the Royal Canadian Flying Club Association.

In the summer of 1915 Curtis applied, as a civilian, for flying lessons at the Curtis Flying School in Toronto. The RNAS would not accept anyone who did not possess a private pilot's license. The Flying School could not take any more students, however, so Curtis joined the Canadian Army. In April 1916 he had just completed an officer's train-

*Curtis.*

ing course when the Navy wrote to inform him that his application was before them and asked him to report for an interview.

It was arranged that Curtis would take flying lessons and pay for them himself—$400.00 for 400 minutes of flying time. The instruction was given flying back and forth in front of the hangar on a six-acre field where the class lined up and took turns one by one. To communicate with the pupil in flight, the instructor throttled back the engine and shouted at the pupil, and those on the ground could hear what was said. The comments were, for the most part, more amusing than instructive. Those students that passed the tests were shipped in batches to England for further instruction. "Further instruction" that at the time did not include aerobatics. This was typical of all the air services and is in no way an implied criticism of any of them, but merely a reflection of the casual approach during aviation's raw youth. The British Government refunded Curtis £75 and paid his passage to England.

Curtis learned the stall the hard way—he crashed. Having walked away from that he was ready to try the next step: "The first time I tried to loop was just before crossing the Channel to France. I dived to pick up speed, but when I was upside down I unintentionally let the joy stick go back to the neutral position as a result of which I was floating along upside down, my weight hanging in the belt. It was quite frightening. When I recovered my position and equilibrium I climbed to 7000 feet, flew over a large forest which I thought would be softer to fall on than the hard earth and looped six or seven times, until I was satisfied that I could do it."

130

One wonders at times if the luck to which veteran fighter pilots refer to as being one of the attributes of success was not more necessary during the training than during the fighting.

Having mastered the loop and survived the stall, Curtis went on to the next stage of aerobatics, the spin—incredible as it may seem, at the Front: "My first spin was involuntary and was over the German lines while flying tail man on an inside turn. It took me 2000 feet to get out of the spin and half an hour to regain my position in the formation."

*Curtis. His Camel of No. 10 (Naval) Squadron bore white stripes as unit identification and a white "A" for "A" Flight. The white rings on the wheel covers were personal marks.*

In the fall of 1917 Curtis was learning the trade of fighter pilot in the toughest school in the world—the Western Front. An aggressive pilot, he tended to take advantage of his luck, and although some of his escapes were hair-raising, he came back for more with invincible enthusiasm. Soon he was feeling that he could take on anybody. On November 5 he led five Camels of "A" Flight on a high offensive patrol up to the lines at Nieuport. The flight took off at 12:30 and climbed to 10,000 feet where Curtis shaped a course northeast along the coast. After a penetration of perhaps five miles he turned back to the lines where a flight of eight Albatros was spotted on a level somewhat above that of the Camels.

They looked like a good target so he headed up into them: "Two of the German formation did a roll as we approached. This should have warned me that they were above average, but it did not and I pulled up and opened fire. It seemed that four of them started firing at me at the same time. In some unaccountable manner I found myself upside down, heading for the earth with a lower right wing that had buckled upwards about two or three feet out from the fuselage. I had had toe straps put on my rudder bar so that I could both push and pull with one foot in case I was shot through the other leg. Well, I found myself trying to keep my body inside the fuselage by pulling up for all I was worth with my toes from the ankle forward. My belt had too much elastic in it and was of very little use. I was hanging on to the fuselage beside the machine gun holes for all I was worth.

"The Germans kept shooting at me in turn, one burst after the other—I was shouting at them to leave me alone, you dirty so and so's.

"At 2000 feet I went into the clouds and they left me. In a few seconds I reached into the fuselage, got hold of the spade grip of the joy stick and pressed the blip switch, which cut the engine off. I pulled back gradually and regained my position and control of the machine less than 1000 feet up.

"I was four or five miles over the lines. I did not want to be a prisoner but did not know whether the wing would stand the strain of carrying the weight of the aeroplane with the engine pulling. I opened the throttle rather gingerly and kept increasing the power, all the time watching to see whether the wing would hold on or not. It did, and I crawled back over the lines at a few hundred feet. As I neared the lines the German ground forces opened up with rifle and machine gun fire. They put holes in the wings and fuselage but did not hit a vital spot. I was able to crawl back to my own aerodrome a sadder and a wiser pilot.

"I actually looked in the mirror to see how grey my hair was and was quite surprised to find that the color had not changed a bit. I don't know what constitutes being badly scared but I will never be that frightened again if I live to be a hundred."

For a time the Camels of "A" Flight bore the white blazes shown in the accompanying photograph. For a very short time. The extravagant decoration was ordered removed by the Wing Commander as soon as he saw it.

\*　　　　　　\*　　　　　　\*

DURING GENERAL NIVELLE'S disastrous offensive in Champagne in the spring of 1917, a young man named Paul-René Fonck attracted attention and interest of the the Storks by his flying and obvious *élan*.

Fonck had been called up on August 22, 1914, winning his first citation exactly one year later. The citation read in part: ". . . in spite of the most unfavorable weather, flying at very low altitude over the enemy positions to gather the required information, daring the most violent enemy fire, in the course of which the aeroplane was riddled with bullets."

*Fonck.*

He was nervy enough, this Fonck, according to his squadron mates, but he never liked the idea of being a sitting duck for anybody, ground-gunners or air-gunners. He took along a carbine during the first year of the war when, for the most part, the opposite numbers of the French and German air services were content to wave when they chanced to meet. Fonck never shot anybody down with a carbine, but he tried. He was glad when machine guns were finally issued to the Caudron squadrons. By the time of the Champagne offensive, the Albatros squadrons were looking at the Caudron aeroplanes as easy victories and the Nieuports and Spads were having a hard time protecting them.

Even though his bus was a lumbering ungainly thing, a kind of flying wire entanglement, Fonck was determined to fight with it. He was a pilot of deftness and address, and it is likely that no one else could have succeeded in such an uninspired apparatus as the Caudron.

In March 1917, Fonck was flying a reconnaissance patrol with another Caudron G.4 when they were attacked by a wedge of five Albatros. Fonck and the other pilot, Sergeant Raux, managed to stay together until they approached the French lines when Raux was wounded, his observer killed, and his aeroplane set afire. Raux dived toward the lines and three Albatros followed him down. Fonck followed the three single-seaters and shot down the rearmost. The machines were within reach of French ground fire at this point and the German fighters prudently withdrew. The wounded Raux brought his burning Caudron in under control before the French front line—the shell-torn earth of no-man's-land was no place to land save in an emergency—and crashed the machine directly opposite a first-aid station. The Germans and French interrupted the war while stretcher bearers went out to retrieve the body of the observer and the badly hurt Raux.

This particular adventure brought Fonck to the attention of his superiors who decided he had the makings of a *pilote de chasse*. Accordingly, he was instructed, when he was due for a leave, to report to Le Plessis-Belleville for a ten-day conversion course to single-seaters. On April 25, 1917, having successfully made the conversion, he reported to *Groupe de Combat XII,* the Storks, then stationed at Fismes.

The Storks—*les Cigognes*—their record was unique. Under the leadership of *Commandant* Brocard, these four squadrons were the finest in France. Spa 3,

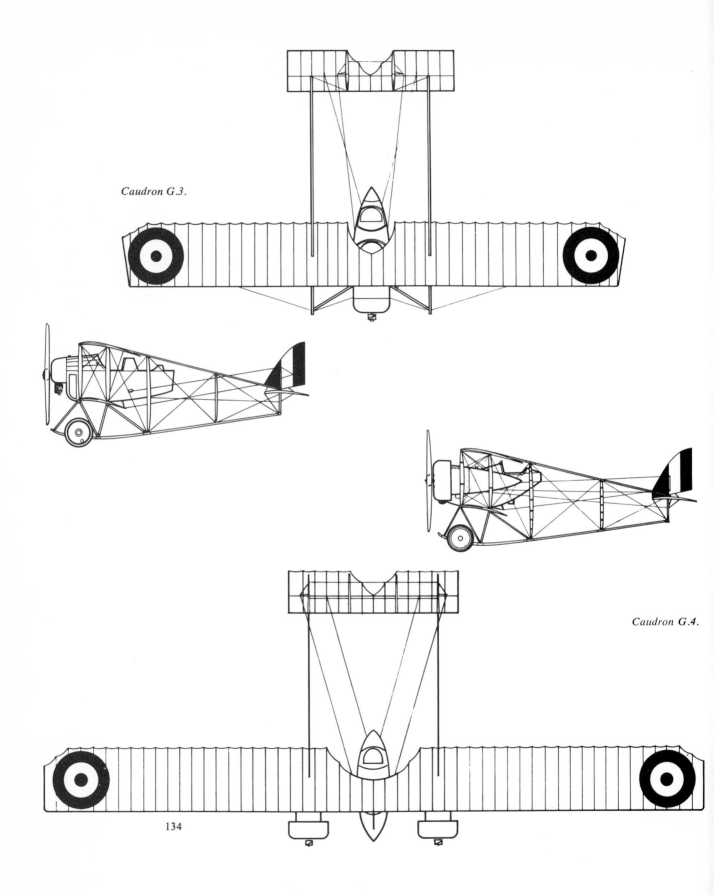

*Caudron G.3.*

*Caudron G.4.*

134

with Auger, Papa Dorme, Guynemer, Heurtaux; Spa 26, *Lieutenant* de la Tour; Spa 73, *Capitaine* Deullin, his coolness was legendary; Spa 103, the youngest squadron of the group, had originally been a bombing squadron, but its pilots fought so well they had been converted to fighters *en masse* . . .

The leader of Spa 103, to which Fonck was assigned, was *Capitaine* d'Harcourt, an elegant gentleman, whose sharpest orders seemed like personal pleas for favors no one could refuse.

The Storks had their traditions. Guynemer started one that everyone else picked up. He would buzz the field after a successful fight and "blip" his engine: BRMM! BRMM! BRMM! as if to say, *"j'en ai un"*—"I got one!"

Everyone but Dorme, of course. Papa Dorme would fly back and land with no fuss and climb casually out of his machine. Usually, one could not tell whether he'd been in a scrap by looking at it, because he never brought it back with holes in it.

"Oh, yes," he would reply to questions. "I left one of 'em flaming at such-and-such a spot." He would never say more. He never entered a claim. All of his confirmed victories were reported by someone else, ground observers or squadron mates. One day, a German radio broadcast announced that Dorme had shot down a German aeroplane. Dorme hadn't said anything about it. He was always the same, calm when he went out, calm when he came back, even after, on one occasion, having lost his lower right wing through collision with a German single-seater near Bapaume. Dorme habitually did his cruising about ten miles behind the enemy lines, and his comrades insisted that his score must have been at least 50.

Such were the Storks.

Brocard gave a crisp first interview to Fonck. "The only thing you are here for is to shoot down *Boches*. Report to 103." That was all.

Fonck's enthusiasm carried him clean out of the fight the first time he went up as a Stork.

Familiarizing himself with the Spad and the lay of the land, he was circling above the city of Rheims, lost in a daydream about the ancient and historic events associated with the name of that city. He spotted a German two-seater about 3000 feet below him, and dived on it immediately, plunging past the machine before he could even find it in his sight. By the time he had regained altitude the surprised *Boche* had cleared out, leaving Fonck alone to curse himself for having acted like an irresponsible schoolboy.

The French, like the British and the Germans, had regularly scheduled patrols to fly, depending on the requirements of the army corps whose fronts they were to cover. Unlike the British and the Germans, however, the French never officially discouraged solo patrols except at the discretion of local commanders of squadrons or groups, so long as these independent and individual undertakings did not conflict with the commitments of the squadron or group.

Fonck was out alone on May 5, 1917, just ten days after having joined the Storks, and two days after having scored his first victory with them. (That first victory had made up for his blunder over Rheims.) He was just north of Laon, picking his way through a sky completely filled with large, irregular patches of cloud. There were no solid layers, just puffs and balls of cloud all around. As he turned a corner, so to speak, he stumbled into the midst of a fight. Five Albatros and an equal number of Nieuports were wheeling in and out of the clouds in a tightly packed melee where each instant, it seemed, brought the risk of collision. A *Boche* flashed in front of him at point-blank range, just as if it had materialized out of the air. Fonck fired without taking time to think and the machine abruptly dived straight down through the clouds. He threw a burst in the direction of two Albatros on the tail of one of the French scouts, then he was in cloud. He lost contact with the fight as suddenly as he had found it, and almost as soon. He dived toward the ground looking for a sign of the machine at which he had first fired. It had crashed in a wood near Laon.

Fonck was not overly superstitious, but he did set great store by a mascot he had, a stork given him by a Madame Herriot of Lyon. One man of the squadron was superstitious about the number 13, however, a pilot named Girval. He once commented on the fact that there were 13 pilots of the squadron at a dinner at Villers-Cotterets. "For the Chinese," he said, "thirteen at the table means that one of the number will die within the year. For us, however, this can have little significance since a year from now certainly more than one of us is going to be dead." Poor prophetic Girval; of the thirteen, he was the first to go.

One of the next was Papa Dorme, shot down on May 25, 1917. Dorme defied the odds many times and got away with it, but it wasn't the odds that caught up with him, for his last fight was an even match.* *C'est la guerre,* said the Storks, it being an unwritten but inviolable law that losses were not to be discussed except clinically. None of them expressed any grief over the death of the big, calm, smiling man—he was only a few years over the average age in the *Groupe,* but those few years earned him the "Papa."

Fonck was on leave at the time and, safe from the eyes of the rest of the men, gave way to a very human grief, but showed nothing of it when he returned.

The German two-seaters enjoyed one advantage when they came over the lines early in the morning. If they came over at dawn, they had the sun at their backs. Thus, it was difficult for the French *chasseurs* to surprise them unless they hunted far on the other side of the German lines; but even so while the sun was low, it was almost impossible to catch the Germans unawares since an attack out of the sun had to be delivered at roughly the same level as that at which the two-seaters were cruising. A fast diving attack was not impossible, but it was ineffective as far as surprise was concerned. Still, there were ways to get them. If you had sharp eyes, you could spot aeroplanes a mile away before their pilots saw you, and then it was a matter of stalking them, knowing what they were going to do, and good shooting.

---

* *Kroll and von Schleich are both credited with this victory.*

Fonck was the best shot at the Front, probably, for he brought down most of his opponents with bursts of no more than eight or ten rounds, and as few as three. He had a remarkably keen eye, and an intuitive sense of what any pilots, French or German, were going to do in any situation. He was never surprised, never at a loss, always a step ahead. That is, after he learned all the ropes.

He learned fast, which is why he learned at all, because by the spring of 1917 when Fonck became a *pilote de chasse,* a lot of good men had gone down. The war in the air had turned serious, deadly, and only a professional could compete with any hope of success.

Fonck nearly got caught one day in June 1917 when he was out on a dawn patrol, looking for two-seaters. It was bright and clear up at 18,000 feet and the low sun was dazzling. Down below, the earth was still wrapped in darkness and the armies lay quietly in the trenches finishing breakfast before beginning the day's work of slaughter and futility.

Fonck spotted two Albatros scouts. Below him, they were brilliantly lit up against the darkness of the ground. He went for them and was astonished when they instantly split up, one apparently running for the lines, the other turning to come straight at him. This one was no amateur then. Just as Fonck was about to close with the second Albatros he suddenly thought, "Trap!" He looked behind and saw that the first had not run but had circled around in back of him. Close. Fonck turned hard, turning inside the first, catching him broadside with a burst that raked him fore and aft. Fonck turned to look for the other man, but he was gone. There was nothing to show for a few seconds of violent action but a long column of smoke that wound away toward the ground and lost itself in the darkness below.

In July, the Storks were transferred to Dunkerque. On the eve of the departure the Germans paid a farewell visit and bombed the field. Stores were packed and the aeroplanes, most of them, were in the stages of last-minute overhaul. No one got off the ground. The pilots were confined to the shaking of fists and the shouting of implacable threats of reprisal.

*Target practice near Hetomesnil.*

The next day, those pilots whose machines were undamaged took off to fly to the new field. Fonck left in threatening weather and passed a gloomy and monotonous hour cross-country to Le Crotoy, where he had learned to fly in April 1915. He was given a warm reception but could not escape a feeling of melancholy. No familiar faces.

Constructed according to his specifications, Fonck had his own gun sight installed on his machines. Looking through it, he saw two concentric circles etched on the lens, a large one and a small one. Their diameters covered respectively ten metres and one metre at a distance of one hundred metres. Thus, when he had an aeroplane in his sight, and knew the wing span or the fuselage length (which was more generally the case) he was able precisely to evaluate distance and judge the moment to fire.

138

The Germans were making the most of team fighting in the fall of 1917, exploiting the development of the *Geschwader*. The Storks lost some of their best men—Guynemer, Heurtaux, Auger—killed or wounded.

Fonck selected new men for a team of his own, much as had Boelcke, with the backing of *Capitaine* d'Harcourt. He lectured them, flew with them, tried to teach them everything he knew. They went out on daily patrols, venturing farther afield every day. He started them out on *Drachen* and when this stirred up the German single-seaters, his men received their baptism of fire. When fights developed this way he had his work cut out for him to keep an eye on his pupils and keep his own tail clear. He scored no victories but his men learned the ropes.

*Fonck.*

Soon he had a team that could work smoothly. They flew a V-formation of nine to 12 aeroplanes in flights of three or four machines grouped likewise in V's. Patrols of Allied machines would frequently meet over Flanders during this period and join forces on the spur of the moment, French, British, and Belgian, to go looking for trouble across the lines.

September 11, 1917, had been a black day for the Storks. It was the day *Capitaine* Guynemer had failed to return. Since no one had actually seen him go down, it had been almost impossible not to hope that he might have been in a hospital somewhere, or even a prisoner. Days had passed, however, and hope had evaporated.

Some time later it was learned that the Germans had officially credited an officer named Wisseman with having shot Guynemer down.

Fonck was told the news by *Commandant* Brocard whose broad shoulders seemed for once to be bending under the load. Fonck had his Spad rolled out and took off alone, partly in the hope of finding a *Boche,* and partly just to be alone. Within ten minutes he spotted a German photo-reconnaissance two-seater directly over the French lines. He climbed in a wide circle around the aeroplane, keeping it just a speck in the distance. When he had the height he wanted, Fonck turned toward the two-seater, coming up to it high. The observer was leaning over the side with his heavy box camera poised in a rack. The pilot gazed either straight ahead or at his instruments, oblivious to everything else. Fonck dived, steeply. He watched the two-seater grow in his sight, the details of the machine and its crew standing out clearly in the bright sky. Leather helmets. Black crosses edged in white. He tightened his grip on the control stick, his finger on the firing button. The tracer bullets flared out and hit the enemy machine in the engine then walked back along the fuselage to the pilot's cockpit. Pieces flew back in the slipstream. Fonck let up on the firing button. As he flashed past the aeroplane he saw it was starting to burn. It reared up in a half loop and as Fonck leveled out of his dive, the observer, who had fallen out of his rear cockpit at the top of the loop, dropped past Fonck's wing tip, arms flung out, hands clutching at the empty air. The two-seater, now flaming like a torch, roared down after him, its passage marked by a long black pall of smoke.

Such, for Fonck, were the funeral ceremonies for Guynemer.

## "THE SUPREMACY OF THE AIR"

*"Despite the victory, and even if it is a hard-wrested victory, there is always that sad regret, that human sympathy for the victim, who was, after all, another pilot like oneself . . ."*

HERMANN BECKER

"IF VON RICHTHOFEN liked a man it was for purely material reasons . . . His estimate of a man was formed by what that man achieved for the cause, and whether he happened to be a good fellow or not was a secondary consideration. But once you had proved your worth, he supported you by every means in his power and with his whole personality. If you were a failure he dropped you without a second's hesitation, without the flicker of an eyelid." Thus did Ernst Udet isolate one of von Richthofen's salient characteristics—mountainous dedication. During much of his career his ordinary feelings were buried under it and he rarely permitted familiarity. Away from the squadron or in private, as when he celebrated his birthday with Count von Holck, he relaxed and allowed friendly sentiment to show itself.

"Each time we came back von Richthofen told us what we had done right and where we had made mistakes. Thus I noticed, to my great astonishment, that he never lost sight of us even when fighting for his life." In this way, Carl-August von Schoenebeck describes the effect and value of another of von Richthofen's attributes, the ability to see what was going on around him. Whether his clear-headedness was the result of sheer determination or whether he was by nature unexcitable will probably never be known; those who knew him in the climactic years of his life were not psychologists.

Carl-August von Schoenebeck emphasized the value of von Richthofen's ability to see everything that was happening: "We knew we could depend on him like a rock. If things were going badly, if we were ever in a hole, he'd notice it and pull us out. It gave the *Jasta* a great feeling of safety."

Born in Bernstadt, in Silesia, on January 19, 1898, von Schoenebeck entered the service in May 1915 when he joined the Guards Grenadier Regiment at Karlsruhe/Baden. His interest centered on flying, however, and he managed eventually to transfer into aviation. In December 1916 he was sent to *F.E.A. 3* at Gotha and reached the Front with *Fl. Abt. (A)203* at Rheims in April 1917. In

*Peter Grosz*

*Carl-August von Schoenebeck before a captured D.H.4*

*Erwin Boehme.*

June he reported to *Jasta 11,* having come to the attention of von Richthofen who perceived that he had the makings of a first-rate fighter pilot. (A few weeks past his twentieth birthday, in March 1918, von Schoenebeck assumed command of his own squadron, *Jasta 33.*)

When he arrived at *Jasta 11,* von Schoenebeck had no single-seater experience and his instruction was undertaken by von Richthofen personally. In this way von Schoenebeck was close to the man; his impressions of the *Rittmeister* are still vivid after 48 years: "He was about average height, stocky, dark blond with blue eyes. A voice of middle range, his manner of speech clipped, clear and concise. He had a noble way of speech and never swore or used foul language of any kind. There was always a discussion after a flight and during these dissections he was calm and self-controlled and spoke with much humor, no matter how dangerous the action might have been. One could not help but feel and be touched daily by his extraordinary energy and will power. He shone with calm in the most critical moments which quite naturally exercised the most salutary influence on all of us."

When von Schoenebeck took over his own yellow-nosed *Jasta 33* in the Péronne/St-Quentin sector, he took along some weighty words from von Richthofen: "The leader is the deciding factor for the success of every squadron. Even the best fighter pilots can prove their full worth only if their leader makes proper use of them."

In September 1917 von Richthofen finally went on convalescent leave. While on leave he was exhorted by the Kaiser, OHL, and *Kogenluft* to stay off active flying duty and accept a position as a technical advisor so as to preserve his life in the interests of the air service and the Fatherland. His reply—negative—was expressed in virtually the same terms as had been used by Guynemer, who disappeared at precisely this time: "I should consider myself a despicable person if, now that I have achieved fame and wear many decorations, I should consent to exist as a pensioner of my dignity . . ."

On October 23 he returned to the Circus.

About the first of December, von Richthofen learned of the death in action of *Leutnant* Erwin Boehme. Born in Holzminden on July 23, 1879, Boehme was in the army before the war; was, in fact, a professional soldier. He had entered the air service about the same time as von Richthofen and had been chosen by Boelcke for *Jasta 2* at the same time as von Richthofen since they were serving in the same unit on the Russian Front. It was Boehme with whom Boelcke had collided and von Richthofen was one of those who had dissuaded him from taking his own life afterward. From August, 1917, Boehme had commanded *Jasta Boelcke,* achieving a score of 24 victories and being awarded the *Pour le Mérite* on November 29—the same day he was killed over Zonnebeke. Next to von Richthofen, Boehme had been the last survivor of Boelcke's original squadron. Boehme was dead; only one left. How much longer now?

144           \*                \*             \*

ALBERT DEULLIN was born in Epernay, in the province of Champagne, on August 24, 1890. His military training was with the 31st Regiment of Dragoons, to which unit he returned on Mobilization in August 1914. He spent the winter with the Dragoons in Lorraine, unhorsed like all the cavalrymen. One winter in the trenches was enough for Deullin and he applied for a transfer to aviation on the strength of a citation he had won. In April 1915 he was released for flight training and in July was assigned to MF 62, flying every kind of mission—reconnaissance, artillery-spotting, photography, observation, bombing.

He was cited again in February 1916 for his work in the Farmans, and was selected as a good prospect for *chasse* during the air campaign at Verdun. The organization and simultaneous expansion of fighter aviation under Tricornot de Rose at Verdun brought a number of good men into the single-seaters, and Deullin was one of the best. At the beginning of March 1916 he took a conversion course to fighters and the end of March scored his first victory. He flew with N 3 (later Spa 3) through the summer and fall of 1916, scoring a total of ten victories and acquiring a reputation as a calm, masterful pilot who was as detached and methodical as a surgeon. In February 1917 he was assigned to another Stork Squadron, Spa 73, as commanding officer.

Deullin was considered one of the outstanding pilots of the *Armée de l'Air,* and he was as good at teaching as he was at fighting. During 1917 he took the trouble of writing down his ideas on *chasse* for the benefit of the rookies: "You must be, above all, adept at manoeuvring. You will try for surprise by means of the sun and clouds . . . [When you have spotted your target and have studied him to determine your exact moment of attack,] try to remain undetected by placing yourself in his blind spots. Fire only after having taken careful aim, and then at point-blank range and in short bursts. While attacking, guard yourself against surprise from the rear."

Deullin stressed the importance of vigilance by pointing out that it was not enough to look around before the attack, one must look around *during* the attack. "The sky is free? Beware! It will not perhaps be so in ten seconds. Never lose sight of the fact that an aeroplane flying at right angles to you is very difficult to see and will very frequently escape your notice. All the while you are attacking, watch out for the arrival of a second adversary; constantly glance behind you, calculating whether or not you have time to push your attack to the end before you will yourself be attacked."

Deullin was shot down several times, wounded three times, once seriously, but he always came back. The Storks regarded his coolness as being the equal of Papa Dorme's. A pilot engaged in a duel with an enemy single-seater must be able to outwit his opponent as well as out-fly him; thus, while one must keep one's own head, it is good to try to make the opponent lose his. "If you cannot get into a position to fire, fire anyway. The enemy might think he is being attacked by a third machine . . ."

Deullin shot down several two-seaters by patient stalking. He would wait for them to come up to the lines, himself patrolling at his Spad's ceiling which was a shade over 20,000 feet. He would hold his station about five miles on the German side of the lines so the two-seaters would pass under him at middle height, still climbing on their way to the Front. Waiting for them to pass, he would dive down a mile behind them, unseen except by the most alert and sharp-eyed observers, leveling out directly behind them at an altitude slightly lower than that at which they were traveling. Climbing slightly and making good use of the extra speed built up in the dive, Deullin would overtake the two-seaters, keeping hidden in the blind spot behind the tail. He would fire at point-blank range.

Deullin summed it all up this way: "Use your head—reflection, patience prudence. Think out each attack fully; differ your attacks if necessary; watch out for surprise, and, no matter what happens, lead the dance with celerity."

By practicing what he preached, Albert Deullin survived the war.

On July 28, 1917, while the Storks were stationed in Flanders, an American volunteer joined the group, assigned to Spa 73 under Deullin. The American was Charles J. Biddle of Andalusia, Pennsylvania. Born March 13, 1890, Biddle graduated from Princeton in 1911, and received a law degree from Harvard in 1914.* He entered the French *Armée de l'Air* by way of the Foreign Legion, and some of his experiences as a student pilot at Avord have already been described.

Biddle was escorted up to the lines for the first time to have a look around and came back from his first patrol with a vivid impression: anywhere below 2,000 feet the fighters are in the trajectories of the big shells, and when one of these goes sizzling by, the Spad rocks like a canoe caught in the wake of a motor boat.

By the middle of September, Biddle had flown enough time with the Storks to develop some confidence, but was not beyond making greenhorn's mistakes. He came across a two-seater while flying alone, having become separated from the rest of the patrol, and from simple unfamiliarity was uncertain whether it was French or British or German. He thought it was German, but since he was above it, waited until it passed under him and he got a good look at the crosses on the wings. "I then turned around," Biddle described the subsequent action in a letter home, "and went for him from above, which by the way, is a fool method to attack a two-seater, as it gives the machine gunner, who sits behind the pilot, a beautiful shot at you. Usually the best way to do it is to get under his tail where he often does not see you and can't shoot without hitting his own tail. I guess I was a bit too anxious, however, and spoiled my own chances. I could see the machine gunner blazing away and could not get to close quarters without giving him a much better chance at me than I had at him. I aimed ahead of him about the distance I thought was right and gave him a rip from my machine gun. I could see the tracer bullets and they looked to me as though I hit him, but I could not be sure. At all events he started for home without a second's hesita-

* *Since 1924 he has been a partner of Drinker, Biddle and Reath, of Philadelphia.*

146

tion, full motor and diving slightly . . . I manoeuvred a little and gave it to him again and I hope I touched him up, for the machine gunner seemed to me to stop shooting. I went after him a third time, this time from behind his tail; we were both streaking it through the air at a scandalous pace. I had my machine nosed down a bit and going full out, was overhauling him and had just begun to shoot again when my machine gun jammed from a broken cartridge so that it was impossible to fix it in the air. We had been going for Hun territory all the time so that we were by this time several miles behind the German lines. With my machine gun out of commission there was of course nothing to do but go home."

One day late in September, Biddle and three squadron mates attacked a flight of German single-seaters and again Biddle became separated from the rest of the patrol, this time because of the westerly wind. He suddenly found himself facing no fewer than seven enemy scouts, two of which were close enough to send their tracers past him "in regular flocks" while he high-tailed it for home. When he got back to the aerodrome he examined his aeroplane, expecting, as he said, "to find about a dozen holes in it."

He was rather disappointed not to find any, and concluded: "I guess those *Boches* must have been very poor shots, or more probably I am just very green and thought that I was in more trouble than I really was."

The American Charles Biddle and his commanding officer Albert Deullin went out hunting together one morning in November. Biddle was excited about the opportunity to study the methods of the *Capitaine* and was determined to do a good job of flying as rear guard. He stuck to Deullin until the beginning of a diving attack on a flight of single-seaters. In a letter Biddle described the action: "In my capacity as rear guard I was necessarily several hundred yards behind, and about the time that I started to follow the captain I caught sight of another Hun coming in behind me and on the same level. He was a good way off, but started to shoot at me, so I had to turn and chase him. When I started after him he also turned and started to run but I had no more begun to follow him when still another put in an appearance above me, and I had to get out. In the meantime the captain had gotten close to his man but had to stop shooting at him to defend himself against a couple of others and in doing so lost sight of the Hun he had attacked. As soon as we landed he told me he could not understand why the fellow had not fallen, for he had seen at least ten of his tracer bullets fired at point-blank range apparently go right into the pilot's seat. Sure enough, a few minutes later confirmation came in that a Hun had fallen at that time and place. This made nineteen for Captain Deullin."

Biddle was learning his business from a professional—". . . watch out for surprise, and, no matter what happens, lead the dance with celerity."

In January 1918 Biddle accepted a transfer into the U. S. Air Service and took the oath as an officer. In Paris, awaiting a permanent assignment, he ordered a new uniform and occupied his time translating *Capitaine* Deullin's notes on fighter aviation to show to American officers in charge of training.

*           *           *

IN LATE SUMMER, 1917, a Bavarian named Rudolf Stark was flying with *Jasta 34* stationed near Verdun. Flying over familiar ground which he had covered many times as a two-seater pilot, Stark was nevertheless a greenhorn—*ein Neuling*—as a fighter pilot.

One day on patrol with two squadron mates, Stark was left behind when the other two spotted a French Caudron and went for it. At just that moment, Stark caught a glint in the air above him and looked up to see a Nieuport diving on him. The Frenchman opened up with his machine guns and Stark desperately went into a hard turn, his ears filled with the sound of bullets cracking through the fuselage behind him. The Frenchman was on his tail and stayed there, putting short bursts into the machine. A blow on his shoulder caused Stark to lose control of his aeroplane for an instant and it dropped in a spin. He recovered, and as he straightened out, the rattling behind him began again. He turned this way and that trying to work his way close to the German lines where he hoped the threat of German ground fire would drive away his tormentor. He was dizzy from his frantic stunting when he thought he was safe and risked a look around. No Nieuport in sight. He made his way home and landed. The aeroplane was not so badly shot up that it collapsed on landing—in fact, it was hardly shot up at all. There were sixteen holes in the fuselage, but that didn't account for all the noise. His shoulder strap had been shot loose and one end had been flung out of the cockpit, the buckle rattling against the plywood fuselage during the wild aerobatics.

*Leutnant* Rudolf Stark eventually became an Ace with six confirmed victories, but he had to master his imagination first.

*Stark.*

*Imperial War Museum / London*

Peter Grosz

In the summer and autumn of 1917 one of the most elegant aeroplanes of the war was issued to Bavarian squadrons to replace the heterogeneous collection of types they were then flying. These squadrons were under the direct supervision of the Bavarian Military Administration rather than the Prussian Government and General Staff in Berlin. In the *Luftstreitkräfte* the most obvious result of this provincialism was that provincial *Jastas* took second place in the distribution of equipment. They flew minor types such as the Roland fighters or they flew cast-offs from other squadrons. When the Albatros D III was available in large numbers the Bavarian squadrons were given the second-hand Albatros D I's and D II's. They did not receive any Fokker Triplanes until *J.G. 1* released some second-hand ones.

When the slim and graceful Pfalz D III went into production the Bavarian squadrons finally got brand-new aeroplanes—the Pfalz Aeroplane Works was a company controlled by the Bavarian War Ministry. Located at Speyer on the Upper Rhine, the factory was in the heart of one of the areas of Europe traditionally associated with woodworking and the wooden construction techniques used by Pfalz were brought to a high point of development. The fuselage of the D III

149

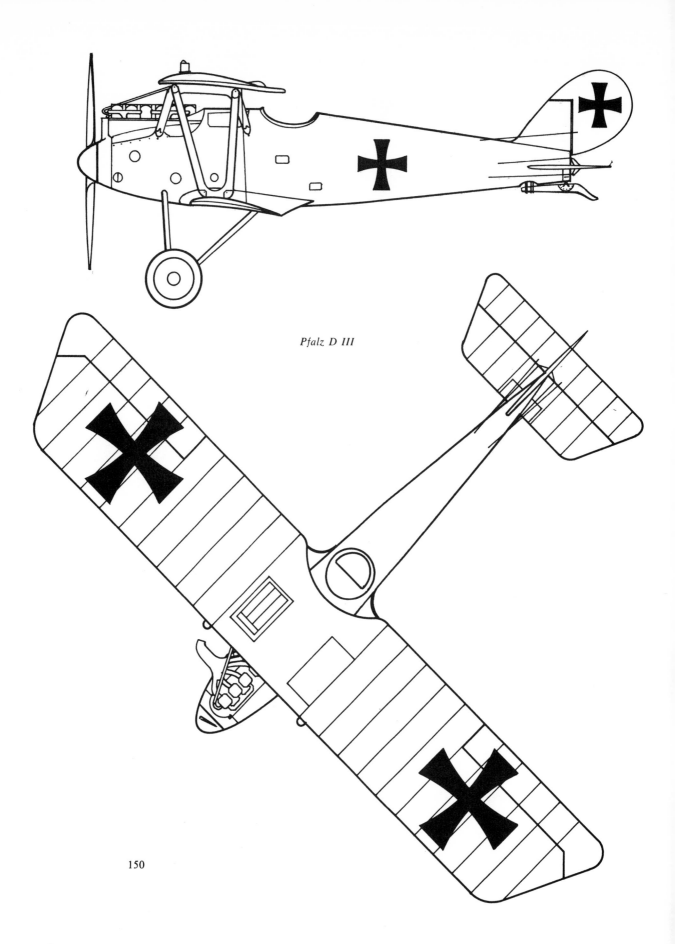

*Pfalz D III*

150

was of the semi-monocoque method, its basic shape being defined by light ply-wood "O" formers connected by half a dozen spruce longerons. To this skeleton was attached the shell which came in two pieces like the halves of a walnut shell. These halves were made separately by wrapping and gluing six layers of paper-thin wooden strips around master pattern forms. The strips were three to four inches wide and were wrapped spirally in opposing directions, the joints reinforced by cloth tape. The halves were fitted to the skeleton and screwed in place, then covered with fabric and doped. The technique was time-consuming compared to the welded steel tube technique regularly used at the Fokker works, but it was marvelously strong.

The armament was two synchronized Spandau machine guns and the engine was the 160-horsepower Mercedes. While the top speed and rate of climb were comparatively slow, the Pfalz D III offset these drawbacks to a large extent by its manoeuvrability, which was good, its responsiveness, which was better than that of the Albatros fighters, its ability to hold together in a dive, which was perfect, and its cockpit view, which was excellent.

Rudolf Stark was flying a Pfalz D III when he first joined a fighter squadron, *Jasta 34* at Verdun. In March 1918 the *Jasta* was transferred to a new base at Le Cateau, about fourteen miles east of Cambrai, to take part in the March Offensive. During the last half of the month the weather was soft and springlike, fairly clear in the afternoon, but frequently misty in the morning and evening.

One evening Stark was out over Péronne when his motor suddenly started to act up. It would sputter spasmodically then run for a moment then misfire and sputter again a few times. This was no place to be out alone with a bad engine so Stark headed for home, nursing the aeroplane along and trying to hold his height. At this awkward moment two British two-seaters appeared out of the mist ahead of him. Knowing that he was an easy victim and that the best form of defense is an attack, he banked slightly to take a sight on the nearer machine and fired. After only a few rounds the guns jammed. The machines turned toward him and, wild with rage, Stark decided to ram one of them. His engine was alternately stopping and starting, then suddenly it caught on and roared up to full power and his guns began to fire—he hadn't taken his finger off the firing button. The observer in the British machine collapsed and the pilot lurched forward. Stark pulled back hard on the stick and just managed to clear the two-seater which passed under him and dived straight down. The other British machine had turned wide and by the time it came around to join in, Stark had lost himself in the mist, his engine sputtering again. Losing height, he nursed the ·aeroplane along, looking for some place to set down safely, until he spotted the aerodrome of *Jasta 79* at Villers-le-Sec. He landed and the mechanics there went to work on his engine.

His first victory; hardly the way he had pictured it. It had happened much more quickly than he had supposed it would, all over in a few seconds, such an utter fluke it was difficult to feel proud of it.

*         *         *

*Udet.*

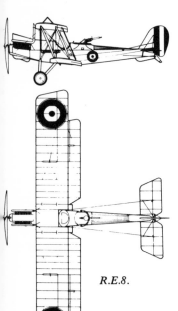

*R.E.8.*

IN AUGUST 1917 Ernst Udet was appointed to the command of *Jasta 37* at Wynghene in Flanders, where, if one climbed high enough, one could see the silver band of the sea shimmering on the horizon.

In the evening of March 15, 1918, it was pouring rain at le Cateau. Udet was squelching about in the mud directing the "unpacking" of *Jasta 37* which had been brought in by train that day from Wynghene. He felt a tap on the shoulder and turned around to find the *Rittmeister* smiling at him. Udet saluted and von Richthofen responded with a casual gesture and some light remark about the pleasant weather.

The two of them stood there in the rain, in the mud, sizing each other up. Rain trickled down their faces.

"How many have you shot down now, Udet?"

"Nineteen confirmed, one awaiting confirmation."

"Hmm."

There was a pause while von Richthofen dabbed at the mud with his stick. "Well, that about qualifies you to join us. Would you care to?"

Care to? The request couldn't be processed fast enough for Udet. On March 26, 1918, he reported for duty at *Jasta 11* at ten o'clock in the morning. At noon he flew his first patrol as a member of the big Circus.

It was a patrol of *Jasta 11* and it was led by von Richthofen who wanted to have new men in his flights their first times out so he could see how they shaped up. They took off and headed west from Avesnes-le-Sec toward Albert. Flying low, about 1500 feet, the patrol came across a British R.E.8 spotting for an artillery shoot. Udet was flying wing man to *Vizefeldwebel* Edgar Scholz; he looked at Scholz for a signal or some indication of how the R.E. should be dealt with. Scholz jerked his chin toward the two-seater and Udet promptly pulled out of the formation and went for it. He made one fast pass from the front and blasted the R.E.'s engine into flames with a burst at point-blank range. When Udet eased back into formation, Scholz waved to him. The *Rittmeister* nodded over his shoulder.

The Triplanes droned on; the pilots swiveled their heads around looking for another target. Ahead of them a tree-bordered road wound across the countryside, lined with Allied troops. That was a target von Richthofen wouldn't pass up. He led the Triplanes down abruptly in a steep dive to tree-top height. One after another the machines leveled out over the road and went down it, the trees blurring past on each side. Small arms fire came up from the troops on the ground and the fabric covering of wings and tails popped as bullets went through. The pilots depressed the firing buttons on the control columns and by gentle adjustments with stick and rudder directed streams of machine gun bullets up and down the road. At the end of the run von Richthofen turned, worked over the troops again, then returned to altitude and led the flight home. Udet noticed the time— it was only 12:30.

The *Rittmeister* strolled up as Udet was climbing out of his machine. "You always attack your man from the front, Udet?" he asked. Udet answered that it was a method that would work well on some occasions.

152

Nodding, von Richthofen turned to go. "By the way," he said over his shoulder, "you can take over *Jasta 11* as of tomorrow."

Udet was acting C.O. of *Jasta 11* until the first week in April, when an infection in his ear grew so bad he was almost literally blind with pain. He did not want to report it for fear of being taken off flying duty. On returning from a flight during which he scored his twenty-fourth victory, Udet stumbled past von Richthofen without even seeing him and headed for the dispensary. The first-aid orderly was poking around trying to decide what to do with the ear when the door opened and von Richthofen strode in. "What's wrong with you, Udet?" he demanded. The orderly promptly answered that there was a very serious infection that required medical care. "Leave for you," said von Richthofen, "now."

The next morning von Richthofen and Udet walked out to the two-seater in which Udet was to return to the rear. Udet climbed in. The pilot took off and banked around the field. Udet waved; von Richthofen waved back and smiled.

*Pour le Mérite holders (from left): Wüsthoff, Reinhardt, Manfred von Richthofen, Lowenhardt, and Lothar von Richthofen.*

\*　　　　　\*　　　　　\*

ON APRIL 1, 1918, the Royal Flying Corps and the Royal Naval Air Service were combined into an independent body, the Royal Air Force. In January, an Air Ministry had been set up with Lord Rothermere as Secretary of State for Air, and Major General Sir Hugh Trenchard as Chief of the Air Staff. Major General Sir John Salmond was appointed RAF Commander in Chief on the Western Front.

\*　　　　　\*　　　　　\*

*From left: Gerstenberg
(chief of German antiaircraft
defense at Ploesti during
the Second World War),
Hauptmann Carganico,
von Richthofen, and Hans
Joachim Wolff.*

*The Rittmeister (left)—a rare
grin of elation over his
62nd victory.*

WHEN THE BATTLE OF CAMBRAI opened, *Jagdgeschwader Nr. 1,* the Richthofen Circus, was moved in by train, set up and operational within two days. On November 23 and 30, von Richthofen scored his last victories of the winter of 1917-18. During the first half of December he visited the Pfalz works at Speyer on the Rhine to look over some new machines, but was unimpressed with what he saw and returned to *J.G. 1* where he spent Christmas. Bad weather restricted flying to a few sorties through most of November and December and January of 1918. In January von Richthofen, as an advisor in aviation matters, went to Poland with the German delegation negotiating the Treaty of Brest-Litovsk. He took the opportunity to do some hunting, then stopped at Adlershof aerodrome for a series of technical conferences and finally returned to *J.G. 1* the first week in March 1918.

He started active flying at once and began to score the way he had in the spring of 1917. He shot down five machines from March 12 to 25; on the twenty-sixth he shot down two; on the twenty-seventh, three. On March 28, he scored a single victory, then on April 2, 6, and 7 he scored four more. In 25 days he had shot down 15 aeroplanes, 12 of them fighters—Brisfits, Camels, and S.E.5's, the best fighters the British—or anybody else—had. He had been out of the fight for three months and only semi-active for five before that. The better part of a year had gone by since the *Rittmeister* had scored like that. His return to action was spectacular. *Der Rote Kampfflieger* was still the champion. Nobody could deny that.

March 20, 1918, was a gloomy day of rain and heavy cloud. Toward evening the rain began to let up and the *Rittmeister* led a patrol of *Jasta 11* from the field at Cappy, near Péronne, to the Front, which ran at that time roughly on a line from Albert to Montdidier. The squalls of the day had left thick banks of cloud ranged along the Front at various levels, and while circuiting one of these the *Rittmeister* came upon a patrol of six Camels of No. 3 Squadron RAF. There had been 12 Camels in two flights, but in trying to rise above the clouds the two flights had become separated, so six Camels faced 15 Triplanes. The Camel leader spotted the Circus and turned to face the attack. The two patrols came together head-on.

After the first pass von Richthofen turned onto the tail of one Camel and literally blew it up with a burst into the fuel tank. He turned instantly and was on the tail of a second Camel, sending splintering bursts into the center section and struts. The pilot, 19-year-old Second Lieutenant D. Lewis, flung his Camel about frantically to escape the fire of the red Triplane. His goggles were shot off. His tanks were hit and his machine flamed but did not explode like the other one. Lewis dived to the ground as von Richthofen broke off. Lewis hit the ground hard and was thrown clear. Scorched, stunned, cut and bruised, Lewis got unsteadily to his feet. He was standing between two blazing wrecks, von Richthofen's last two victories.

The *Rittmeister* roared over, a hundred feet off the ground, and waved.

*       *       *

THE INDEPENDENT Royal Air Force had been established by the nominal amalgamation of the RFC and the RNAS, but there was little outward change in the field save for the renumbering of RNAS squadrons which simply added 200. Thus No. 9 Squadron RNAS, stationed at Bertangles north of Amiens, became No. 209 Squadron RAF.

Leading the Camel-equipped No. 209 was Squadron Commander C. H. Butler; Deputy C.O. was Captain A. Roy Brown, a Canadian.

On the morning of April 21, 1918, ground mists hampered operations, and the squadron took off on a high offensive patrol over an hour late. From 9:35 to 9:45 a.m. three flights of five Camels each took off at five-minute intervals. Brown was leading the first flight and was in overall command of the patrol. The other two flights were led by Captain O. W. Redgate and Captain O. C. Le Boutillier, an American. Among Brown's men were two Lieutenants named Mellersh and May. Lieutenant F. J. W. Mellersh (later Air Vice-Marshal Sir Francis Mellersh) was an experienced man, his final score was nine confirmed victories; Second Lieutenant Wilfred R. May was on his first offensive patrol. He eventually won the D.F.C., a Captaincy, and seven confirmed victories, but on April 21 that was all ahead of him. He had everything to learn, and had been told to keep out of a general scrap should one develop. His instructions were to stay over a fight and watch, keeping his eye on the air around him, and dive and run for home if he got into trouble.

After some three-quarters of an hour of patrolling, Le Boutillier's flight broke away to chase a brace of Albatros two-seaters, one of which was shot down in flames while the other escaped in the clouds. The other two flights, led by Brown, reached the end of their beat several miles south of the River Somme near Corbie. Two machines dropped out with engine trouble and returned to base. Brown now led a half-strength squadron of eight aeroplanes in a northerly direction toward the Somme, Le Boutillier and his flight following a minute or so behind.

April 21, 1918, dawned cold and misty at Cappy, but as the morning grew old the sun began to shine through. The wind began to pick up and was soon blowing hard. It played an important part in the day's events because it was from the east rather than from the west. The Circus had been augmented by the temporary addition of *Jastas 5* and *46* which, like *4, 6, 10,* and *11* of *J.G. 1,* were under the command of von Richthofen. By the time the mists had cleared enough for a patrol to be mounted it was almost noon German time (10:30 British time). The *Rittmeister* led the patrol, which was to consist of the Triplanes of *Jasta 11* and a mixed bag of Triplanes and Albatros D V's from *Jasta 5.* One of the members of the first *Kette,* or flight, of *Jasta 11* was Manfred's cousin *Leutnant* Wolfram von Richthofen, for whom this was the first patrol. The second *Kette* of *Jasta 11* was led by *Leutnant* Hans Weiss who was flying a white Triplane. The flights shaped up in the air, then headed west along the Somme valley.

Wolfram von Richthofen had been given the same instructions as Wilfred May. Wolfram followed his orders; Wilfred didn't, with what results will be seen.

As Brown led his seven men north toward the Somme at about 12,000 feet, von Richthofen led his 20 Dr I's and D V's west at about 3000 feet. West of Cérisy, a hamlet on the left bank of the Somme, the British antiaircraft artillery opened up at the Circus machines. Brown spotted the white puffs and headed toward them, almost immediately catching sight of the German formations. He waggled his wings and dived to the attack. At the same moment the German pilots saw the Camels and rose to meet them.

From 12,000 feet seven stubby olive drab Camels howled down. May stayed behind—to watch. The attack fell first on the *Kette* led by Weiss. Head-on was the best way to meet an attack. That way one's own machine presented the smallest target and one could bring one's own guns to bear. The flashy Circus machines—red, yellow, white, green, blue—reared up and the patrols came together. Machine guns crackled as the flyers squeezed off their first shots simultaneously. Curling lines of tracer smoke speared through the air. The machines closed at a combined speed of two hundred miles an hour. When they came together at the first pass they broke up or down, left or right, or went through the enemy formation, then whipped around in an instant to try to get on a man's tail. The fight was a sudden, whirling explosion; a tight vicious merry-go-round. With motors full on and racketing, the aeroplanes spun around one another like a flock of noisy butterflies. Captain Le Boutillier and his flight caught up and plunged into the fight. A blue-tailed Triplane dived straight down, Mellersh right after him. Two Triplanes dived after Mellersh. The deafening dance continued. No man held a straight course or a steady bank for more than a second lest another man get on his tail or nail him with a deflection shot the way a hunter kills ducks by leading them. The ear grows accustomed to a steady loud noise and soon one ceases to hear it. The pilot flies along in a kind of deafening silence. So the fighter pilots of the Great War heard nothing while in the air, not the engines of other ships in formation, nor their own voices raised in shouts of anger, joy, or despair, but only the clatter of machine guns; and in a fight if they heard machine guns they knew they were the targets of the shooting.

Lieutenant Mellersh had been so hotly chased that the only way he could escape was by throwing his Camel into a spin and letting it drop. His pursuers were put off by the spinning of the machine and Mellersh pulled out almost at ground level and hedge-hopped for British territory. He landed safely at Bertangles. About two miles north of Corbie the Somme, canalized as an improved waterway, makes a right-angled turn roughly south. As Mellersh passed over the course of the river he recognized Roy Brown's Camel over that right-angle bend; north of the bend he saw a red Triplane going down.

Wilfred May, circling at 12,000 feet as Brown led the Camels down, had watched the fight begin with the head-on clash; saw the centrifugal explosion of machines as they came to grips; saw the whirlwind of action as they turned and began chasing tails; saw the fight settling lower and drifting west in the wind. A German machine rose up out of the fight and arched back down into it. May watched. The first Hun he had ever seen. God. What would he do if one of them came at him? Another one! He dived at the machine. It was too much to ask any spirited young man to stay out and watch. He followed the Hun down, fired and missed, went on down into the scramble. Suddenly Fokker Triplanes seemed to be coming at him "from all sides." He had the impression that he was at the center of a ring of German machines that had only one target. He "seemed to be missing some of them by inches." In his excitement he held his guns open and fired one continuous burst, hoping to spray all of them, until his guns jammed. So far he had forgotten everything he had been told. At this point he remembered one thing—how to get out. He wrenched his machine into a spin and dropped away toward the earth. He caught a quick glimpse of the sun as he leveled out and promptly set a course west. He looked about as he headed home, saw no machines pursuing him, and began to feel pretty good that he had gotten away.

*Leutnant* Hans Joachim Wolff of *Jasta 11* along with *Leutnant* Karjus double-teamed a Camel during the fight, then Wolff looked around quickly to check up on his comrades. Wolfram was not in the fight, Weiss and Scholz were over Sailly-le-Sec. Where was the leader? Chasing a Camel, heading west. Had the *Rittmeister* forgotten the wind was blowing hard to the west today? Most probably he had. That wind could cause trouble . . .

While Wolff was watching the *Rittmeister* press into enemy territory, getting closer to the ground all the time, a Camel came up behind him and shot 20 holes in his machine. Wolff reacted instantly and so saved his skin, and then looked again for the red machine, but it was nowhere in sight. Wolff began to feel the first forebodings of disaster.

Roy Brown saw May drop away from the fight. Brown had shaken off two pursuers on the fringe of the battle and was turning to wade in again. He glanced in May's direction and saw that the Camel had leveled out low and was heading west over British territory. He also saw that a red Triplane was sitting on May's tail.

May didn't know he was being pursued until he heard the rip of machine guns. Frantically he turned and dived, coming out directly over the village Vaux-sur-Somme, where the tiles were nearly blown off the roofs by the passing of his machine and the red Triplane. They thundered over the village and skimmed the hill behind it, the guns of the Triplane snapping short bursts at 30-foot range. May turned as he reached the Somme and headed down the river valley.

The *Rittmeister* was behind and slightly above May, outmanoeuvring and out-guessing him at every turn, so that every evasion May tried brought him closer. May was losing height, in a few seconds he would be trapped between the rows of bare trees lining the banks of the Somme. He went around the right-angled bend in the river, but von Richthofen beat him to it, cutting the corner by leaping over a hill, and May was as good as in the bag.

When Brown spotted the red Triplane on May's tail his reaction was in-stantaneous and unstudied—he headed for it. He put his nose down in a shallow dive and covered the distance in a minute, sailing straight downwind from 1000 feet to about 200 feet, coming out slightly above and to one side of the Triplane. As the two machines ahead of him zig-zagged, Brown sped on a direct line to a point over the river, where he turned and made a pass at the Triplane, going on down in the same shallow dive after firing one burst. All three machines were so low that Brown lost sight of the other two behind the trees. Now the other two machines were going the opposite direction from Brown, who banked and caught sight of them again, the red Triplane apparently still pursuing May very closely. The process was repeated, Brown on a straight course quickly overtaking the zig-zagging machines ahead of him. It is conjectured that he fired a second burst, for it was at this point that observers in the air (Lieutenants Mellersh and May, and Captain O. C. Le Boutillier) saw Brown's Camel close to the Triplane, saw the red machine abruptly swerve, wobble unsteadily, and descend. It went down on a more or less even keel and landed right side up a little bit less than a mile northwest of Vaux-sur-Somme. The undercarriage collapsed under the impact, but the machine was otherwise intact.

Most of the chase took place close to the ground and several ground-gunners took a shot at the red Triplane as it went by. Three Australian soldiers in particular were honestly convinced that one or the other of them had brought it down. They were Sergeant C. B. Popkin, Gunner W. J. Evans, and Gunner Robert Buie.

According to the reports of six medical officers, one small-caliber bullet killed von Richthofen, going in either in the right chest or right armpit and coming out under the left nipple. It may or may not have glanced off the spinal column. Depending on whether it did or did not the bullet could have come from the side or somewhat from the front. Depending on whether von Richthofen was level or banked right or left when he was hit, the bullet could have come from above, below, or from anywhere in between. The case for Brown, to whom the RAF gave official credit, is as strong as it is for anyone else, and there were three witnesses in the air who saw him close to a red Triplane. Whether the red Triplane referred to in Brown's combat report was indeed von Richthofen's machine is a critical point, and one for which no absolute proof seems to exist. Numerous officers and men of the Australian Corps, in whose lines von Richthofen fell, insist that his low-flying machine came under ground fire only. Brown, who did not mention von Richthofen by name in his combat report, merely said that he had put a long burst into a "pure red Triplane" which was firing on May and which was seen to go down and crash by May and Mellersh.

On this day in April, Marshal Foch sent four divisions of the *Détachement d'Armée du Nord* into the front lines in the Flanders sector to help stiffen the British defense and particularly to help defend the commanding eminence of Mont Kemmel. Otherwise, there was little to report. There was a brief lull in the Ludendorff offensive. It was a Sunday.

The following afternoon the *Rittmeister* was buried with military honors by No. 3 Squadron, Australian Flying Corps.

*A Canadian historian, Mr. Frank R. McGuire, who has spent many years collecting and correlating documents relevant to the death of Manfred von Richthofen, has published a carefully prepared summation of these in Cross & Cockade Journal, Summer, 1963, vol. IV, no. 2.*

BY 1918 tactical formations were fully developed and it might be observed that most of them were still valid in the 1939-1945 war. Broadly speaking, there were three basic formations: line, echelon, and "V." In a line formation the machines flew side by side, like men marching shoulder to shoulder; in an echelon the machines were arranged on different levels, as if they were on steps; in a "V" formation—well, a "V" is a "V." In the line the leader flew at one end or the other; in echelon, at the bottom; in a "V" formation, he flew at the point.

An excellent and widely-used formation was evolved by *Leutnant* Werner Junck, the leader of *Jasta 8* from March 1918 to the end of the war. In this formation called *"Juncksche Reihe"* or "Junck's Row," the leader flew at the bottom of a string of machines, each of which was above and to the side of the one in front. In this way the whole *Jasta* was arranged in a diagonal echelon upwards. Each man could see and follow the man in front of him and guard his tail against attack. The last man was an experienced man who was not likely to be taken by surprise from the rear. A defensive circle could be formed quickly in the event of attack, and the formation was flexible so that any manoeuvre up, down, or to the sides could be performed by any machine without danger of collision. This was a variation on the more or less universal "V" formation flown by both sides.

In the RFC, and later RAF, one of the outfits that played an important part in the development of fighter tactics was No. 84 Squadron under Major Sholto Douglas, now Lord Douglas of Kirtleside. Sent to France in September 1917, the squadron set up at Flez near St-Quentin and immediately began to take effect. Serving as a flight commander was Captain Hugh W. L. Saunders, a six-foot South African who finished the war with 19 confirmed victories. Saunders, who was as easy-going as he was big, always used the term "dingbat" to describe anything for which he did not know the name. Major Douglas once cracked that he didn't know what Saunders was and must therefore call him a "dingbat." And Dingbat Saunders it remained.

Serving in Saunders' flight was another South African named Lieutenant A. W. Beauchamp-Proctor. Just five feet tall, Proctor was a peppery puppy compared to Dingbat Saunders, who has described him as "a very brave young man—a poor pilot but a magnificent shot." Proctor was one of the great Aces of the war, his score at the Armistice being 54, which put him fifth on the roster of British Aces and earned him the Victoria Cross for his consistently daring and effective work.

Saunders and Beauchamp-Proctor developed various tactics and Saunders recalls: "No. 84 Squadron played an important part in the development of fighter tactics—especially in squadron formation tactics which became the normal method of operation during 1918. We operated in three flights of five aircraft each echeloned upwards and backwards with gaps of 1500 to 3000 feet between flights. The bottom flight led and normally went into the attack first. The two other flights provided cover and only joined in the fight when the situation justified such action. These tactics were further developed during World War II when the use of R/T (radio) enabled the leader to control his flight or squadron and direct pairs of fighters into particular enemy aircraft.

*Beauchamp-Proctor.*

160

"Balloon strafing became highly developed in No. 84 Squadron. It was quite a dangerous game, for the balloons normally flew at 1500 feet or below and were protected by nests of machine guns. The most successful tactic developed by Proctor was for the flight to approach in a steep dive covered by another flight from attack from above. The leader, usually Proctor, dived right up to the balloon firing to the last moment before zooming away. Of his fifty-four enemy aircraft destroyed, Proctor got 16 balloons."

On August 22, 1918, Proctor attacked a string of seven balloons, flamed two of them, and drove the observers in the rest over the side to take to their parachutes.

In June 1921, while practicing for an RAF aerial pageant, Proctor was killed when his Snipe spun into the ground at Upavon.

In May 1918 George Vaughn joined No. 84 Squadron, being assigned to Saunders' flight. Saunders remembers Vaughn as an aggressive young man, "one of a number of U. S. pilots who came to 84 Squadron to gain fighter experience before joining U. S. fighter squadrons then forming in Europe. Vaughn was by far the most successful. He was a first-class shot and courageous. He got his first enemy aircraft on one of his earliest patrols."

Asked about this first victory, Mr. Vaughn smiled and said that he'd gotten a strip torn off by Saunders because of it.

It happened on the morning of June 16, 1918. The German March Offensive had driven No. 84 Squadron out of its flying field at Flez, near St-Quentin, and the squadron had moved to new quarters at Bertangles where several British units were located. At 8 o'clock in the morning, No. 84 took off from Bertangles to fly fighter escort to the D.H.4's of No. 205 in a bombing attack on a German aerodrome at Foucaucourt. Saunders was leading five S.E.5a's of his flight at about 12,000 feet in a wide sweep to the southwest after leaving the target. Vaughn was flying at the rear of the "V" formation, keeping what he supposed was a sharp eye out for enemy scouts. His first inkling of trouble came when he heard the shots going through the rear of the fuselage and the sound of machine guns overhead.

A Pfalz D III with a bright yellow body had dived on the British machines and had apparently selected Vaughn as his target because he was at the rear of the flight. Having delivered his burst, the German pilot zoomed and turned away. Shocked and enraged at the thought that somebody had taken a shot at him, Vaughn broke formation and went for the Pfalz. The S.E. had the edge in speed and Vaughn quickly caught up as his adversary dived to 5000 feet. *Combat Report No. 205* for No. 84 Squadron gives Vaughn's brief narrative of the events after the attack: "I did a right-hand climbing turn, and came out on the tail of one E.A. which had turned east. I opened fire when at about 100 yards range, expending 200 rounds from my Vickers gun. I was then within 50 yards of E.A. who started to throw out clouds of smoke. After falling some 500 feet, E.A. burst into flames.

"This is confirmed by Lieuts. Manzer, Mathews, and Fyfe of this squadron; also by the bombers whom we were escorting, No. 205 Squadron."

161

In the heat of the moment Vaughn had imprudently chased his man several miles into German territory. "I remember the occasion," says Saunders, "when Vaughn followed the enemy aircraft well over the lines to a very low altitude . . . It was a dangerous thing to do and frequently resulted in the victor being shot down from the ground."

The flight reassembled after the brief flurry of action and Saunders led his men back to the aerodrome. Once on the ground, Saunders indicated that he would like to have a word with Vaughn in private. "Now, that was a good show, Vaughn, but . . ." The reprimand was friendly enough and was delivered in a bantering tone ("I gave him a pretty good raspberry," says Saunders), but the advice was taken to heart by Vaughn. By the time he transferred to the U. S. Air Service, Vaughn had won six victories with the RAF and a well-deserved British Distinguished Flying Cross. On August 29, 1918, he transferred into the U.S.A.S., reporting as the commander of "B" Flight to the 17th Aero Squadron at Auxi-le-Château. On September 22 he led three other members of the 17th to an attack on a formation of 18 enemy fighters. He shot down two of them, his squadron mates shot down two more, and the enemy formation was dispersed. This was one of the actions that earned him the American Distinguished Service Cross. George Vaughn finished the war with 13 confirmed victories, an Ace in both the Royal Air Force and the United States Air Service.

*When George Vaughn joined the 17th Aero Squadron, he brought along a souvenir of the RAF, his cut-down fleece-lined flying boots.*

162

REED MCKINLEY CHAMBERS was born at Onager, Kansas, on August 18, 1894, and attended public school there. While he was still a boy his family moved to Memphis, Tennessee, where, in 1916, he enlisted in the Tennessee National Guard, serving eventually as a Regimental Sergeant Major. In April 1917 he transferred as a Sergeant into the Aviation Section of the Signal Corps and received his basic flying instruction. Chambers was a natural pilot, and at Rantoul Field, Illinois, where he completed his training, he became an instructor with a total of 22 hours in his logbook. He was sent overseas early in 1918, assigned to the 94th Aero Squadron as a flight commander on the first of March. At the same time Lieutenants Edward V. Rickenbacker, Douglas Campbell and Alan Winslow arrived at the aerodrome at Toul, as did the new commander, Major Raoul Lufbery.

The establishment of the 95th Aero Squadron in the same vicinity had preceded that of the 94th by only a few weeks, and these two squadrons, the nucleus of the 1st Pursuit Group, were the first American fighter squadrons in the field.

The American fighter squadrons established in France from February 1918 to the end of the war were equipped with French machines, the Nieuport 28 and the Spad 13. The 28 was issued first. It was the last of the Nieuports to be used in the war and was flown mostly by the Americans, very few being issued to French *escadrilles*. It was quite different from any of the previous Nieuport designs except for the fact that a rotary engine was used, the nine-cylinder 160-horsepower Gnôme-Rhône Monosoupape. The fuselage was rounded in cross section, as opposed to the usual slab-sided Nieuport practice; the wings were equal in span and chord with parallel interplane struts, as opposed to the usual sesquiplane layout with "V" struts. The ailerons were located in the lower wing. The 28 developed a serious fault soon after it was introduced at the Front. In a prolonged dive or during violent manoeuvring the fabric on the wings was sometimes peeled off. Apparently normal condensation resulting from daily climatic change attacked the glue with which the plywood of the leading edge was bonded, causing the plywood eventually to delaminate. The loosened plywood worked against the fabric, putting a severe strain on it so that the fabric might split from the overload it took in

*Nieuport 28*

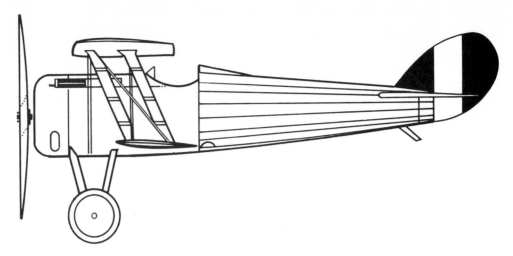

diving or rough handling. Once the fabric was split the slipstream got under it and ripped it away. The problem was a critical one, but fortunately few fatalities resulted from it, and by the summer of 1918, when the problem had been overcome, most U. S. squadrons flying the 28 had switched to Spads. Roughly 300 of the 28's were purchased by the AEF and it has the honor of being the machine with which the first "all-American" victories were achieved.

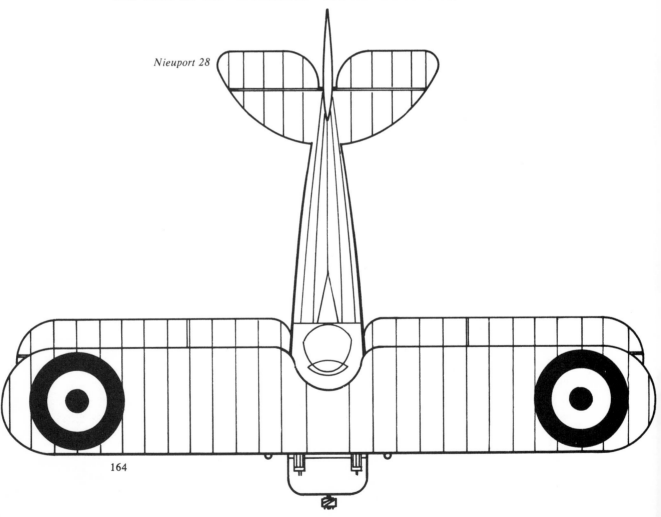

*Nieuport 28*

On March 29, James Norman Hall arrived at the 94th. Hall was another of those rare birds, a fighter pilot who was a college graduate, having taken his Ph.B. at Grinnell College in 1910. When the war broke out he was on a bicycle trip through England and he promptly enlisted in the 9th Battalion of the Royal Fusiliers. He spent most of 1915 in the trenches at Loos, Messines, and "Plugstreet" Wood, where he served so creditably that he was selected for officer's training. He was suddenly given an honorable discharge, however, and returned home to find that friends of the family had arranged the discharge because his father was seriously ill. When his father recovered, Hall returned to Europe in the summer of 1916 and on October 11 enlisted in the French air service. He trained at Buc, Avord, and Le Plessis-Belleville and was assigned to the *Escadrille Lafayette* on June 16, 1917. He was wounded and brought down ten days later during a fight against heavy odds and spent the summer in hospital. On October 3, 1917, he returned to the *Lafayette* and stayed with the outfit during the period of transition, in early 1918, when it was absorbed into the U. S. Air Service as the 103rd Aero Squadron. Hall was commissioned a Captain on February 7, 1918, and as an experienced pilot was brought into the 94th as a flight commander. In May, with his score standing at six confirmed victories, be became one of the victims of the Nieuport weakness. While diving on an enemy machine near Pont-à-Mousson, the fabric on the upper wing tore off and he fell a considerable distance out of control. He had just succeeded in regaining his equilibrium when he was hit by ground fire and crashed near Pagny-sur-Moselle. Hall spent the rest of the war as a prisoner. Repatriated after the Armistice he settled in Tahiti where, in collaboration with Charles Nordhoff, he later wrote the *Bounty* Trilogy.

By the time Hall joined the 94th as a flight commander the squadron had already made its first flight over the lines. On March 19, Major Lufbery took Lieutenants Campbell and Rickenbacker across for a look. Eagerly questioned by their squadron mates on their return, Rickenbacker and Campbell said it was pretty interesting but there had been no German planes. Lufbery smiled and said he'd seen half a dozen.

Gervais Raoul Lufbery was the classic soldier of fortune. A bit old to be a fighter pilot, he was 30 when he was accepted for flying training. He was born in 1885 in France, in Clermont-Ferrand, the capital of the ancient province of Auvergne. It is said he must have inherited the moody disposition of the people of those mountains, if not from his parents, who did not raise him, then from relatives who did. His father had adopted American citizenship before the boy was born and gone to America to try his fortunes when the boy was six. Lufbery's mother had died when he was one, and so he was left with relatives when his father sailed for America. At 19, Lufbery decided he would see the world and set off for the U. S. by way of the Balkans, Turkey and North Africa. He arrived in New York on the same day that his father sailed to Europe on business and they never met again. Lufbery banged around the U. S. and Cuba, and on the strength of his father's citizenship joined the army for a two-year hitch in the Philippines, 1908-1910.

Discharged from the army he roamed about India, Japan and China. In 1912, in Saigon, he met and joined up with a compatriot, the famous pre-war exhibition flyer, Marc Pourpe. Although completely unschooled, Lufbery was bright enough to be able to pick up anything he set his mind to, and in a short time became chief mechanic and factotum to Pourpe. Together they barnstormed Europe and Africa. They were in France when the war broke out and Pourpe offered himself to the *Service d'Aéronautique*. He was accepted but Lufbery was not. Well, everyone knew the war was going to be over by Christmas anyway. Lufbery joined the Foreign Legion, but was soon transferred into the air service as Pourpe's chief mechanic. For Pourpe, the war *was* over by Christmas—he was killed in action on December 2, 1914.

Lufbery's energy and ability had come to the attention of his superiors and it was suggested that he take flying training. He accepted gladly and was sent to flight school at Chartres in May 1915, receiving his wings in July and posted to VB 106 in October. For six months he flew almost daily bombing missions in the Voisin squadron. In the meantime, the *Escadrille Lafayette* was coming into being through the efforts of Norman Prince and Dr. Gros. Lufbery, on the basis of his hitch in the U. S. Army, was approached with a view to interesting him in joining the new American squadron. Lufbery accepted, and after a conversion course at Le Plessis-Belleville was transferred into the *Lafayette* in April 1916.

Lufbery was a born mechanic, but, unlike many other born mechanics, such as Fokker and Voss, was not a born pilot. He had to work hard at flying, but, because he had the kind of perseverance that counts, he eventually became a superlative pilot. He scored his first victory on July 30, 1916, and his fifth, to become an Ace, on October 12, 1916, during the famous raid on the Mauser works at Oberndorf. It was following this same raid that Norman Prince was killed in a landing accident.

Edward F. Hinkle, who designed the Sioux Indian insignia for the *Escadrille Lafayette,* recently said in an interview for *Cross & Cockade*: "Lufbery was a wonderful mechanic and his 'plane was always the best in the *Escadrille*. Anyone would rather have a second-hand Lufbery machine than a new one, anytime."

During 1917 Lufbery flew regularly and without interruption, a skillful professional who knew everything there was to know about guns, aeroplanes, tactics, engines. He was awarded the *Médaille militaire* and the *Croix de Guerre* with ten palms. He was awarded the Military Cross by Britain, the first man in the American service to be so honored, and he was named a *Chevalier* of the *Légion d'Honneur*. He was also given a snazzy roadster by the Hispano Suiza company.

When the U. S. Air Service began to pull itself together, Lufbery was commissioned a Major and promptly taken out of the fight. He fidgeted behind a desk at Issoudun for a time while the American brass hats slowly came to the realization that they knew nothing about the war, or how to run it, that everybody else but America had had four years of experience. Finally Lufbery was assigned to the 94th as C.O.; the brass hats went on to find other blunders to make. Taking Lufbery out of action for a short time did no real harm, but putting untrained Americans in did. Untrained Americans fell in droves in the fall of 1918.

Assuming command of the 94th, Lufbery began the task of instructing the green Americans in the business of air fighting. He succeeded, but exactly how he succeeded no one knows. Lufbery wasn't much of a talker, and never encouraged shop talk. Douglas Campbell remembers that he didn't like to talk, and never said much, that he was businesslike and intense. Perhaps he did it by sheer intensity, putting an education by implication into every well-chosen word. When he did talk, his remarks were short, terse, and always delivered at the appropriate moment.

Eddie Rickenbacker describes Lufbery as "a taciturn man, but if he felt that you had the qualities and the interest in becoming a real fighter pilot he would go out of his way to give you the benefit of his knowledge,

"He did this with me by taking me out alone with him on his lone patrols with instructions to follow his maneuvering, which would teach me to see all corners of the sky very quickly. However, he always advised me to watch him and if he got into trouble not to join him but to go on home.

"I know of several other youngsters in whom he took the same interest, but, of course, his greatest ability was in teaching by example and achievement."

The first score for the squadron and for America was a simultaneous double victory by Douglas Campbell and Alan Winslow on April 15, 1918. Lufbery had assigned Captain David M. Peterson, another *Escadrille Lafayette* veteran, to lead two other men, Chambers and Rickenbacker, on a patrol between Pont-à-Mousson and Saint-Mihiel. Lieutenants Winslow and Campbell were to stand by from 6 to 10 a.m. The patrol took off about 6 o'clock, found the lines, but as it was a cloudy day not unmixed with fog, found nothing going on. They eventually gave up and headed toward home.

167

In the meantime, the *Flugmeldedienst* had spotted the three Nieuports and requested an interception from a neighboring *Jasta*. Two German scouts, an Albatros and a Pfalz D III, were sent up but not only could not find the Americans, they lost themselves in the process. The Germans were finally spotted by ground observers and were reported by telephone to the 94th aerodrome at 8:45 when they were no more than 15 miles away. Campbell and Winslow had their aeroplanes warmed up and took off. The two Germans came out of the mist near Toul and headed for the field, possibly to try to identify it or stage an impromptu shoot-up. Winslow, with Campbell right behind him, came up behind the Albatros and opened fire.

"I was just a stupid kid," says Campbell today. "We knew there were two aeroplanes. When I saw Winslow attack one, I should have been looking around for the other one." The Albatros had turned hard when Winslow opened fire. Winslow went after him. Campbell turned too, and it was lucky he did for just at that moment the Pfalz had come up behind him and started shooting. Campbell threw his machine violently to one side when he heard the sound of machine guns. He saw the Plafz then and for a moment was occupied in keeping out from in front of the other man's guns. He ducked down and came up underneath the aeroplane and put one burst into it, seeing several of his tracers go into the engine. The Pfalz immediately went down in a dive and Campbell dived after it. He had seen Winslow's victim go down out of the corner of his eye. He put one more long burst into the Pfalz and it began trailing flames.

Both German pilots were taken alive. Their machines had come down one on either side of the aerodrome, Campbell's victim within five hundred yards of the hangars. The two Americans landed within four minutes of having taken off.

It wasn't always that easy. Chambers once came back with 80 holes shot through his aeroplane. He had made a terrific attack on his target, but returned with nothing more to show for his effort than the 80 bullet holes.

On one other occasion an enemy aeroplane was intercepted over the field, but this time the tables were turned. Instead of a novice, it was a veteran who went after it; instead of winning a victory, the 94th suffered a stunning loss.

At about 10 a.m. on Sunday, May 19, an Albatros two- or three-seater appeared over the area, apparently on a photography mission. Antiaircraft guns opened fire, but did not succeed in bringing the machine down or chasing it away. Major Lufbery jumped into a Nieuport and took off alone. The men of the squadron confidently expected Lufbery to make short work of this affair. He attacked several times, without any apparent effect while the German rear gunner fired back. Then suddenly fire streaked back from the engine of the Nieuport. Long flames swirled over the cowling, seeming to engulf the whole ship. The body of Lufbery was seen to fall away from the burning aeroplane and plunge down.

Fire in the air was one of the things that his boys had asked Lufbery about. Reed Chambers remembers his saying that he would *never* go down a flamer. He didn't.

*          *          *

IN FEBRUARY 1918 *Oberleutnant* Adolf *Ritter* von Tutschek was promoted to *Hauptmann* and placed in command of *Jagdgeschwader Nr. 2,* composed of *Jastas 12, 13, 15,* and *19. Hauptmann* von Tutschek's own squadron, *Jasta 12,* of which *Leutnant* Hermann Becker was deputy C.O., was staff squadron. At that time the squadron was stationed at Toulis, 18 kilometres or about 11 miles, north of Laon. The accompanying photograph shows the field at Toulis at this time when the squadron was switching from Albatros D V's to Fokker Triplanes. The machines of *Jasta 12* had uniformly painted black tails with individual insignias in black and white on the fuselages. The machines of von Tutschek had all-black bodies and tails. The fourth and fifth machines from the bottom, a Dr I and an Albatros D V respectively, were von Tutschek's. The sixth machine, a Triplane with a black and white quartering, was Becker's.

*Hermann Becker.*

169

*Hauptmann* von Tutschek was a wiry and impulsive Bavarian who was a skillful leader, liked and admired by his men. On August 11, 1917, he had been seriously wounded and out of action for the rest of the year, the *Jasta* being led in his absence by *Oberleutnant* Blumenbach. In December 1917 von Tutschek had visited the Pfalz works at Speyer, along with von Richthofen and others, to evaluate new designs, then in February 1918 had returned to the Front at the head of his old *Jasta 12* and the newly-formed *J.G. 2.*

The photograph of the men of *Jasta 12* was taken at Toulis as they posed on the steps of their *Kasino*. From right to left they are: *Oberleutnant* Krapfen-bauer (*Geschwader* adjutant), *Leutnant* Koch, von Tutschek, *Oberleutnant* Blumenbach, *Leutnants* Staats, Hoffman, Muller, Becker (with Dackel in his left arm), Bock, and Officer-Candidate Ulrich Neckel.

*Hermann Becker.*

In February and March von Tutschek shot down four more machines, but on March 15, 1918, fate caught up with him over Laon. Just inside the German lines the wreckage of his Triplane was found with no visible evidence of bullet damage, and von Tutschek himself had not been shot. On his right temple was a superficial injury that seemed inconsistent with crash injuries, and it was conjectured that a spent bullet or a ricochet had hit him there and stunned him and his machine had fallen out of control bearing him to his death. His men, at any rate, were convinced that he had perished undefeated—except by fate.

Hermann Becker was in Berlin that day, requisitioning stores for the squadron, and he heard the news of the death of his comrade and commander the next day from the chauffeur who met him in Marle to drive him back to the aerodrome. His only thought was that perhaps it wouldn't have happened if he had been with his flight near von Tutschek. "Too late, too late," he said bitterly, "Fate attacked too fast."

*　　　　　*　　　　　*

BY THE END of May both Douglas Campbell and Eddie Rickenbacker were Aces. On June 6 Campbell was wounded in an attack on a photographic two-seater. He began his attack with a diving pass and worked the enemy machine from 18,000 down to 3000 feet. The German pilot was very good and his manoeuvring prevented Campbell from closing up in the blind spots. Thinking the gunner was finally out of ammunition, Campbell went right in for a shot and as he turned away the gunner put a burst into the Nieuport. One explosive bullet hit a few inches behind Campbell and a large piece of shrapnel lodged in his back. He broke off and headed home. The wound was not serious, but the first all-American Ace was out of action for the rest of the war.

He was out at a time when every loss was critical. Allied reinforcements were moving up and every man was desperately needed. The U.S.A.S. had two full-time jobs on its hands, the fight for aerial supremacy and ground attack; sorties were flown throughout the daylight hours. To hold up the German advance, bottleneck targets such as bridges were singled out, and when the Germans put up a stiff defense for these targets, violent air battles resulted. In general, the Germans were outfought in the air long before they were stopped on the ground. When bridges were destroyed the German engineer companies threw pontoon bridges across the rivers and the troops continued to move up. At Commercy, one such pontoon bridge was a priority target, and Reed Chambers led the 94th in that day. The bridge was lined with troops and Chambers signaled the squadron to form in a line behind him. The troops opened up with rifle and small arms fire as the Spads came down firing at a mass of human targets packed in a narrow and confining space. At the end of the run the Spads turned around and came back. "It was like cutting wheat," Chambers recalls. When all the ammunition was used up the squadron went home, gassed up, re-armed, and took off again. When they went back, the reception was hotter than it had been the first time, but the horrible job was done, and it was still like cutting wheat.

*Chambers.*

The strain of constant flying and fighting, of high-altitude patrols without oxygen, of too much killing, began to tell. There were mistakes, accidents, needless losses. This was happening on both sides of the line. After flying all day the men would drop exhausted into their cots at night, and then the bombers would come over. Many men lost friends during bombing raids. George Vaughn recalls that he was much more afraid of the bombers than he was of the fighters: "You just don't know where the bombs are going to land. You're helpless."

Some things happened that could only be ascribed to nervous exhaustion. Reed Chambers, a cool customer if there ever was one, was tormented by a nightmare: a face. The face would appear vague and distant, and would slowly come nearer until it seemed as if the face and Chambers were literally nose to nose, staring at each other. That's all, just staring. Then Chambers would wake up, his sleep spoiled. Who was it? Chambers was not superstitious, but it was a torment not to know to whom this disembodied face belonged. Was it a man he had killed? Or was it the man waiting for him in the sun?

*Cook. Coblenz aerodrome*
*in 1919, a Fokker D VII*
*claimed by U. S. as*
*reparations.*

Brigadier General Everett R. Cook (ret'd.) was deputy Chief of Staff of the 8th and 12th Air Forces, 1942-3, and of the U.S. Strategic Air Force, E.T.O., in 1944. In the summer of 1918 he was Captain Cook of the 91st Aero Squadron, flying French-built Salmson two-seaters in the St-Mihiel offensive. The following is an excerpt from an unpublished manuscript:

"Just at this time a rather unpleasant incident happened which nearly cost us a team. We had an early morning mission. 'Pop' Seymour from Peekskill, New York, was my observer. We were supposed to get out just before dawn—about four o'clock—and go over for a real early look at the Germans in their back areas. We were headed north toward the lines at about 4000 metres.

"Over Nancy we spotted a German plane coming into our lines. The French antiaircraft were firing at him. To our left over our balloon lines we saw a Nieuport evidently out in the early morning looking for meat in the form of *Boche* ships. We were late, as we had had trouble getting our altitude and we were anxious to get in and out before the patrols got up.

"Our mission took us right in behind the German plane and we thought at the time that we would at least see a good fight and maybe get in a passing shot at the Hun ourselves, although that was secondary. Our attention riveted on the German plane was suddenly diverted by a burst of tracer bullets passing in front of us and hitting our right wing. A glance upward revealed the Nieuport diving on us firing. Without thinking I kicked the ship around and we went into each other both firing.

*U. S. Air Force photograph*

*Salmson 2A2.*
*at gunnery range.*

173

"He went off to the side and down in a steep dive. I thought I had gotten him, but didn't care much. We kept on going and in a minute he was back trying to get under our tail. We immediately went into a spiral so that we could watch him. Pop Seymour, my observer, had his rear guns trained on him and kept asking me through the telephones. 'Must I shoot him . . . must I shoot him?' It had occurred to me that this might be an instance of an Allied plane being flown by an enemy, of which we had heard stories which we later came to believe were entirely mythical.

"We wanted to be sure, so I said, 'Wait, let's see what he does.' Finally he seemed to recognize our cockade insignia painted on the wings. By this time I had stalled the ship and we fell off in a spin. When I pulled up the pursuit plane was gone. We gained our altitude and finished the mission. When we landed we reported the encounter. Suppositions were at first that some German was flying in a captured Nieuport. However, Major decided to find out, so taking me with him he went over to the pursuit field to investigate.

"When we got there we found that it was Reed Chambers, an old friend from Memphis, my home town. He had reported the incident as a combat with an enemy machine. It came out later in Army reports as such. He must have been surprised and nervous when he saw a machine coming out of the sun and didn't stop to investigate. He was some shot at that, having me cold in the air. 'If he ever meets a *Boche* in the air he will have to do better or he will never get one,' I wrote in my diary.

"The same pilot later became one of the greatest American pursuit pilots on the Front, winning recognition for a string of *Boche* victories, and later succeeded to the command of Rickenbacker's squadron."


In June 1918 Captain Charles J. Biddle was appointed commanding officer of the 13th Aero Squadron, U.S. Air Service.

On August 16 he became an Ace when he brought down his fifth machine, a Rumpler, near Nancy. After jockeying for position he came up under the two-seater and with a short burst mortally wounded the rear gunner. The German pilot had no choice but to surrender and Biddle escorted the aeroplane down to an open meadow where both machines landed.

A crowd from the city quickly gathered around the American and his prize and a French General demanded that a photograph be taken as a souvenir of the occasion. A little girl gave Biddle a tiny bouquet of flowers she had picked and he accepted it, thanking her in French. As the photograph was about to be taken, Biddle started to hide the flowers behind his back, but he saw the little girl watching him. Afraid that he might hurt her feelings by hiding the flowers, he self-consciously posed with them in his hand, "feeling like a June bride," he said.

*        *        *

Photograph from Charles J. Biddle.

*Becker.*

IN SEPTEMBER Hermann Becker and *Jasta 12* were equipped with the Fokker D VII, "the best German scout machine of the war," according to Becker. Between the end of April 1918 and the Armistice, some 3000 D VII's were delivered to first-line squadrons. The aeroplane had been selected for mass-production as a result of the excellent performance it had given at competitive trials held at Johannisthal in January. In order to launch production as quickly as possible, the Albatros works was ordered to construct D VII's under sub-contract. This was a moral victory for Tony Fokker; the crowning irony is that the Albatros works produced more D VII's than the Fokker works.

With two standard power plants, the 160-horsepower Mercedes D III or the 185-horsepower BMW IIIa, the Fokker D VII had a top speed of about 120 miles per hour. Both the Mercedes and the BMW (Bavarian Motor Works) were six-cylinder, in-line, water-cooled engines. The fuselage of the D VII was of welded steel tubing covered with fabric all over except for sheet metal panels around the engine. An experimental all-wood model was built by Albatros just to show that it could be done in the event of a steel shortage. The all-wood model, 40 pounds heavier than the standard steel tubing model, merely showed how difficult it was to improve on the products of the Platz/Fokker combination.

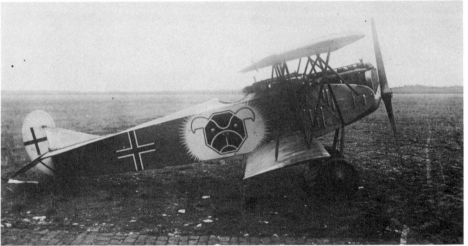

Peter Grosz

The D VII had cantilever wings like the Dr I, "one-piece" structures whose spars ran all the way through from one end to the other. Thus the bottom wing, instead of being made in two panels with one panel bolted on each side of the fuselage, was one piece attached to the bottom of the fuselage. The two wings together made a "cell" that was unusually strong.

The D VII was easy to fly, completely devoid of any tricky habits, responsive and manoeuvrable all the way up to its ceiling, and when it stalled, stalls were straight forward with no tendency to whip around into a spin. The D VII was said to make good pilots out of poor ones. It was not so manoeuvrable as the Sopwith Camel, or Fokker Triplane, but it was as manoeuvrable as the Spad or the S.E.5, and its ruggedness, speed, and consistent performance up to ceiling made up for any deficiencies.

176

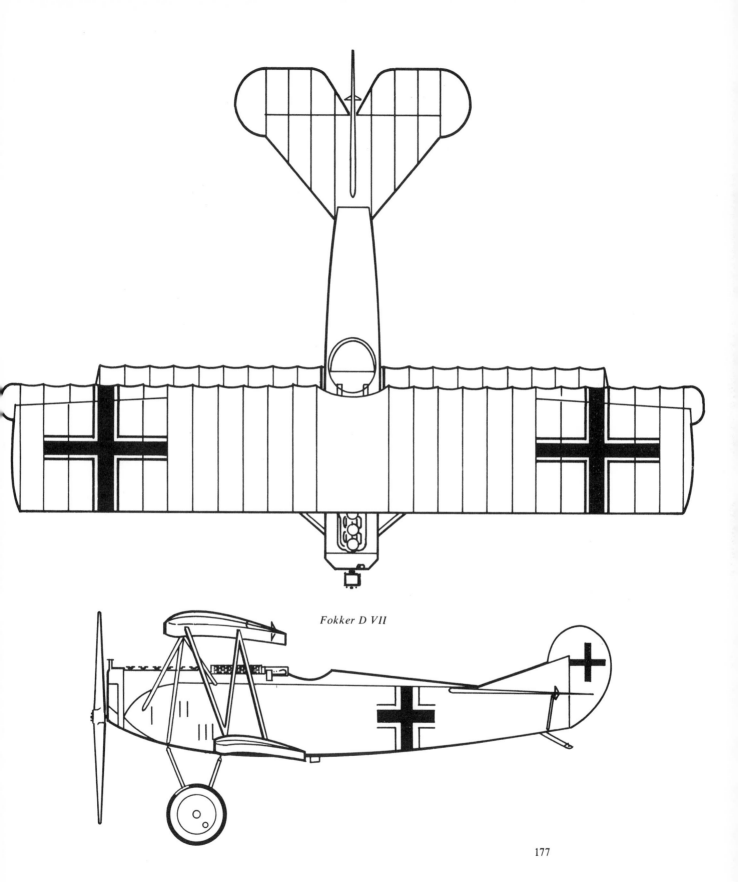

*Fokker D VII*

Late one day in September, *Leutnant* Hermann Becker was leading his men home to the field at Giraumont (near Conflans-en-Jarnisy, 25 miles east of Verdun) —seven Fokker D VII's in V-formation, the flanking machines ranged in echelon upward from the leader. They were returning from a hunt over Verdun and were heading east. Ahead of them Becker spotted another flight of seven machines at about the same height traveling in roughly the same direction. Keeping an eye on them, Becker held to his course and slowly overtook the other machines. They were two-wingers, big ones. Two-seaters. As the Fokkers closed the distance between them, the other machines suddenly turned north. Americans! D.H.4's. Becker fired a red flare and opened his throttle. He brought his nose up a trifle and turned north on an interception course. Following his signals the men to right and left spread out into a line abreast and began to close with the DeHavilland machines whose rear gunners swung their Lewis guns around and opened fire as the Fokkers bore in. At point blank range the Germans started shooting. The D.H.'s dropped or dived one by one and disappeared in the clouds below. Becker waved his formation back into a V and led them down through the clouds. Penetrating the wall of cloud they became aware how dark it had grown—it was virtually night on the ground. A familiar pattern of railroad tracks gave assurance that they were over Conflans. Looking about, Becker was amazed to see all seven D.H.'s wrecked on the ground as if they had gone down in formation.

Back at the aerodrome the flight was received with great excitement. The ground crews had heard the aeroplanes but had not been able to see them. They had heard the noise of the machine guns and had seen a few torches falling without being able to make out what they were. They had been wildly jubilant when, a moment later, all seven Fokkers of the flight had buzzed the field.

Hardly a week later they intercepted a flight of eight DeHavillands just south of Briey, shot down five of them and "captured" one, forcing the machine down on their own field at Giraumont. Pilot and observer were guests in the squadron *Kasino* before being led away as prisoners.

Only the Americans could have absorbed, or would have sustained, losses like that. All the D.H.'s were from the same squadron. The loss of 13 machines and 26 men would have obliterated two *Fliegerabteilungen*.

\*　　　　　　　　　\*　　　　　　　　　\*

OF THE 95 Congressional Medals of Honor awarded by the United States for service in the Great War, four went to members of the Air Service: Captain Rickenbacker of the 94th Aero Squadron, Lieutenant Frank Luke of the 27th, and Lieutenants Harold Goettler and Erwin Bleckley of the 50th.

The 50th Aero Squadron was a D.H.4 squadron that took part in the battle for the Argonne Forest in October 1918. Based at Rémicourt, its job was the usual two-seater job of observation.

*D.H.4*

On October 2, Major Charles Whittlesey, commanding the First Battalion, 308th Infantry, 27th Division, and supported by the Second Battalion under Captain (acting Major) George McMurtry with additional detached units, began an advance through the Argonne Forest on the American left flank. His object was to penetrate the forest and dig in on the far slope of the Charlevaux Valley. Whittlesey and his 550 men were the only Allied troops in the sector who had attained their objective by night. The next morning he realized the awful truth that the Allied offensive had stalled and he and his men were surrounded. The only contact with the rear was by means of carrier pigeons, so Whittlesey sent off a message to Division requesting artillery support and supplies to enable the two battalions to hold out until direct contact could be re-established. The first organized enemy attack began, and in a few hours Whittlesey's men suffered 50 per cent casualties. The survivors did not sleep that night, but lay huddled and cold waiting and watching. In the morning the enemy fire began again.

The New York editor who received the short story about the trapped Americans sent back to the correspondent at 77th Division headquarters for more details on the "Lost Battalion" and played it up as a human interest story. Like many catch-words it was a little bit wrong but was chosen because it was easy to say. It was actually not a question of one "lost" battalion, but two; and they were not lost, geographically speaking. *They* knew where they were. The confusion lay with the rest of the Americans who were trying to find them.

On October 4 the 50th Aero tried to supply Whittlesey and his men by air drop. They flew over the area but could not spot any Americans, who were naturally lying low. The 50th crews kept trying to find the men, but without luck. The suspense continued through the next day. On October 6 the squadron flew a series of missions during which the aeroplanes flew so low that two of them were shot down and a third came home with a badly wounded pilot. Lieutenants Goettler, pilot, and Bleckley, observer, had made a number of trips without getting wounded but without finding the Americans either. They had made passes at 500 feet, then at 200. At 200 feet they were flying through the ravine, and the German soldiers on the high ground were firing *down* on them with rifles, machine guns and pistols.

50th Aero Squadron.

Goettler and Bleckley volunteered to make one more try. They would find the Americans by process of elimination. They would fly so low that they would draw the fire of the Germans on the floor of the ravine who had hitherto held their fire so as to avoid revealing their positions.

It was a dangerous method, but it worked. And that is why Lieutenants Goettler and Bleckley of the 50th Aero Squadron, U.S.A.S., were awarded the Congressional Medal of Honor posthumously. That evening the trapped Americans, and the Germans surrounding them, saw the big two-seater with the "Dutch Girl" insignia on the fuselage skim the trees and drop into the ravine. The Germans opened up with everything they had and the D.H. plowed through a curtain of fire. At the end of the ravine the machine zoomed, turned, and came back. Both men were hit many times and the D.H. itself was shot up so badly that tatters of fabric were streaming back in the slip stream, the engine was misfiring, and pieces were flying off. Bleckley slumped down in the rear cockpit and Goettler struggled weakly to get the nose up to clear the trees at the end of the ravine. The D.H. lurched up and over the obstacle and dropped heavily into the French front lines. Goettler was dead; Bleckley pressed the map into the hands of a French officer and then he too was dead. Clearly outlined on the bloody map was the one spot where there had been no ground fire, the one spot where the "Lost Battalion" had to be.

The next day a hastily organized expedition broke through and brought out the survivors.

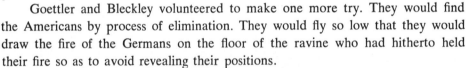

EDDIE RICKENBACKER'S operational career was interrupted by a troublesome mastoid condition. Shortly after his promotion to Captain came through in the middle of June he was hospitalized and didn't get back to the Front until the end of July. On September 25 he assumed command of the 94th.

Rickenbacker was, and is, a competitive man. He wanted his squadron to be the best in the U.S. Air Service, and to do that he knew that every man had to be on his toes. He wanted precise reports from the ground crew on all aeroplanes that were not in flyable condition and if the reports did not coincide with his opinions it was tough on the mechanics. Rickenbacker could listen to an engine and tell you what was wrong with it. To the pilots he preached team tactics—it didn't matter who got the credit so long as the 94th had high score. The victory scores of rival squadrons were posted to keep the men informed of what was expected of them.

This was his way, and it worked. He made the squadron click like a professional team. On his first day as C.O., however, he achieved his outstanding success not as a member of the team, but on a voluntary solo patrol. The action

*Rickenbacker*

U. S. Air Force photograph

181

earned him the Congressional Medal of Honor and it served to give ample indication that now that he was an acting Major he did not intend to run the squadron from behind a desk.

High over Etain he spotted two Halberstadt CL II's on an observation mission. He was above them and in the sun, an ideal setup for a fast diving attack. He looked around to see if he could spot an escort and caught sight of five Fokker D VII's above and behind the two-seaters. Since he was alone he figured he hadn't been spotted because he was up-sun from both flights. He worked around behind the wedge of escort D VII's and entered a steep dive, planning to get the rearmost machine and escape by continuing his dive. The speed of the dive would take him away fast before the other fighters could jump on his tail. He caught the last man completely by surprise. One short burst at close range and the pilot slumped in his seat, the Fokker falling away abruptly in a spin. To Rickenbacker's surprise, the remaining Fokkers scattered instead of coming around to chase him, so he eased out of his dive and went for the two-seaters. The observers were good shots and they were ready for him, so it wasn't as easy as the first attack. As he closed behind the two-seaters, both observers opened up and gave him a good spraying. He dived below the machines and came up under one of them, but the pilot was a *vieux routier* like his observer and quickly kicked his rudder to swing the tail out of the way and give the observer a shot. Rickenbacker heard bullets whistling past again and broke away. He looked for the escort fighters—this was taking too long. No fighters around yet. He tried once more. Regaining his height he came in from the side, from a position diagonally ahead of the lead ship. That way the lead ship masked him from the fire of the other two-seater and Rickenbacker kept himself in a blind spot since the observer in the lead ship couldn't fire through his own wings. Rickenbacker fired a long burst into his target and fell away fast in a sideslip. The two-seater went down in flames as Rickenbacker zoomed back up into the sun. The escorting Fokkers returned to the scene finally, but he had given them the slip.

\*         \*         \*

*The "Hat in the Ring"—94th Aero Squadron.*

WHEN HELLMUTH VON ZASTROW began flying an *Eindecker* during the Battle of Verdun he had already begun work on *Palmström als Flieger,* a burlesque on aviation derived from the works of Christian Morgenstern (1871-1914). Morgenstern created a family of personages, human and fabulous, who appear repeatedly in his verse, most of which is amiable satire cloaked deceptively in nonsense. One of his poems is about an architect who stole the spaces between the pickets of a fence and built therewith a great house. Palmström is one of his characters, so *Palmström the Aviator* seemed a good title to Hellmuth, since a more inept type for an aviator than Palmström would be hard to imagine.

*Der Monoplan* is one of Hellmuth's parodies that expresses his own wry humor and seems a prodrome of the sense of futility that later produced such a bitter satirist as Berthold Brecht:

### THE MONOPLANE

A monoplane there was anon
With landing wheels to land upon.

An Army pilot who saw the thing,
Came quickly there one evening

And flew the 'plane away, but found
He'd left the wheels upon the ground.

The monoplane felt perfectly silly,
Its wheels all knocked off willy-nilly;

An unseemly sight of disarray.
The Inspector-General had it hauled away.

The pilot, meanwhile, had to scram
From *B.A.O.* to *B.A.M.*

During the rainy weather of the spring and summer of 1916, Hellmuth continued his project, working on it at odd moments and while grounded by bad weather.

Hellmuth flew an *Eindecker* as a scout and escort pilot until June 1916. On August 26 he was transferred to *Jasta 2* as Oswald Boelcke's adjutant, a position he held during the late summer and fall when Boelcke successfully launched German fighter aviation and then needlessly lost his life in an accident.

Hellmuth was promoted to *Oberleutnant* and from early 1917 to the end of the war served in the Office of the Inspector General for Air in Berlin, where further disillusionment awaited him, for his job was to help clean up the Augean stables of graft and profiteering that war creates everywhere.

Hellmuth von Zastrow survived the war, but succumbed a short time after to depression and illness.

One of Hellmuth's poems was cast into Latin by his cousin Theobald who thus made light of his classical education:

## THE ALBATROS

The Albatros on the field awaiting,
  A splendid start is contemplating.
    The Albatros.

The Albatros, a thirsty machine,
  Quaffs water, oil, and gasoline.
    The Albatros.

The Albatros dreams that it will soon
  Soar through the sky and chase the moon.
    The Albatros.

The Albatros has met its doom—
  The Albatros fall down go boom.
    The Albatros.

Albâtros in planitie stat
startumque magn' expecticat,
    Albâtros.

Albâtros capit oleum
aquamque et petroleum,
    Albâtros.

Albâtros habet somnium
se culmen rer' ess' omnium,
    Albâtros.

Albâtros mane mortuumst:
Pilotus terrans aufgebumst.
    Albâtros.

Theobald could indeed joke about the way an Albatros might fall down go boom because it happened to him twice and he got away with it both times. The Albatros C III in the accompanying photograph was one in which he was a passenger at Schneidemühl in April 1917. During a training flight, the engine conked out and the pilot tried to stretch his glide to make a landing on the field. That he didn't make it is apparent from the photograph.

*Theobald von Zastrow.*

In August 1917 Theobald was posted to *Fl. Abt. 31* at Slonim in Russian Poland 180 miles east-northeast of Warsaw where he flew a number of missions over the Russian lines as an aerial photographer. The weather was good during the summer and Russian fighter opposition was nil, so the German two-seater crews had an easy time of it, with a sense of "joy-riding" that was absent from the Western Front. The terrain behind the Russian lines with its natural and man-made features became as familiar as their own home towns.

One day at the end of August the C.O., *Hauptmann* Bohnstedt, called Theobald to his office and informed him that he was to fly a bombing mission against the railroad marshaling yard at Shilitschi. Long columns of freight cars were stacked up there and if the switches could be destroyed, vast quantities of materiel would be bottled up.

Theobald and his pilot climbed into their machine and took off at 8:00 a.m. The weather was clear and sunny and at 3500 metres the air was calm. Between Theobald's feet on the floor of the rear cockpit of the D.F.W. C V sat a large box camera with a 25-centimetre lens and six glass plates stored in slits at the rear of the box. Touching his right knee were ten 7½-kilogramme (16½-pound) bombs, arranged horizontally in a rack. Preparatory to dropping these, Theobald would arm them by pulling the pins in their noses. This would free the screw-type fuse which was actuated by centrifugal force, the necessary spinning motion of the bomb being imparted by fins in its tail which also helped to stabilize the bomb in its fall. Behind him was the Parabellum machine gun, mounted on a circular track that ran around his cockpit.

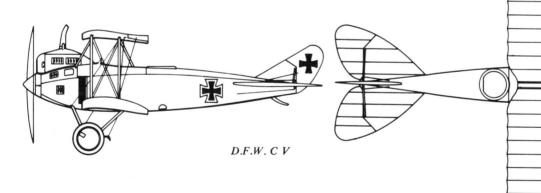

*D.F.W. C V*

Coming in at 3500 metres, Theobald squinted at the target, armed his bombs and dropped them all in a single salvo. He tapped his pilot on the shoulder and the pilot began a wide circle that brought them back over the target in a little less than two minutes. Theobald hoisted the camera and leaned it on the cockpit side, holding the pistol grip and "trigger" in his right hand. He leaned over and pointed the camera down. He found the target zone in his view finder and when his "bombardier's instinct" told him the moment of impact had arrived, he squeezed the trigger. Quickly, he inserted the plate cover and

185

withdrew the negative, storing it in the rear of the camera, slid a new plate into position and shot again. He exposed several plates, then tapped the pilot on the shoulder to signal that they could go home.

On landing at the field near Slonim, Theobald turned the camera and plates over to the sergeant in charge of the processing laboratory and awaited results in the *Kasino*, washing down a roll with a small glass of vermouth. The lab sergeant ran in excitedly and said, *"Herr Leutnant,* I think you really hit something here," and ran out. Theobald raised his eyebrows and shrugged.

It wasn't long before he was advised that *Hauptmann* Bohnstedt wanted to see him. He reported to the C.O.'s office and took his cue from the *Hauptmann* himself, who was regarding him with half-concealed amusement. "I thought that something there looked funny, *Herr Hauptmann,* so I decided to hit it instead." Theobald was shooting a transparent line and he knew the C.O. knew it. Bohnstedt pushed a photograph across his desk. Theobald picked up the print and looked at it, but for several seconds had no idea what he was looking at. Then slowly it became clear. He spotted the bomb bursts, gray cotton puffs a mile from the switchyard. There must have been a strong cross-wind near the ground—missing by a mile was a bit too much even without a bombsight. The smoke and dust of the explosions formed a cloud that was roughly circular when seen from the overhead as in the photograph, but reaching out from the cloud was a long thin shadow that stretched over the ground across buildings, railroad tracks and into the countryside. It was from a column of smoke that must have been a thousand feet tall, and the morning sun had caused the extraordinary shadow that gave the only evidence as to what had happened. Theobald's lucky miss had blown up an ammunition dump.

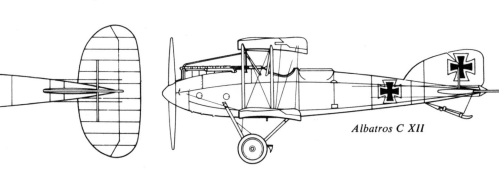

*Albatros C XII*

The end of September 1917, *Fl. Abt. 31* received a few machines of the new Albatros two-seater model, the C XII. The C XII had a plywood-covered fuselage and fabric-covered wings like the Albatros fighters and was powered by a 260-horsepower Mercedes D IVa engine. It was the most elegant two-seater of the time; its performance was excellent and dependable after a few teething troubles had been eliminated.

One of these troubles was the susceptibility of the carburetor to freezing at high altitudes, and one of the victims of this unfortunate tendency was *Leutnant* Theobald von Zastrow.

186

On October 1, 1917, at five o'clock in the afternoon, Theobald and his pilot, *Leutnant* Röchling, were on top of the world. They were up on a joyride, familiarizing themselves with their new aeroplane. The weather was beautiful, the air was sparkling, and at 16,000 feet the bright feathery cirrus clouds above them seemed close enough to touch. It was cold at that height, so cold that after a while it began to chill their exuberance and Theobald tapped Röchling on the head to indicate that he wanted to go down. At that moment the motor sputtered. It caught briefly, then began sputtering again. Röchling pushed the nose down hard, hoping the dive would force the propeller to windmill and keep the motor going. To no avail—the motor died and the propeller stopped dead.

Theobald grabbed his map and began making some fast calculations. Röchling levelled out and headed toward Slonim in a shallow glide. Theobald figured that with their altitude they should be able to make the German lines with a couple of miles to spare. Neither of them had given a thought to the fact that their off-duty flying might just as well have been over German territory—most of their flying had been over Russian territory and it just seemed natural to head that way when they started. Now that familiar ground below began to look pretty dangerous.

In the unnatural quiet, with only the sound of the wind, Theobald and Röchling discussed the situation. They might have landed immediately, for 25 miles behind the Russian lines there was a chance that they would not be spotted, and they were certainly far behind the concentrations of troops at the Front. Possibly they could fix whatever was wrong, then take off and fly home. Had they but known it, they probably could have started up the motor with no trouble at all, but they didn't know that the source of the failure was nothing more serious than an iced-up carburetor. They decided to keep going for the German lines.

They had lost about half their height and were still ten miles behind the lines when they passed over a small lake, the aspect of whose surface made Theobald's scalp prickle. The western half of the lake was smooth as glass while the eastern half was ruffled. That could only mean a westerly wind, a wind blowing from west to east—in other words a headwind. They could never make it. He shouted his discovery to Röchling. They were low now, and vast tracts of woodland stretched in all directions. Suddenly shots cracked out from the woods below as Russian soldiers spotted the German aeroplane skimming the trees. Röchling was hit and jumped in his seat. He was hit two more times and Theobald, fearing he might lose control of the machine, unbuckled his safety belt and tried to reach into the front cockpit to take the stick. At that moment the landing gear snagged on the topmost branches of the trees and the aeroplane nosed over, catapulting Theobald out of his seat. "Like the cork from a bottle of champagne," said one Russian officer who witnessed the crash.

Theobald came to a few moments later, feeling that he must have swallowed most of the marsh he landed in. Outside of a huge bruise on his leg, he was unhurt. Russian soldiers stood all around with rifles pointed at him. The

*The Cavaliers' Club, Fliegerabteilung 31 at Slonim, summer, 1917. At left, Röchling; to his left, Theobald von Zastrow.*

aeroplane was lying upside down on the ground, Röchling still strapped in his seat. Röchling was shaken up but not hurt in the crack-up, and he was groggy from his bullet wounds. He was fumbling for his cigarette lighter to fire the aeroplane. Since he was still strapped in, it was fortunate that he couldn't find the lighter.

Theobald and Röchling were split up. Röchling received excellent care and was exchanged after the signing of the treaty of Brest-Litovsk. Theobald was sent to a prisoner of war camp near Moscow. Transferred somewhat later to another camp, he escaped during the disorders attendant on the Revolution and made his way back to German territory by hopping freights. There were few railroads in western Russia but he knew them all, having flown over them many times. On February 15, 1918, he returned to *Fl. Abt. 31* to the general amazement of his comrades, all of whom had supposed him dead.

There was a rule that one who had escaped from capture was permanently relieved of duty at the Front, and Theobald was accordingly posted to the *Geschwaderschule* at Paderborn as an instructor in aerial gunnery and photography.

In the spring of 1918 *Fl. Abt. 31* was transferred to the Western Front, being based at an aerodrome at Puxieux in the St-Mihiel salient, a few miles west of Metz. *Hauptmann* Bohnstedt was desperate for experienced men, for the game on the Western Front was immeasurably rougher than it had ever been on the Eastern, and he asked Theobald if he wanted to volunteer to return to the squadron. Bored with his teaching job, Theobald accepted the invitation and reported to Puxieux at the beginning of August.

Missions, as before in *Fl. Abt. 31,* were mostly photographic reconnaissance, inspired by the necessity of keeping a watch on the build-up of American forces, but Allied air opposition made a big difference. The only way the German two-seaters could operate with reasonable safety was to go singly, or at most in pairs, make one photographing pass and come back fast. It was rare that fighters could be spared for escort.

Shortly after returning to the squadron, Theobald was sent out with a new pilot to photograph some American positions flanking the salient. They got their pictures and were returning home at a medium altitude when suddenly a single-seater rushed in from the side. Theobald was looking around to guard against a surprise attack, but between the time that he had scanned that piece of sky and returned to search it again, a dark gray Nieuport 28 had materialized out of nowhere. The aeroplane didn't fire, but rolled slightly to one side, flashed under the D.F.W.'s tail and was gone. Theobald hadn't had time to fire. Why the Nieuport didn't fire, we'll never know.

Theobald had still had one good look at the Nieuport as it crossed behind him. The insignia painted on its side had brought back to him, in this incongruous place, the memory of a Christmas from his childhood at Sengerhof. His father, Baron Heinrich, was a collector. He collected for the fun of collecting and never concerned himself with the value or purpose of his collections which sometimes lacked both. Once, he had brought home a china figurine of Uncle

Sam, over two feet tall and acquired Heaven knows where or how. The figure, complete in every detail—from red-and-white-striped trousers and blue coat, to goatee and stovepipe hat with red and white stripes and blue hat band—had eventually been pressed into service at the parish church one Christmas to substitute in the traditional *crèche* for the figure of one of the Magi which had been accidentally broken. Theobald immediately recognized the Uncle Sam hat painted on the fuselage of the Nieuport and concluded that the aeroplane was flown by an American, and that the insignia probably represented an American squadron.

Thus *Fl. Abt. 31* was introduced to Captain Rickenbacker's 94th Aero Squadron.

In September 1918, *Fl. Abt. 31* moved to Doncourt, about 20 miles east-southeast of Verdun, and switched to Halberstadt CL II two-seaters. The Halberstadt was an excellent aeroplane, almost as fast and manoeuvrable as a single-seater. Its small size made it look like one from a distance, and many Allied pilots, making a "surprise" attack from the rear, were surprised themselves to find this wasp had a sting in its tail. In a CL II, Theobald and a veteran sergeant-pilot were once attacked by a swarm of American fighters. Theobald never fired a shot—it would not have been possible to do so even if he had not been hanging on with both hands, for the pilot threw the ship around like a fighter. He looped and spun so that none of the attackers got a shot in, and finally dived in a split-S to the safety of the German lines.

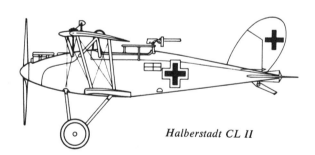

*Halberstadt CL II*

In October Theobald was sent to *F.E.A. 4* at Posen as a gunnery instructor. The transfer was *Hauptmann* Bohnstedt's gift to an old comrade, one that Theobald has always felt saved his life, for things were bad on the Western Front and most German aviators believed it was only a matter of hours. Every mission was regarded as the one from which there would be no return. Theobald served the final weeks before the Armistice at Posen, one of the few who survived the entire war, or the horrors of the peace that followed.

*　　　　　　*　　　　　　*

THE ADMINISTRATOR of the *Aéro Club de France* for the past 20 years is an Ace of English extraction, Robert Waddington. The French branch of the family was established around 1800. The grandfather of Robert Waddington was a professor at the *Collège de France* and *Membre de l'Institute,* and one of his cousins was Ambassador to London, and Representative for France at the Congress of Berlin in 1878.

Robert Waddington entered the army as a private in the 141st Infantry Regiment, in which he served until the end of 1914. In 1915 he transferred to the flying service as an air gunner. His brother was already in the air service, a Voisin pilot later killed in action near Ostend in June 1916.

*Waddington.*

On the death of his brother, Robert Waddington applied for pilot training, his application bearing the words, "Requests to replace his brother killed in aerial combat." His pilot's commission was signed by General Pétain.

Waddington received his pilot training at Buc and Avord, his aerobatics at Pau. He flew in Spa 12, then Spa 154, and finally Spa 31. His machines always carried the number 13.

Asked if he had ever met a German pilot, he said, "I did not have the opportunity to converse with a German pilot during the war but one time only, having shot down a German single-seater in French territory near Rheims. I was able to meet the pilot who was only slightly wounded. The interview was perfectly correct, I would even say cordial, as was the custom in aviation between conqueror and conquered. The German pilot, shaking my hand, said simply, 'You were the stronger,' and, 'Good luck.' "

His first success, although it was not registered as an official victory, was in April 1917 on the Aisne front, not far from Berry-au-Bac. He attacked a German reconnaissance two-seater at about 3500 metres. The Germans defended themselves very well, the pilot snapping his machine about in tight vertical banks to prevent Waddington getting into the blind spots, the observer-gunner triggering off short, accurate bursts that kept him at a distance. Two or three more Spads arrived on the scene and all took turns harrying the German until finally, at about 800 metres, the pilot and gunner mortally wounded, the machine out of control, the two-seater spun down and smashed into the ground.

Several times a day—three, in good weather—the *chasseurs* were out over the trenches, taking off for the first patrol before dawn, and landing for the last time after dark. At 500 metres the sun was blinding in the morning while the earth below was still dark. In the distance one could see the *Drachen* bobbing at 200 or 300 metres over the German trenches.

Periodically, GQG requested that certain balloons be destroyed because they were causing particular trouble. The *chasseurs* would then take off at dawn,

190

climb all the way to ceiling going toward the sun, turn, and with the sun on their backs, dive at the balloons. The dive from height, if they were lucky, gave the pilots the advantage of surprise and they made their attacks before the balloons could be reeled in. The speed of the dive, again if they were lucky, threw off the ground gunners, and the Spads could get away by hugging the ground after pull-out, although sometimes, and this happened to Waddington, they had to run through a curtain of enemy fire at the end of the dive.

He flamed one balloon with a burst of only six rounds. He knew exactly because the guns jammed after that first burst.

One day during a balloon attack Waddington narrowly escaped disaster. In company with Jacques Ehrlich, also of Spa 154, he was beginning his firing pass. Ehrlich, wishing to close up to Waddington, misjudged the distance because Waddington had inadvertently placed himself in the sun, whose rays dazzled Ehrlich. The two Spads came together and Ehrlich's propeller tore off half of Waddington's wing, the propeller itself being splintered in the collision. Ehrlich switched off instantly and glided toward the lines, landing safely in French territory. Waddington's Spad plunged down in a vicious spin from which he managed to recover at only a few hundred feet from the ground. He too switched off, and with his aeroplane barely under control, came in for a safe landing in a vineyard near Rheims. A truck from the aerodrome collected Waddington and his Spad, and the mechanics replaced the wing on the aeroplane, which he flew again the following day.

One of Waddington's last fights took place on October 2, 1918, following his transfer to Spa 31. Flying over the plains of Champagne he and *Capitaine* Reverchon spotted and attacked a squadron of eight Fokkers. At the start of the fight *Capitaine* Reverchon was hit, his aeroplane set on fire, and man and machine disappeared in a terrific explosion when they hit the ground in the midst of the shell craters. Waddington got one of the German fighters under his guns for a split second and the Fokker burst into flames, another blazing torch falling from the same piece of sky as *Capitaine* Reverchon.

Waddington was sorely beset, and his aeroplane was being shot to pieces. He dropped away in a tailspin then in a series of "falling leaves" to throw off the Germans pursuing him. Almost over the French lines the Fokkers withdrew; their bullets had been rattling like hail all through his aeroplane. He piled up on the sandbags barely 60 feet inside the lines, miraculously unhurt. Not counting the hits in the motor, there were over 200 holes in the fuselage, wings and tail of the Spad.

In the closing months of the war, the single-seat fighters were nearly all equal and all good. Man had taken his biggest step since he had learned to walk—he had stepped into the sky. In the 15 years since Kittyhawk, and really in the four since the outbreak of the war, aeroplanes had progressed from powered gliders—unpredictable and almost uncontrollable—to dependable, adaptable, modern airplanes. Since that time, airplanes have grown bigger and more powerful, but the difference is merely quantitative, not qualitative. For his business in the

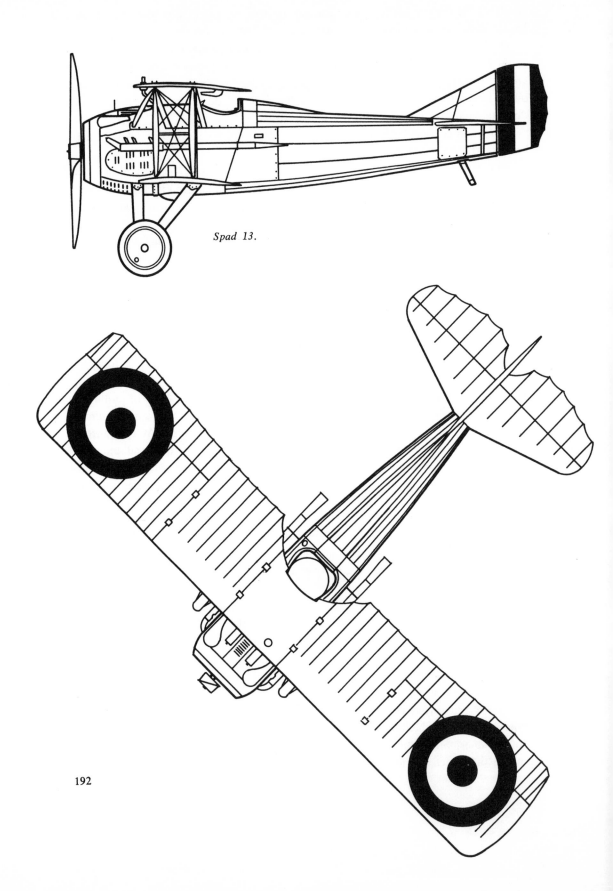

Spad 13.

192

air, open-cockpit biplanes like the Spad, the S.E.5, and the Fokker D VII gave a man everything he needed to span distance, challenge height, and laugh at the cloud-dappled face of the land. The pilot listened to the sound of the wind in the wires and knew his speed without guessing; he felt the sun and the wind on his cheek and from that knew his bearing and whether or not he was flying cleanly, without skidding or slipping. He felt a sense of oneness with the machine that was an extension of his brain and hands and feet. His limitations were the machine's limitations. It would take him as high as there was oxygen to breathe, and it would dance there, over all but the highest clouds. He could dive and zoom, loop and spin, and feel a harmony with the wind, and a closeness to the elements over which he triumphed. The realization of his oldest dream came and went in a day, and we shall never have such wings again.

The following footnote is from Robert Waddington: "One of the best tactics of defense in the case of a combat against a number of enemy machines was the spiral climb. With a 220-horsepower Spad, whose climb was superior to that of the Fokkers, an experienced fighter pilot could attack alone a large enemy squadron—I have often done it. Picking a target, the *chasseur* dived on him from above, fired one or two bursts in the descent and zoomed with acquired speed into a spiral climb, quickly putting himself out of range of the enemies' guns. On several occasions, after attacks of this kind, I have escaped from large squadrons, even though my attack brought me close enough to see the faces of my adversaries under their helmets and goggles."

*       *       *

AFTER THREE YEARS of captivity Roland Garros escaped from the citadel of Magdeburg and succeeded in returning to France by way of Holland in February 1918.

"I am a novice now!" he said in a newspaper interview. "What am I beside those who had not even flown before my capture? I used to say that the progress which would be achieved in three years would surpass imagination, but I never thought I would be the first victim of that progress . . ."

On his return to active duty, Garros had literally to start over again, and he was sent to the aerobatic school at Pau. He returned to the Front in Spa 26, commanded by *Capitaine* de Sévin, where he threw himself into his flying. He would break away from his squadron mates while on patrol, heading straight toward any machine he saw, and on several occasions he had to be rescued.

On October 5, 1918, the fourth anniversary of the first aerial victory, that of Frantz and Quénault, Garros departed on a patrol with *Capitaine* de Sévin never to return. The *Capitaine* could not give a precise account of what had happened, only that Garros had abruptly gone hareing off at a moment when de Sévin was not able to follow him. In the far distance an aeroplane was seen to fall in flames then break up in the air.

A dispatch from the Wolff Telegraph Bureau, Germany's major news agency, was published in the Swiss newspapers on October 17: "A Wolff-note announces that the aviator officer Garros was mortally brought down in the German lines on October 5. Before the war, Garros was one of the best-known French aviators. He was taken prisoner April 18, 1915, and escaped in February 1918. Upon his return he was first occupied in the construction of aeroplanes and later returned to the Front."

Some days later, French troops entering Vouziers found his grave in the southwest corner of the civil cemetery there.

\*        \*        \*

ON NOVEMBER 2, 1918, *Leutnant* Hermann Becker was cited for the *Pour le Mérite*. On November 10, the Kaiser abdicated and fled to Holland. Becker never received the award, but, in his own words, *Man hatte auch ohne diese seine vaterlandische Pflicht erfüllt,* "Even without these (awards) one has performed his duty to the Fatherland."

\*        \*        \*

AT THE BEGINNING of 1918, *Capitaine* Jacques Leps was appointed to the command of Spa 81. He held this position to the end of the war, leading the squadron to 30 confirmed victories and 20 unconfirmed, for the loss of only one man, a pilot killed during a strafing attack on a column of infantry. Leps' own score was 12.

The distinctive insignia of Spa 81 was a running hare pursued by a greyhound. It was designed by an American, *Brigadier* Bayne, who served under Leps and was accidentally killed one day while stunting over the field.

On November 11, 1918, Leps was sitting in the cockpit of his Spad, his prop turning over, the squadron lined up beside him, engines running. He had completed his last checks, was ready to go. The squadron's mission was to fly escort for a bombing raid on Metz; it was to be a big show.

Leps raised his hand to give the signal. Running toward him was a clerk from his administration office, waving his arms and making great gestures. Leps watched the man run up. Confirmation. The Armistice. *C'est finie la guerre.*

For one thousand five hundred days, Leps had known nothing but the war. From the first day to the last day there had been nothing in his daily life but the life he was holding on to at the moment. There had been no future, no "after the war," only now. The war had taken him so young, so profoundly, he realized with a shock that he could no longer imagine a life of peace.

He switched off the engine; it sputtered and stopped. One by one the rest of the squadron switched off. The hot engines ticked and pinged as they began to cool. Leps unfastened his seat belt and climbed out of the cockpit.

That night the early-rising sickle moon entered its first quarter.

\*        \*        \*

# BIBLIOGRAPHY

*L'Aéronautique Pendant La Guerre Mondiale.* Paris, M. de Brunoff, 1919.

Biddle, Charles J., *The Way of the Eagle.* New York, Charles Scribner's Sons, 1919.

Bodenschatz, Karl, *Jagd im Flanderns Himmel.* Munich, Knorr & Hirth, GMBH, 1935.

Bonnefon, Paul, *Le Premier "As" Pégoud.* Paris, Berger-Levrault, 1918.

Bordeaux, Henry, *Chevalier de l'Air; Vie Héroique de Guynemer.* Paris, Librairie Plon, 1918.

Brzenk, Hans, *Wir Jagten den Feind.* Berlin, O. Schlegel, 1939.

Buist, H. Massac, *Aircraft in the German War.* London, Methuen & Co., Ltd., 1914.

Chambe, René, *Dans l'Enfer du Ciel.* Paris, Editions Baudinère, 1933.

Cocteau, Jean, *Dans le Ciel de La Patrie.* Paris, "Société Spad," 1918.

*Cross & Cockade Journal of the Society of World I Aero Historians,* a quarterly, is the first and only periodical devoted exclusively to the study of the aviation of the Great War in all its aspects. Quality of original research and seriousness of purpose evinced in every issue of *Cross & Cockade* are beyond praise. The business office of *Cross & Cockade* is 10443 South Memphis Avenue, Whittier, California.

Cuneo, John R., *Winged Mars, Volume II, "The Air Weapon," 1914–1916.* Harrisburg, The Military Service Publishing Company, 1947.

Douglas, (William) Sholto, Lord Douglas of Kirtleside, *Years of Combat.* London, Collins, 1963.

Eberhardt, Walter von, *Unsere Luftstreitkräfte 1914–1918.* Berlin, C. A. Weller, 1930.

Falls, Cyril, *The Great War.* New York, G. P. Putnam's Sons, 1959.

Fokker, Anthony, *Flying Dutchman.* London, Routledge, 1931.

Fonck, René, *Mes Combats.* Paris, E. Flammarion, 1920.

Gibbons, Floyd, *The Red Knight of Germany*. New York, Garden City Publishing Co., Inc., 1927.

Gray, Peter, and Owen Thetford, *German Aircraft of the First World War*. London, Putnam & Co., Ltd., 1962.

Hawker, Lieut. Col. Tyrrel Mann, *Hawker, V. C.* London, The Mitre Press, 1965.

Hegener, Henri, *Fokker—the Man and the Aircraft*. Letchworth, Harleyford Publications Limited, 1961.

Lamberton, W. M., *Fighter Aircraft of the 1914–1918 War*. Letchworth, Harleyford Publications Limited, 1960.

Mortane, Jacques, *Navarre, Sentinelle de Verdun*. Paris, Editions Baudinère, 1930.

Mortane, Jacques, *Roland Garros*. Paris, L'Edition Française Illustrée, 1919.

Neumann, Georg Paul, editor, and others, *The German Air Force in the Great War*. London, Hodder & Stoughton, Ltd., 1920.

Nowarra, Heinz J., and Kimbrough S. Brown, *Von Richthofen and the Flying Circus*. Letchworth, Harleyford Publications Limited, 1958.

Robertson, Bruce, and others, *Air Aces of the 1914–1918 War*. Letchworth, Harleyford Publications Limited, 1959.

Schweckendieck, O., *Der Kampfflieger*. Hamburg, Hanseatische Verlags-Anstalt, 1938.

Stark, Rudolf, *Wings of War*. London, John Hamilton, Ltd., 1933.

Stewart, Oliver, *The Story of Air Warfare*. London, Hamish Hamilton, 1958.

Taylor, Sir Gordon, *The Sky Beyond*. Boston, Houghton Mifflin Company, 1963.

Tuchman, Barbara W., *The Guns of August*. New York, The Macmillan Company, 1962.

Udet, Ernst, *Mein Fliegerleben*. Berlin, Verlag Ullstein, 1935.

"Vigilant," *Richthofen, the Red Knight of the Air*. London, John Hamilton Limited, 1934.

# INDEX

References to pages on which illustrations appear are in *italics*.

## A

Ace, first: 33
A.E.G. B II: *25*
Aerial supremacy
  of Fokker *Eindecker:* 57-59, 65, 83, 87
  French: 58
  regained by Germans (1917): 93, 95
  won by RFC (1916): 88
Albatros aeroplanes: 9, 25, 34, 87, 108, 111, 113, 115, 133, 137, 138, 168
  C I: 27
  C III: *53, 184*
  C XII: *186-188*
  D I: *73, 74, 76*, 78, 149
  D II: *74*, 85, 86, 117, 149
  D III: *93, 94*, 95, 109-110, 119, 149
  D V: 128, 156, 157, *169*
Alexander: 108, 109, 120
Allmenröder: 95, 109-110
Andrews: ix, *83*, 85-86, 125
Argonne, Battle of the: 179-180
Auger: 135, 139
Australian Flying Corps: 159
Aviatik aeroplanes: 9, 15, 24, 25, 28, 33, 46, 48
  B I: *14*
  B II: *49*

## B

Baer: *72*
Ball: 88, 90-*91*, 92
Balloons: 32, 36, 139, 161, 190-191
Barès: 23, 36
Bayne: 194
B.E. aeroplanes
  2a: *xv, 12*, 79
  2b: 79
  2c: *42*, 77, 80, 88, 90
  2d: 83, 96
  8: 79
Beauchamp-Proctor: *160*-161
Beauvricourt, de: 27
Bécherau: 62
Becker: ix, 114-115, 128, 141, 169, *170, 176*, 178, 194
Bernis, de: 23, 34, *35*, 38, 39, 52
Biddle: ix, 3-6, 55, 72, 146-147, 174-*175*
Birkigt: 69
Bishop: *90*
Bleckley: 179, 180
Blériot: 7, 11, 69
Blériot aeroplanes: *xv*, 7, 9, 45
  training in: 4-6
  Penguin: *4, 5*, 29, 32
  XI: *5*, 79
Blumenbach: *170*
Bock: *170*
Boehme: *144*
Boelcke, Oswald: 9, *25, 27*, 30, 31, 41-*43*, 53, 73, 75-77
  awarded *Pour le Mérite:* 44
  death of: 78, 125
Boelcke, Wilhelm: 25
Bohnstedt: 185, 186, 188, 189
Boillot: 117

Bombings :42, 44, 50, 185-186
  Mauser factory raid: 106-108, 166
  plan for strategic raids on Britain: 53
Boyau: 117
Bozon-Verduraz: 119
Brest-Litovsk, Treaty of: 155
Bristol aeroplanes
  Baby Biplane: 80
  F.2 "Brisfit": *97-99*, 155
  Scout: 41, 80, *81*, 82, 88
Brichambaut, de: 22
British air units
  organization of: 96
  RNAS squadrons renumbered, 156
  No. 11 Wing: 108
  No. 2 Squadron: xv
  No. 3 Squadron: xv, 155
  No. 5 Squadron: 83
  No. 6 Squadron: 79
  No. 11 Squadron: 88, 90, 91, 97
  No. 13 Squadron: 88, 90, 96
  No. 15 Squadron: 83
  No. 19 Squadron: 95
  No. 20 Squadron: 65, 120
  No. 22 Squadron: 65
  No. 23 Squadron: 65
  No. 24 Squadron: 65, 78, 83, 85-86
  No. 25 Squadron: 65
  No. 40 Squadron: 95
  No. 48 Squadron: 97
  No. 56 Squadron: 92, 128-129
  No. 84 Squadron: 160-161
  No. 205 Squadron: 161
  No. 209 Squadron: 156-159
  No. 3 Wing (RNAS): 106
  No. 1 Squadron (RNAS): 104
  No. 8 Squadron (RNAS): 92, 104
  No. 9 Squadron (RNAS): 156
  No. 10 Squadron (RNAS): 104, 106, 108-110, 120, 130-132
British military aviation
  number of aeroplanes (Aug., 1914): xiii
  *See also* Royal Flying Corps
Brocard: 46, 118, 133, 135, *136*, 139
Brown: 156-159
Browning: 26
Butler: 156

## C

Cambrai, Battle of: 155
Campbell: ix, 163, 165, 167-168, 171
Carlin: 7
Carganico: *154*
Caudron aeroplanes: 50, 148
  G. 3: *134*
  G. 4: *42*, 133, *134*
Chadwick: 72
Chambe: 34, 38-39
Chambers: ix, 48, 163, 168, *171, 172*, 174
Champagne offensive: 126, 133
"Circuses," defined: 96
Collishaw: ix, 106-*107*, 108-110, 120-121
Color markings
  British: 108

German: 87
Constantinesco: 121
Cook: ix, *172*-174
Cronyn: 129
Cunnell: 120
Curtis: ix, *130, 131*-132

## D

Dackel: *170*
Dahlmann: ix
Davies: 106
Decoin: 117
Deperdussin: 69
Deullin 135:, 145-147
D. F. W. aeroplanes
  B I: *25*
  C V: *185*, 188
D. H. (DeHavilland) aeroplanes
  2: 65, 78, 82-*84*, 85-86, 129
  4: 161, 178, *179*-180
Doisy: *see* Pivolo
Dolan: *72*
Dorand aeroplanes: 113
Dorme: 135, 137
Douglas: 160

## E

Ehrlich: 191
Engines: 108, 121
  Anzani: 4, 11
  Argus: 73
  Beardmore: 65
  BMW: 176
  Gnôme: 11, 82-83
  Gnôme-Rhône: 163
  Hispano Suiza: 69, 100
  Mercedes: 73, 93, 126, 151, 176, 186
  Oberürsel: 65, 126
  Rhône: *121*, 126
  Wolseley Viper: 100

## F

Falkenhayn, von: 12, 40, 75
Farman aeroplanes: *see* Maurice
  Farman aeroplanes
Faure: 13, 15
F. E. aeroplanes
  2b: *65, 66*, 77, 78, 88, 120
  2d ("Fee"): *120*
  8: *95*
Felloneau: 117
Festner: 95
Fitzgibbon: 108, 120
Foch: 159
Fokker: 10-12, 40, 60, 126, 166
Fokker aeroplanes: 57-59, 66, 83, 85, 93, 176, 191
  D III: 85
  D VII: *172, 176*-178, 182
  Dr I (Triplane): 121, 126-*127*, 128, 149, 152, 155-159, *169*, 170
  E I: 27, *41*, 50
  E II: *41*
  E IV: 65
  M.5: *11*-12, 40-41
Fonck: 29, *133*, 135, 137-*139*
Franchet d'Esperey: 15

Frantz: ix, 13, 15, 26
French, Sir John: xiv
French air units
    organization of: 96
    *Groupe de Bombardement IX:* 106
    *Groupe de Combat XII* (Storks):
        69, 118, 133, 135-139
    HF 19: 34
    MF 8: 22, 34
    MF 62: 145
    M-S division (Villacoublay): 23
    M-S 3: 46
    M-S 12: 23, 34, 37-38
    M-S 23: 19, 28
    M-S 49: 32
    N 3: 69, 77, 145
    N 31: 77
    N 67: 59, 62, 64
    N 77: 117
    N 124 *(Escadrille Lafayette):* 72,
        106-107, 165-167
    Spa 3: 69, 133, 145
    Spa 12: 190
    Spa 26: 69, 135, 193
    Spa 31: 190, 191
    Spa 48: 117
    Spa 73: 69, 72, 135, 145-147
    Spa 81: 111, 194
    Spa 103: 69, 135
    Spa 154: 190, 191
    VB 106: 166
    Voisin 24: 13
French military aviation
    number of aeroplanes (Aug., 1914):
        xiii
    training: 3-6

G

Garros: 18-*20*, 26, 28, 30, 33, 42
    capture of: 31-32, 40
    escapes and is killed: 193-194
Gatling: 26
German air units
    organization of: 25, 58, 76, 96, 114
    *Brieftauben Abteilungen*
        (Carrier Pigeons): 43, 53, 114
    *Festungsfliegerabteilungen:* 16, 29
    *Fliegerabteilung 29:* 29
    *Fliegerabteilung 31:* 185-189
    *Fliegerabteilung 57:* 114
    *Fliegerabteilung 60:* 17
    *Fliegerabteilung 62:* 25, 30, 41, 43
    *Fliegerabteilung 69:* 53
    *Fliegerabteilung (A)203:* 143
    *Fliegerabteilung 206:* 48
    *Fliegerabteilung 227:* 109
    *Flieger-Bataillon Nr. 1:* 16, 29
    *Fliegerersatzabteilung 2:* 16, 114
    *Fliegerersatzabteilung 3:* 143
    *Fliegerersatzabteilung 4:* 189
    *Fliegerersatzabteilung 7:* 18, 53
    *Fliegerersatzabteilung 8:* 114
    *Jagdgeschwader 1* (Richthofen
        Circus): 96, 155-159
    *Jagdgeschwader 2:* 96, *169,* 170
    *Jagdgeschwader 3:* 96
    *Jagdgeschwader 4:* 96
    *Jasta 2 (Jasta Boelcke):* 76-78, 85-86,
        87, 144
    *Jasta 3:* 87, 125

*Jasta 4:* 96
*Jasta 5:* 156-157
*Jasta 6:* 87, 96
*Jasta 8:* 160
*Jasta 10:* 96, 124
*Jasta 11:* 87, 92, 95, 96, 97, 109, 110,
    120, 144, 152-159
*Jasta 12:* 114-115, *169,* 170
*Jasta 13:* 169
*Jasta 15:* 169
*Jasta 19:* 169
*Jasta 33:* 144
*Jasta 34:* 151
*Jasta 37:* 152
*Jasta 79:* 151
*Kampfeinsitzer Kommandos:* 58, 75
*Kagohl 1:* 114, 124
*Kagohl 2:* 53, 114
German military aviation
    "B" and "C" class machines: 25-26
    color patterns for squadrons
        established: 87
    Flight Report Service established:
    independent air service established:
        75
    number of aeroplanes (Aug., 1914):
        xiii
    prewar: 9-12
Gerstenberg: *154*
Girard: 24
Girod: 117
Girval: 137
Goettler: 179, 180
Gros: 72
Grossetti: 62
Guerder: 46
Guignand: 59, 64
Guynemer: 45-47, *68,* 71, 88, 113,
    117-*118,* 135
    death of: 119, 139

H

Halberstadt aeroplanes: 125
    B II: 73
    CL II: *26,* 182, *189*
    D I: 73
    D II: *73,* 129
    D III: 85
Hall: *72,* 165
Happe: 106, 108
Harcourt, d': 135, 139
Harvey-Kelly: xv, 12
Hausen, von: 117
Hawker: 65, 79-80, 82-83, *85*-86
    inventions of: 82
    killed: 86
Henderson: xiv
Heurtaux: 135, 139
Hindenburg, von: 75
Hinkle: 166
Hoeppner, von: 75
Hoffman: *170*
Hoidge: 129
Holck, von: 53, 67, 143
Hotchkiss: 26

I

Immelmann: *27,* 29, *30,* 31, 42 *44,* 53
    death of: 66
    develops tactics: 43

J

Junck: ix, 160
Justinus: 49-50

K

Karjus: 156, 158
Kirbach: 115
Kirmaier: 85, 125
Kleinhenz: 95
Kluck, von: xiv
Knight: 78
Koch: *170*
Krapfenbauer: *170*
Krefft: 95
Kroll: 137*n*

L

Lafayette Flying Corps and *Escadrille:*
    *72,* 106-107, 165
Le Boutillier: 156, 159
Le Révérend: 23
Leefe-Robinson: 97
Leps: ix, 1, 62-63, 111-*113,* 194
Lewis, D.: 155
Lewis, Isaac Newton: 26
L'Hermite, de: 117
Lieth-Thomsen, von der: 75
Loerzer: 96
"Lost Battalion": 179-180
Lowenhardt: 153
Ludendorff: 75
Lufbery: 107, 163, 165-*167*
    death of, 168
Luke: 179
L. V. G. aeroplanes: 9, 25, 51-52
    B II: *30*

M

Machine guns: *30*
    Browning: 26
    deflection system for: 19, 21
    first: 13
    Fonck's gun sight: 138
    Hotchkiss: *26,* 28
    Lewis: *26,* 60, 65, 80, 82, 89, 100
    Maxim: 27
    Parabellum: *26,* 27, 60
    Prideaux belt: 82
    Spandau: *27,* 73, 151
    synchronized (interrupter gear):
        40, 66, 69, 121, 123, 151
    Vickers: *27, 28,* 69, 89, 100, 121
McCudden: 129
McKeever: 97
McMurty: 179
Mansfield: 12
March Offensive (1918): 151, 161
Marne, First Battle of the: 34
Martinsyde Scout: 79
Mateu: 69
Maurice Farman aeroplanes: 22, 34, 50
    Longhorn: 23, 79
Maxim: 26
May: 156-159
Mayberry: 129
Mellersh: 156, 157, 159
Moinier: 36
Morane-Saulnier aeroplanes: 18-19,
    34, 52
    "N" monoplane: 19. *28,* 32-33
    *parasol:* 23-*24,* 27, 35-37, 46

Morgenstern, verse of: 17, 183
Mouronval: 117
Muller: *170*
Muspratt: 129

N

Nash: 108, 109
Navarre: 22-24, 34-39, *51*-52, 59-60, 62
    awarded *Légion d'Honneur:* 39
    shot down: 64
Neckel: *170*
Nieuport aeroplanes: 88, 117, 148
    *Bébé:* 59-*60, 61, 64,* 65, 68, 83, 89
    17: *89, 90,* 106
    28: *163, 164,* 165, 168, 171, 188-189
Nivelle: 126, 133

O

Olieslagers: 67

P

Page: 108, 120
Parachutes: 7
Pégoud: 7, *8,* 9, 10, 51
    death of: 32-33
Pétain: 57, 58, 190
Peterson: 167
Peuty, du: 108, 118
Pfalz aeroplanes: *58,* 155, 170
    D III: 128, *142, 149, 150,* 151, 161,
    168
Pivolo (Doisy): *34*-35, 37, 64
Poinsard: 22
Pourpe: 166
Platz: 126
Plumer: 109, 121
Porr: *27*
Prince: 72, 107, 166

Q

Quénault: 13, 15, 26

R

Raux: 133
R. E. aeroplanes
    5: 79
    8: *26, 152*
Reid: 108-109, 120
Reinhardt: 153
Reverchon: 191
Rheno: *72*
Rhys-Davids: *129*
Richthofen, Lothar von: 95, *153*
Richthofen, Manfred von: 17-18, 53,
    67, 76, 78-79, 95-96, 97, 109, 115,
    124, 128, 143-144, *152-153, 154-*
    155, 170
    commands *Jagdgeschwader:* 96
    death of: 156-159
    receives *Pour le Mérite:* 87
    shoots Hawker down: 86
    shot down and wounded: 120
Richthofen, Wolfram von: 156, 158
Rickenbacker: ix, 163, 165, 167, 171,
    179, *181*-182
Roland aeroplanes: 149
    CL II: *91*
Röchling: 187-*188*

Rose, de: 39, *58,* 59, 83, 145
    death of: 67
Rothermere: 153
Rounds: *72*
Royal Air Force, formed: 153, 156
Royal Flying Corps: xv, 42 becomes
    RAF, 153: 156
    obsolete planes of (1917): 93, 95
    organization of: 96
    praised by French: xiv-xv
    prewar training for: xiv
    wins aerial supremacy (1916): 88
    *See also* British air units
Royal Naval Air Service
    becomes part of RAF: 153, 156
    *See also* British air units
Rumpler aeroplanes: 9
Russian Front: 53, 75, 76, 185-188

S

Saboteurs, landing of: 38
Saint-Sauveur, de: 59, 63
Sallier: 22
Salmond: 153
Salmson 2A2: *173*-174
Sardier: ix, *116*-117
Saulnier: 19
Saundby: 85-86
Saunders: ix, 160-162
Savary aeroplanes: 13
Schaefer: 95
Schleich, von: 96, 137*n*
Schoenbeck, von: ix, 143-*144*
Scholz: 152, 156, 158, 159
S. E. aeroplanes
    5: *100-101,* 128-129, 155
    5a: 100, 161
Sévin, de: 193
Seymour: 173-174
Sharman: 108, 109, 120
Siegert: 21
Skene: xv
Solo patrols: 125, 135
Somme, Battle of the: 67, 88, 91, 114,
    124
Sopwith aeroplanes
    Camel: *56-57,* 121, *122-123,* 130-
    *131, 132,* 155-159
    1½ Strutter: *106*
    Pup: 100, *121*
    Triplanes: 95, *104-105,* 108-110, 120
Spad aeroplanes: 85, 95, 111-*112,* 113,
    117-19, 126, 146-147, 190-193
    origin of name: 68-69
    A.2: 62-*63*
    7: 68-*70, 71,* 95
    13: 69, 128, 163, *164,* 171, *192*
    17: 69
Staats: 170
Stark: *148,* 151
Stempel: 58
Strolh: 117
Sykes: xv

T

Tactics
    of Ball: 90
    of Becker: 115
    of Deullin, 145-146, 147
    first "dogfights": 59

Fonck's V-formation: 139
German organization for: 58, 76
Immelmann and Boelcke in
    development of: 43
of RFC for aerial supremacy: 88
three basic formations developed:
    160 of Waddington: 193
Tarascon: ix, 77-*78*
Teubern, Ehrhardt von: ix, 29, *30,* 31,
    42, 43, 44
Teubern, Walter von: ix, *27,* 29
Thieffry: 67
Thierry: 45
Thomsen: 43, 76
Tour, de la: 135
Trenchard: 153
Turnure: *72*
Tutscheck, von: 96, 114, 169-*170*

U

Udet: 48-50, 143, *152*-153
    suicide of, 48
United States air units: 75
    organization of: 96
    1st Pursuit Group: 163
    13th Aero Squadron: 174
    17th Aero Squadron: 162
    50th Aero Squadron: 179-180
    91st Aero Squadron: 173
    94th Aero Squadron: 163, 165-168,
    171, 179, 181-182, 189
    103rd Aero Squadron: 72, 165

V

Vaughan: ix, 48, 100-*101,* 161-*162,* 171
Verdun Battle of: 53, 56-63, 67, 114
Vergnette: 19
Vickers aeroplanes
    F.B.5: 88
    F.B.9 "Gunbus": *88*
Voisin: 13
Voisin aeroplanes: 43, 166
    L.2: 13, *14,* 15
Voss: *124*-126, 128-129, 166

W

Waddington: ix, *190*-191, 193
Waltz: 125
Weiss: 156-158
Wenzl: 156
Whittlesey: 179-180
Wilhelm II: 34, 43
Winslow: 163, 167-168
Wisseman: 139
Wolff: 95, *154,* 156, 158
Woodbridge: 120
Wuehlisch, von: *27*
Wüsthoff: *153*

Y

Ypres, Third Battle of: 124

Z

Zander: 76
Zastrow, Ernst von: 16
Zastrow, Hellmuth von: 10, *16-17,* 29
    verses of: 183-184
Zastrow, Theobald von: ix, 10,
    184-*188,* 189